POOP
CULTURE

Feral House
PO Box 39910
Los Angeles, CA   90039

www.feralhouse.com

10 9 8 7 6 5 4 3 2 1

Design by Hedi El Kholti

POOP CULTURE

How America Is Shaped By Its
Grossest National Product

BY **DAVE PRAEGER**
Editor, PoopReport.com

TABLE OF CONTENTS

poop
report.com

FOREWORD BY PAUL PROVENZA

WHY ON EARTH would anyone buy and read a book about poop? Why the hell would anyone *write* a book about poop?

Because poop is the very essence of being *human*. Try as mankind has, there's just no denying the universality of poop. As one of the most successful children's books in publishing history says right in its title, "*Everyone Poops*." I myself am working on turning that unlikely source material into a feature film. Call me crazy, but I've given poop a *lot* of thought.

There are those who think this speaks to some prurient interest on my part. Or that it suggests a state of arrested development or some such pseudo-Freudian nonsense. In fact, my interest in the subject—like that of Chaucer, Swift, and the author of this fascinating book—comes from a deep, heartfelt interest in all aspects of the human condition. How poop affects us all is downright operatic in its scope. It informs history, culture, and entire social structures. How we deal with emptying our bowels impacts everything from our most intimate relationships to revolutionary upheavals of powerful empires and the ecological balance of the earth. In ways big and small, poop *really matters*.

Early on in my career as a comedian and actor, I was called in to meet with one of Hollywood's most influential and powerful movers and shakers—a meeting that, if all went well, could change my life. I arrived at his office early, growing increasingly nervous and jittery in the reception area as my appointed time drew nearer. My anxiety and tension grew stronger and stronger, until it gripped me deep within, quite literally wrenching my gut.

The pressure grew too intense to bear, and I quietly requested the men's room key from the receptionist—a degrading ritual perfectly engineered to intimidate and demand supplication from those who await an audience with the high and mighty. Any suggestion of discretion on my part vanished as she bolted out from behind her desk, handed me a key chained to something roughly the size of a zeppelin, and proceeded to mime an elaborate Kafkaesque labyrinth to the bathroom. It was an ostentatious semaphore instantly decoded by everyone in the reception area and the offices along the way. I felt a palpable and knowing disdain as, dead man walking, I passed each of them on my unambiguous walk down The Long Brown Mile.

After a torturous journey through a tortuous gauntlet of humiliation and self-consciousness, I finally reached the glowing fluorescent heaven. I sighed a sigh of impending relief and rushed into a stall, dismayed to discover that I would not be alone in my revelry.

I have no background whatsoever in the field of forensics, but to even a casual watcher of *CSI* it would have been clear that whoever inhabited the black and white wing-tip shoes in that stall next to mine had been there for quite some time, and had been eating very well for much of his life. Whatever self-consciousness I may have felt at allowing my gut to unwrench in the presence of another human being disappeared as my companion wrestled through a complicated labor to birth to his own unwanted offspring.

Something truly epic was taking place next door. Primordial sounds, much like the earth made while cooling, rumbled through already thick, fetid air. Waves crashed against porcelain shores as Zeus himself hurled mighty comets into a humble sea beneath him, lashed by mythic winds and terrifying thunder. An undulating swirl of stench snaked itself almost visibly over the partition in an otherworldly manifestation of everything evil that resided within man.

This was *cataclysmic*. The effects of this event were vast. California's fault lines, I feared, will shudder from the pressure. Weather patterns, I was certain, would be shifting. Milk must be curdling all around the world. The Kennedy assassination may need reinvestigating. And there I sat, a canary in this poisoned gastrointestinal coalmine.

My five senses struggled to survive this bio-terrorist attack, and only an inch of stainless steel panel separated me from ground zero. Yet I had only compassion and respect for this man's heroic struggle. His tortured grunts and agonizing groans moved me empathically, and I was relieved that my relief came more effortlessly. With all the urgency befitting a hazmat situation, I quickly evacuated both myself and the area.

I went back to the receptionist, heaved the key and its anchor back over the desk, and tried to recover. I sat for a while considering grief counseling when an assistant finally came to bring me in to my meeting.

I rose a bit wobbly, and followed him into a huge corner office. Vast windows framed a stunning vista of the city far below, further increasing my unsteadiness. This was the office of a man who, like the view, overlooked all of Hollywood. The height of this office and the prominence of the man inhabiting it were equally dizzying. He came from his desk to greet me and offer an insincere generic apology for the late start of our meeting, when all of Hollywood suddenly disappeared as my eyes whip-panned, rack focused and zoomed in on his black and white wing-tips.

This proverbial Hollywood mover and shaker had been literally moving and shaking Hollywood right next to me.

The meeting unfolded very differently than I expected as all my humility, subservience and deference were overcome by the fact that I had shared with him the lowest common denominator of every living thing in existence. His status, wealth or influence no longer held sway over me, for I had been present as he purged his filthy, stinking colon of the vile detritus of so much overpriced Morton's cuisine. I could not have been more comfortable or at ease in his substantial presence. The biological reality, necessity and inevitability of poop was the great equalizer.

While at first glance poop and its culture may seem like a silly subject for a book, I assure you it's not. "*Everyone Poops.*" And everyone knows they poop. But everyone also has an attitude and a perspective toward poop, too. And most people aren't even aware of that part. And that's where it gets really interesting.

The taboos, the sophomoric jokes, the schoolyard giggling that accompany the subject and act itself of pooping are all part of a cultural and social construct that somehow has framed that most vulnerable, intimate, and *equalizing* fact of daily life for us all with inexplicable shame, guilt, fear and anxiety for a very long time. Why? How? By whom? Is it possible that when the subject is brought out in the open and its universality acknowledged as inevitable and human, the mighty fall? Or is it that the ordinary are raised up higher? Either way, an imbalance tips. Poop is *power.*

Our conscious and unconscious attitudes toward the fundamental, necessary, life-sustaining biological process of elimination are remarkably similar to the squeamishness, fear, anxiety and morality ascribed to another basic human imperative, our sexuality. Is that a coincidence? An accident? Cultural evolutionary progression? Is it simply confusion resulting from the close proximity of pertinent external organs? Perhaps there's something else going on.

It's shocking to think that a book about *poop* can be considered an act of courage. But it is. Most of us have knee-jerk responses to the topic and the fact of pooping that we are not even aware of. Attitudes that, like the awful stench of poop itself, permeate all of society and culture. Attitudes that resonate. Attitudes that, like the pungency of any fart worth mentioning, have serious "hang time." To challenge those attitudes is to challenge some vague power and unseen authority over us all. It is a challenge to all the thoughts and ideas inside each of us that we unwittingly allow to keep us from accepting our very *humanity.*

This book has some very profound and beautiful things to say. It takes a dirty, smelly, unpleasant subject like shit and brings forth ideas that are empowering, dignifying and life-affirming. As one contributor to PoopReport.com (this author's own website) states so elegantly, philosophically and unapologetically:

"I stink, therefore I am."

That is a *perfect* truth.

— Paul Provenza, Director, *The Aristocrats*

THE ORIGIN OF FECES

I HAVE FRIENDS with funny names: Di Uhreea, Poopergal, Pill Pooper, Logjam, the Dumpster, the Big Wiper, Ass Phlegm, Motherload, Hairy Pooter, General Colon Pow, Bunga Din, and C. Everett Poop, among others. I even have enemies with such names as The Holy Shitter, Super Bowel, and The Shitman. I run PoopReport.com, and all these people and many more unnamed participate on my site.

PoopReport.com is dedicated to the intellectual appreciation of poop humor. It's partly for readers to laugh at stories submitted by people whose butts have betrayed them—those who didn't quite make it to the bathroom, and those who made it there but not quite to the toilet, and many other victims of the human bowel's propensity for mishaps. Just about everyone, it seems, has a funny poop story. The human butt is ridiculous. But PoopReport goes beyond humor to discuss poop with a candor rare in today's culture. Freed by anonymity from the constraints of polite society, contributors have intellectualized the topic to a surprising degree, considering it comes from an organization whose logo sports corn-studded cartoon feces. We are scholars as well as jesters, and one of the very few organizations to study poop. This is one of the major contradictions of civilized life: although poop is a part of life for every human being who lives long enough to expel his or her meconium, shockingly little thought has been devoted to its role in our lives.

Its role, we've learned, is huge. It affects us psychologically, manifests in social relations and hierarchy, influences child-rearing, and makes an impact on the environment, art, media, culture, and commerce. Few aspects of human life escape the influence of its ubiquitous and inevitably urgent presence.

STRIP THE PURPOSE of life to its core, and finding food is what's left. You get up every morning and do what you need to do to ensure there will be food on your plate next time you get hungry. Only when you're sure of your next meal do you pursue leisure. The human body is adapted foremost for food-finding. Even things such as love and family and community, from this brutally reductionist point of view, are just means to extend your food-finding network.

If finding food is the most important thing in life, then poop might seem to be the least.

Our most basic understanding of poop is as the food the body doesn't want. A more advanced understanding recognizes that poop is composed of water, dead bacteria, indigestible fiber, undigested fat and protein, and dead cells—a more complex substance than we might guess, but nevertheless worthless. You can fertilize your crops with it, but chances are you're not a farmer, which means poop can't help you find food. It's the furthest you can get from your purpose in life. This book isn't going to argue otherwise.

But poop's total lack of utility does not justify its position in our culture, buried in such negativity that it's afforded thought only on a website frequented by people with names like Obi-Dung Kenobi and Commode-O Dragon.

The taboos surrounding poop are society's response to its physical properties: it stinks, disgusts us, and comes from our private parts. But while the physical properties and our aversion to them are natural, the taboos are a cultural construct: part of a set of rules and rituals about how we should relate to poop and the sights, sounds, and smells which accompany it. These powerful rules have compelled the creation of an infrastructure that supports ubiquitous toilets, and running water to fill them, and toilet paper, and sewers to take the poop away, and municipal sewage treatment plants to collect and process the poop from every home, office, school, restaurant, and place of worship in the country. These rules are powerful enough to engender discomfort about discussing the one thing that George W. Bush, Osama bin Laden, Queen Elizabeth, Rosa Parks, Gandhi, Hitler, Martha Washington, Joan of Arc, Socrates, and Moses have in common with you and me.

Why does it make us uncomfortable? Though we laugh about it on TV, in the movies, and among friends, laughter often signals unease. Outside of moments of levity, poop is a source of awkwardness. We don't like being seen on our way to the bathroom or heard while we're in there. We simply don't like to admit that we poop. Has it always been this way? Could we go back in time and watch ancient Romans slinking between stone columns, peering around corners to elude witnesses, rehearsing some pretext (in case of encountering an acquaintance) of merely looking for the vomitorium?

And with all that trauma, why are some people in our society not embarrassed about it in the slightest? Beyond the jokes and nervous laugher, it's clear that there are two distinct approaches to pooping in our society. Some men and women walk with feigned nonchalance toward the bathroom, hoping no one notices, meeting no one's eyes, ready to pretend to wash their hands should they see anyone they know. But others walk with newspapers under their arms and their heads held high, smiling and whistling and making no pretense about where they're going and what they're going to do when they get there. How can similar people, raised under the same religious and cultural influences, have such divergent views of the same experience?

I CREATED POOPREPORT.COM in 1999, after a friend told a poop story so funny that it needed to be shared with the world. An extensive Web search had an unbelievable result: there were no websites for sharing funny poop stories. So I took it upon myself to pioneer the genre, beginning with a simple rule: post nothing I wouldn't want my parents to see. That meant no pictures of poop and no fetish content. The site wasn't intended to gross people out or arbitrarily challenge taboos. Rather, it was to be a forum for men and women to laugh at the universal absurdity of the digestive system as we analyzed its meaning in our lives.

The site became popular. I've posted at least one reader-submitted story nearly every weekday since then, and attracted a following of men and women of all ages and backgrounds, large enough that the flow of content has never run dry. There are only a few ways in which our butts can malfunction, of course, so many of the stories are variations on a couple of themes. This means that it isn't the plots of the stories that has kept thousands of people coming back day after day; it's the writing. The most popular stories are the ones in which the writer crafts a story that sings. It's funny to read, "I tried to hold it in, but the train bumped and I farted." But style makes it funnier: "Then the train hit a rough spot, and harmony and balance broke loose, and out came the Fart at the End of Time—a ten-second sputtering dung-funk that shook seismographs in California and knocked the Earth slightly off its axis."

For the first couple of years, I was content watching the site grow and interacting with its readers. But the more I learned about the subject, the more I realized how little about it is known. A few books and essays have attempted to analyze poop's role in one particular niche of society or another, but there are no think tanks, university programs, or academic journals. Compared to the mountain of scholarship on, say, sixteenth-century French literature, the paucity of thought on poop's significance in our culture is shocking.

And so I began this book. This is not a history of poop, but a study of today: a snapshot of the ways our butts influence our culture. History is provided for context, but the goal is to understand how poop affects us, how we view it, and why; to understand its impact from the moment it slides out of our butts to the moment it enters the sewage treatment plant; to explore how we've arrived at this strange discomfort and confusion about a natural product of our bodies; to see how this contradiction— the natural as unnatural—shapes our minds, relationships, environment, culture, economics, media, and art.

This book adheres to the same aesthetic as the site: I'm not writing this to gross you out. You won't get sick. There's nothing in this book I wouldn't want my parents to read. You will be shocked (probably) and you will laugh (I hope), but those reactions are to be expected when you confront a taboo. At the end, poop will still stink and be gross, but I expect you'll agree with the readers and contributors of PoopReport.com: it nevertheless deserves our intellectual appreciation.

IN WRITING THIS BOOK, I have had the pleasure of interacting with some of the very few men and women who have furthered serious study of poop. Many thanks go out to Marisol Cortez, Danny Gerling, and Jeff Persels for their insight into the confluence of theory and scatology. I thank Christi Clifford and Messrs. Gerling and Persels once again for helping me craft a loose manuscript into the solid mass you now hold. I'm indebted to those outside the hallowed pages of PoopReport.com who squeezed out some time to answer my questions or confirm some facts: Russell Ganim, Paul Rozin, Wim Delvoye, Gianni Degryse, Terence Dick, Paul Spinrad, Joe Jenkins, Jonathan Isbit, Bruce Logan, Jay Heinrichs, Brian Barry, Don Mills, and Dan Wood, Paul Provenza, Jeff Bergstrom, Patton Oswalt, Jack Sim, John Lauer, and Maureen Ogle. I offer a blast from my dorsal trumpet in honor of Adam Parfrey, Shane Davis, Hedi El Kholti, and the good people of Feral House. And I thank Susie, Eric, Mom, Dad, and my pulchritudinous wife Jenny for having no problem being related and/or married to the Poop Guy.

Finally, I salute with a flush every PoopReporter not listed above. It's not that I don't appreciate you; it's just that you don't have funny enough names.

— Dave Praeger, January, 2007

Cloaca—New & Improved at the Power Plant Gallery in Toronto. Picture courtesy of Wim Delvoye.

Cloaca—New & Improved at the Power Plant Gallery in Toronto. Picture courtesy of Wim Delvoye.

CHAPTER 1

HOW DO YOU DOO

WITH ENVIABLE EASE, poop slid out of the mechanical anus and onto the conveyor belt below.

Most of us know pooping as a struggle. Our bodies are optimized for the hunter-gatherer lifestyle—running around the savanna, eating berries and meat, pooping behind bushes in a squat. Pooping today is a battle against sedentariness, a diet of processed foods, and a rectum that's half-closed in the sitting position (on which more later). For most of us, pooping is a time-consuming, sweat-inducing battle between the life we lead and the life we're built for.

The machine's poop just slid right out. Only a few seconds passed from the moment the wizened head peeked until the tip of the tail dropped off. A single tubular mass, smooth and unkinked (because the machine's sphincter never clenched—because the machine never had to pause to catch its breath and push again, unlike we humans) flowed confidently and with constant velocity, falling a short distance to curl gently on a conveyor belt that then slowly moved the feces away from the artificial digestive system that had created it. Around the glass-enclosed conveyor belt, people crowded for a closer look.

Women in chic suits gaped. Men with white beards and bald heads pushed up their thick-rimmed glasses and leaned in. Young art students peered with genuine fascination, forgetting momentarily that young art students are supposed to be jaded. Critics, benefactors, reporters, collectors—all were enthralled by the foot-long piece of brown waste, 75% water, 8% dead bacteria, 8% fiber, 5% fat, 4% other, chemically indistinguishable from what's moving through your digestive system right now. What forty hours ago had been food from a local restaurant was now poop. The machine hummed, satisfied. The crowd applauded, astounded.

Every day from March 27 to May 23, 2004, art lovers gathered at The Power Plant gallery in Toronto to witness poop springing forth from the bowels of Belgian artist Wim Delvoye's *Cloaca—New & Improved*. Enclosed in steel and glass, this thirty-foot-long representation of the human digestive system functions just like yours. Food goes in through its mouth, gears chew it up, enzymes break it apart, and bacteria digest it, in a process involving the same chemicals and symbiotic organisms as serve digestion in humans. Electronic and mechanical systems play the part of the enteric nervous system, regulating food's passage through glass jars acting as *Cloaca's* stomach, small intestine, large intestine, and rectum, and timing secretions from its liver, pancreas, and gallbladder. Hours later, out the other end comes poop—brown, slimy, smelly, and chemically identical to the human version.

Cloaca—New & Improved is the second in a series of five pooping machines created by Delvoye. At speeds and efficiencies that have improved with each version, the *Cloaca* series all do the same thing: eat, digest, and poop. The first *Cloaca* could process a meal every forty hours; *Cloaca Turbo*, the third version, did it in as little as six. Besides Toronto, *Cloaca* has exhibited in New York, Antwerp, Vienna, Lyon, and Bordeaux.

As a work of art, *Cloaca's* meanings are numerous and profound. *Cloaca* desexualizes poop, sequestering it from gender and allowing analysis without the distractions of genitalia. It proves, in terms of efficacy and miniaturization, the superiority of the human body over today's technology. It reminds us that poop is a phenomenon experienced by every human being. It comments on the nature of modern art.

And, although this is not Delvoye's intention, it provides a great lesson in biology. In this plastic, steel, and glass torso, Delvoye has recreated our flesh-and-blood process. His version differs from ours by a few thousand pounds and a few hundred thousand dollars; but the basics (chewing, digesting, excreting) and the specifics (pepsin, creatine, symbiotic bacteria, and so on) are the same. The only major functional difference is that while we eat to create energy, and poop is the waste, *Cloaca* eats to create poop, and its waste is the energy liberated from the food by digestion.

The digestive tract

The purpose of the digestive system is to turn food into energy. Everything we eat can be broken down into proteins, fats, carbohydrates, and fiber. We can't digest fiber, but we convert the other three components into amino acids, fatty acids, and glucose—simple energy molecules small enough to pass through the walls of the digestive system and into the bloodstream for distribution to every cell in the body.

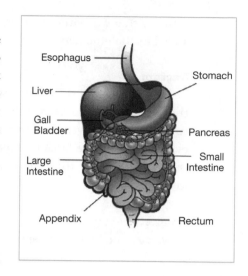

Mouth

Food goes in. Food gets mashed. Saliva is added to help it liquefy.

Esophagus

Food goes down.

Stomach

Food is stored and mixed. As food moves through, water is added to help digestive chemicals turn it into mush.

Small Intestine

An assembly line of specialized chemicals from organs including the pancreas, liver, and gallbladder break food down into molecules small enough to be absorbed through the intestine walls.

Colon (Large Intestine)

Whatever the small intestine hasn't digested spends hours or days working its way through your colon. Hordes of teeming bacteria live symbiotically in your digestive tract, working to liberate the more stubborn nutrients from the molecules that made it this far without being digested. Most of the water added in the stomach is reclaimed here.

Rectum
Technically part of the colon but often considered separately, the rectum is where feces gathers until it is expelled. The rectum contains nerves that inform the body that it's time to evacuate; the more feces that gathers and the longer it waits, the more urgently those nerves implore you to drop off the kids at the pool.

Sphincter
Stays clenched (one hopes) until it's time to let go.

Anus
Poop comes out.

BLACK OR WHITE, man or woman, Christian or Muslim or Jew: pooping transcends all boundaries and embodies shared humanity—collectively understood, appreciated, and feared. It's a pleasure to some and a chore to others; but when it turns bad, its demands can force any of us at any time to abandon all pretense of civilized behavior to meet the exigency of an innocent meal gone wrong. The experience of needing to poop, of pooping, and of having pooped is universal.

Nevertheless, any particular poop represents a never-to-be-repeated confluence of diet, metabolism, and environment. The size, smell, density, and structural integrity of any given Lincoln Log depends foremost on what you ate and your body's response to it, and then on stress, environment, activity, and any other external influences during the digestive period. Like a snowflake, every poop is unique.

Discussions about poop must accept this uniqueness. Some people are thrice-daily poopers and others only triweekly. Some produce floaters; others, sinkers. Some produce elephantine masses, while others create modest Milk Duds. But even though some snowflakes reek of boiled egg and others leave great brown smears, they both still fall under the general definition of "snowflake." And so it is with poop. The baseline for comparison is not the idiosyncratic end product, but the experience—urge, act, and aftermath.

While one pooper's average production may be of a girth to make another pale in fear, both can relate to the struggle against a poop bigger than what one is used to, because the urge, act, and aftermath are alike enough for all. The urge starts as a distant sensation and works its way into consciousness, growing in urgency until it forces compliance. The act is the birth process—depending on how critical the urge, the act may be an exhausting bout of pushing or a simple unclenching of the sphincter or an uncontrollable explosion in one's pants. If the urge was moderate, the aftermath is unremarkable; if the urge was all-consuming, the aftermath is just as intense. The dichotomy between the urge and the aftermath is the first duality of poop. Poop is both pain and relief. The more it hurts to hold it in, the better it feels to let it out. The prelude of anguish, the postscript of tranquility—like childbirth, pooping is fruition achieved through suffering.

AN UNBALANCED SYSTEM: CONSTIPATION AND DIARRHEA

Pooping is normally an unremarkable event, essential to the function of the body. A typical poop—whatever is normal for a given person, whether its end breaches the water or it can be completely hidden by one square of used toilet paper—marks the peak of a metabolism-specific bell curve. From this norm one routinely deviates as diet, metabolism, and environment interact. One may not notice the minor variations, which manifest as a log slightly smaller, or slightly mushier, or slightly more stubborn than the average. But stray far enough beyond the standard deviation and the word "poop" no longer applies.

A cow's digestive system is good at processing plant matter, and not so good at digesting anything else. The human digestive system, on the other hand, can accommodate wide variations in diet, from bran muffins to curry vindaloo. It can convert large simultaneous infusions of fats, carbohydrates, and proteins into the amino acids, fatty acids, and glucose the body needs for energy and maintenance. But it prefers not to. The digestive system seeks equilibrium with your diet: if it recognizes the consistent ingestion of particular inputs, it adjusts itself to produce more or less of certain chemicals and create an environment more or less hospitable to particular bacteria in anticipation of more of the same. This is why corn can come out undigested—the digestive system allocates certain resources to certain tasks, and digesting corn hulls requires a lot of resources to digest. Your stomach will work on the easy stuff first, and digest the corn only if it has resources left over. Nothing to worry about; undigested corn is a merely aesthetic problem.

What a cow lacks in digestive agility it makes up in specialization, wisely restricting its diet to what it can easily digest. Humans aren't so bright. Our systems adjust to anticipate food within parameters based on recent diet patterns, but our penchant for chili cook-offs shows how much we enjoy eating outside those limits. A diet within the margin of error set by the digestive system's adaptations results in regular, top-of-the-bell-curve poops. But for every six meals you eat at McDonalds, there's that seventh at Taco Bell. A digestive system anticipating a gentle dollop of ketchup and mustard tends to react with vengeance when you drown it in hot sauce.

There are two ways to confound your digestive system: overwhelm it with an input it could probably handle in smaller quantities (such as a whole wheel of cheese), or introduce new or unexpected inputs (consider a Westerner's first encounter with Indian food, or first hamburger after a decade of vegetarianism). The result: diarrhea or constipation.

Diarrhea

Government health literature preaches that a healthy adult poops no more than three times per day. Poop number four, according to them, is diarrhea. But we've already established that a normal poop can't be specifically characterized—poop is different for every person. And so is diarrhea. Government guidelines don't tell you when you have diarrhea. Your nose tells you. Your eyes tell you. The back of your underwear tells you.

The digestive process requires up to nine liters of water, which comes from drinking, from saliva, and from secretions in the stomach. In your stomach, the food, water, and various chemical secretions mix into a partially-digested liquid mass (chyme) that your digestive muscles push through the system in undulations (peristalsis). Normally, your intestines reclaim up to 95% of that water, drying out the stool to the point of cohesion as a nice log. Diarrhea occurs when there's too much water left in the stool. The stool doesn't coagulate, but instead comes out in fits and spurts.

According to the technical literature, overly soft stool qualifies as diarrhea even if it coheres. To most people, though, that would fall within the accepted margins of regular pooping. Real diarrhea, to most people, comes with the cramps, the splatters, the explosions, the sporadic sprints to the bathroom to indulge a butt acting like a garden hose. There's no grey area—if it's diarrhea, you know it.

But there's a little-known fact about diarrhea. It's not the problem; it's the solution. Diarrhea is how the digestive system protects itself from intruders. If your body doesn't like what it detects—a particular species of bacteria, or some food it interprets as a threat, or whatever else might set it off—it adds water to your stool to flush everything out. Once it's in the clear, the diarrhea stops. Anti-diarrhea medicine doesn't help you get healthy. It halts the inconvenient symptoms, which is useful if you're due on stage at Carnegie Hall, but it ultimately prolongs your suffering, because the threat your colon wants to expunge is still inside.

Your diarrhea will continue until the threat has been squirted out. The biggest danger is water loss: your body relies on your colon to reclaim the water it's now using to flush itself out, which is why you should drink lots of fluids when you've become a human espresso machine. As long as you stay hydrated, the biggest threat from diarrhea is pain, inconvenience, embarrassment if you stray too far from the toilet, and a sudden increase in your dry-cleaning budget.

Constipation

Too much water in the stool causes diarrhea. Too little can cause constipation.

One of your intestines' jobs is to remove water from the liquid waste that passes through it—ideally, just enough to make a soft but cohesive poop. If the stool spends too long in the colon, it can dry out too much. Stool needs to be pliable to negotiate the colon's twists and turns; if too dry, it can get stuck. This results in little rabbit poops as your log dehydrates and breaks apart like mud on a dried lakebed—if you're lucky. If you're not, the result is a log stuck against your colon wall, too dry to overcome friction.

This is why fiber is so important for the human digestive system. Found in plant matter, fiber is a kind of carbohydrate too complex to digest. Instead, it acts as a bulking agent, absorbing water and giving your peristaltic muscles traction as they work the semi-digested mass through the system. Without fiber, your system has trouble moving things along, which means the poop may dry out too much or too soon. Peristaltic muscles in the upper parts of your colon are used to working with mushy chyme; a dry log at that point might put up a struggle, slowing to a stop.

An unhealthy diet is only one cause of constipation. An unhealthy outlook is another. If you ignore the urge to poop because you're too busy or don't like to poop at school or at work, your colon will nevertheless continue to reclaim water while the poop waits; by the time you're ready, the poop might be too dry to push out. If you abuse laxatives, your muscles can grow too weak to push along a normal stool. Or maybe you have a tumor in your colon, slowing the chyme until it dries out too much. There are many reasons, often cascading and self-perpetuating. Constipation is a vicious cycle, and the dried-out turds it creates are equally vicious on your o-ring.

INTERNAL AFFAIRS: INVESTIGATING YOUR INSIDES

For most people, diarrhea and constipation are rare—uncomfortable but brief slides to the distant slopes of the bell curve.

Both usually respond well to diet change: lots of fiber and water if you're constipated, lots of bland foods and patience if your ass thinks it's a faucet. But for too many Americans, bowel dysfunction is a way of life. From gallstones to hernias to colon cancer to irritable bowel syndrome to hemorrhoids to diverticulitis: the National Center for Health Statistics estimates that 60–70 million Americans suffer some form of digestive malady. For fourteen million people in 2002, it was serious enough to require hospitalization. And according to the American Cancer Society, colorectal cancer alone kills 55,000 people a year. Many factors contribute to these problems—most notably, as you'll learn, the American diet and lifestyle—but when you're suffering from endless constipation or ceaseless diarrhea or oscillating wildly between the two, you're not concerned with what you or your culture could have done differently. You want to know what's wrong and how to fix it. But your digestive system comprises thirty feet of twists and turns from your mouth to your anus. How do you find the culprit?

Stool samples are useful for identifying some causes of diarrhea, such as food poisoning or cholera. Beyond a few illnesses, however, their usefulness is limited. A scene from the 1994 film *The Madness of King George* shows the King's best scientists analyzing his stool, picking it apart and subjecting it to various archaic methods to find clues to his strange behavior. In the eighteenth century, there weren't too many ways to see what was going on inside the body short of cutting it open. Today's medical science has made a lot of progress in that department.

Unfortunately, the methods developed aren't much fun. No matter which way you go about it, if you're going sphincter spelunking, you're in for a rough time.

PHYSICAL EXAM

Every journey up your ass begins with a single step. To evaluate the muscle tone of your anal sphincter and search for tenderness, blood, or obstruction, the doctor uses a rubber glove and a jar of lube, while you try to think happy thoughts.

Discomfort quotient: Just hope your doctor has small fingers. And that he remembers to take off his ring.

COLORECTAL TRANSIT STUDY

To observe food moving through your body, you swallow capsules containing small markers that disperse as they pass through the digestive system. You're x-rayed several times 3–7 days later so doctors can see where the food goes, and when.

Discomfort quotient: Fortunately, you don't have to recover the markers.

ANORECTAL FUNCTION TESTS

If you're subject to chronic leakage or premature release, you may have a weak sphincter. To find out, doctors evaluate your muscle function by inserting and then slowly retracting a catheter or air-filled balloon.

Discomfort quotient: If your problem is indeed a weak sphincter, then you probably won't even notice this test going on. Otherwise... yeah, you'll notice.

BARIUM ENEMA X-RAY

The muscles of your colon don't show up well on x-rays. To search for irregularities in all its nooks and crannies, doctors fill your colon with barium, a chalky white substance. Yes, fill—they pump what seems like a cement-truck-load of it into you, so that the x-ray shows the outline of every lump and fissure. Starting about ten minutes after the procedure, you spend the next couple of days pooping it all out.

Discomfort quotient: For this to work, your colon must be empty. Emptying your colon, unfortunately, is not like draining the oil from your car—although it does become more so after you drink that whole bottle of laxatives they prescribe.

DEFECOGRAPHY

The barium enema x-ray provided a snapshot of the state of your bowels. But that's not enough—your doctor wants to see your muscles in action. Defecographers fill your rectum with a soft paste with a consistency similar to poop, then seat you on a special toilet-*cum*-x-ray machine-*cum*-VCR to make a movie as you poop it out.

Discomfort quotient: The paste has to get into your rectum somehow. Imagine a medical turkey-baster.

SIGMOIDOSCOPY

After a period on a liquid diet and a few enemas for good measure, the doctor sticks a long, flexible tube into your now-empty rectum and lower colon. It's got a light and a camera and, if you're really lucky, an air-hose to inflate your colon to enable a better view.

Discomfort quotient: A sigmoidoscope only goes in about a foot. You'll barely know the doctor is sticking something up your butt.

COLONOSCOPY

This combines the spring cleaning you get before a barium enema with the fun of anal insertion. For this procedure, the doctor may or may not sedate you, but will lay you on your side and feed a camera cable up your ass—all the way up—in search of anything out of the ordinary. And when he finds it, the colonoscope has a set of pinchers to snip off a chunk for later examination.

Discomfort quotient: Take all of the previous, and add another five feet.

CAPSULE ENDOSCOPY: THE END OF INDIGNITY

Colonoscopies may soon join leeches and blistering as a medical archaism. Medical scientists have encased a camera, battery, transmitter, and light in a multivitamin-sized capsule the patient swallows. It tumbles through your system, taking thousands of pictures and uploading them to an external receiver. A few days and twenty-five feet later, doctors can have a complete snapshot of your digestive system, from mouth to squinting brown eye. Though today it's used mostly to examine the small intestine (which is too long and twisty for scoping techniques to navigate), it's clearly the internal imaging technique of the future.

Discomfort quotient: The bad news is that you still need to empty your digestive system with laxatives. The good news is that you don't need to recover the camera once it comes out.

EATS, SHITS, AND LEAVES: MANAGING HUMAN WASTE

For a few canny art collectors, the *Cloaca* experience didn't end when the exhibit closed. Many collectors took home the ultimate *objet d'art*: an actual *Cloaca*-produced specimen, carefully vacuum-sealed in clear plastic to ensure a long display life, accompanied by a menu documenting what *Cloaca* had been fed to sculpt this masterpiece, for only $1,000. Unlike Piero Manzoni's 1961 *Merda d'Artista*, in which only the artist's word guaranteed that the tin cans he so successfully sold really did contain his feces, these souvenirs proudly emphasize every shimmering lump and fissure. Critics who long purveyed clichés about the worth of modern art had their most caustic opinions confirmed: it really is shit.

In Toronto, the Power Plant Gallery carefully preserved the finest specimens *Cloaca* produced, putting them in the freezer until Delvoye could package them for sale. *Cloaca's* digestive process is subject to the same sort of fluctuations as yours—it, too, has an average from which it sometimes deviates. If the food *Cloaca* eats falls within the margins its calibrators anticipate, the result is a nice, solid log. If the balance between protein, fat, carbohydrates, and fiber is off (or if there was an error in calibration), the result is constipation or diarrhea.

In Toronto, when *Cloaca* got diarrhea, a gloved attendant would scoop up the mess, take it into the bathroom, and flush it down the toilet.

The attendant didn't bag it up and throw it in the trash, or toss it out on the sidewalk. Flushing it down the toilet is what you're supposed to do with poop (at least, poop you can't get collectors to buy from you). Our parents spend much of the second and third years of our lives teaching us that poop doesn't go in the trashcan, garden, or garbage disposal. Poop goes in the toilet. That's why there are an estimated 350 million toilets in America today—many more than one per person. That's why Americans buy eight million toilets a year. That's why federal, state, and local investment in the wastewater infrastructure has been $250 billion since 1972. That's why, according to the EPA, over eleven trillion gallons of water are processed by sewage treatment plants every year.

That poop is automatically consigned to the toilet—even when it's picked up off an art exhibit, even when there are probably ten trashcans between the mess and the toilet, even when it's not even human poop—isn't just a quirk of modern culture. It's the culmination of millennia of sanitary conditioning. It's a reaction instilled by both nature and nurture, by parental instruction and social pressure, for our individual and collective protection—and, these days, for our oppression.

Let's start at the beginning.

A long time ago, before toilets, before urinals, before people paid $7 to see a machine do what they did in their bathroom that morning for free, human beings were wanderers. They lived off the land, hunting and gathering just as other animals did. Humans were not at the top of the food chain, as they are today— they were just a point in the circle of life. They took from the land, and pooped where they walked, and their poop returned to the land the resources they took. Organisms in the soil converted the poop into nitrates, and plants absorbed those nitrates as fertilizer, and it started all over.

Humans must meet three needs to survive: food, water, and shelter. About ten thousand years ago, agricultural skills had so advanced that humans could better attain all three by settling in permanent villages that allowed for shared resources and encouraged the specialization of labor. Now only some of the villagers were hunters, wandering around the countryside, pooping where they might. The rest stayed in and around their homes, dropping their poop in closer proximity to where they ate, drank, and slept. In and around these villages, poop began to accumulate.

And accumulating poop is dangerous.

For many forms of life, other species' feces is a reproductive vehicle. Many kinds of seeds pass undigested through an animal's system to disperse wherever the animal may poop; many kinds of parasite eggs, bacteria, and viruses use the same tactics. From tapeworms to typhoid, fecal contact is a disease vector—directly, if you take a bite of your afflicted neighbor's feces, or indirectly, through accidental ingestion (you step in poop, touch your shoe, and then eat without washing your hands), through water contamination, and through diseases carried by the insects and vermin that feces attracts. The more poop lying around, the bigger the potential threat.

Even if early village dwellers didn't know that poop could cause disease (a fact unknown until the 1850s) they knew that it smells bad. Poop is repulsive, and any vermin attracted to something so repulsive must be repulsive themselves. Just like modern ones, early villagers didn't want poop, its smell, or the vermin it attracts anywhere near them. To combat this, social codes arose to regulate the placement of poop.

For most early civilizations, acceptable places were rivers or ravines or even behind a bush, far from anyone's abode. This sequestered the poop from sight and smell—and, hopefully, from the village's food, shelter, and water (assuming they pooped downstream). As long as the ravine was deep enough for decomposition to occur before it filled up, the village was safe. As long as the river flowed swiftly enough to remove the poop faster than people could deposit it, the village was safe. In other words, as long as the method of sequestering enabled poop to disperse or decompose faster than the villagers could produce it, the village was safe.

An adult averages roughly a half-pound of excrement per day. Multiply that by the number of people in a community. Now contrast that to the amount of poop the community's sanitary management choices can disperse or decompose, and it's clear that as a population density grows, so too grows the threat from its accumulated poop. Its safety depends on being able to destroy poop faster than it can produce it. Once a population poops more than it can disperse or nature can degrade, a threat to health appears.

Sanitation is therefore vital for a community's survival: for the good of society, people need to put poop in its place. Taboos implement this imperative, and government enforces it. If you go outside and poop on the sidewalk, you'll be shunned or arrested —not because your half-pound of poop could bring an epidemic, but because society's health depends on keeping poop in its place. Individual dissent is intolerable because mass dissent would be catastrophic. One person pooping on the sidewalk because it's too much bother to walk to the ravine isn't going to bring plague upon the village, of course—but if each villager made that decision, the aggregate might.

This is the second duality of poop. It troubles the individual only until the moment it springs from its brown womb; then it becomes a problem for society.

Many societies knew that poop is more valuable as a fertilizer on the farm than it is in a ravine at the edge of town. Using poop as fertilizer returns humanity to its appropriate place as a link in the food chain. Eastern civilizations recognized this far more often than their Western counterparts. Unfortunately, Eastern cultures didn't know that human poop is only safe and sanitary for agriculture if it's properly composted.

(The composting process is simple: put poop in a pile and let it sit long enough for bacteria to convert it into nitrates and for organic activity to raise the temperature enough to kill lurking pathogens. Then spread it on your fields and enjoy your prize-winning tomatoes.)

As villages grew into cities, poop production inevitably outstripped cleansing capacity. Perhaps the ravine was too inconvenient, or perhaps the river dried up; whatever the reasons, when poop accumulated faster than it could be dispersed, the alternative to removing it was collecting it locally. Some societies restricted their poop to buckets or clay pots, but most eventually gravitated toward communal cesspools.

At its simplest, a cesspool is a hole in the ground. Cesspools span human history from the earliest settlements to pre-plumbing tenements in twentieth-century New York City. They proliferated because they're easy: dig a hole and put poop in it until it's full, and then either empty it or cover it and dig a new one. Conventional wisdom holds that burying poop is a good way to compost it, but that's not necessarily true—cesspools do not allow oxygen to circulate through the material, which limits the prospects of organisms that break the poop down and heat it up to destroy pathogens. Over the years, poop in a cesspool will eventually decompose, but in the meantime, it'll just leach into the lakes, rivers, and—to the chagrin of the 15,000 Londoners who died in an 1848–49 cholera outbreak—wells.

For cities whose residents would otherwise be pooping in alleys and behind buildings, cesspools are a good solution in the short run. In the long run, though, cesspools just concentrate a neighborhood's poop closer to where they eat, drink, and sleep, ensuring that today's solution will be tomorrow's epidemic. Some landowners, perhaps recognizing this, might line the cesspool with a leak-proof material. A lined pit is a privy-vault, named after the little house built above a cesspool for privacy and protection from the elements. (Privacy, in this case, meant protection from passing eyes—cesspools were often shared by families or neighbors, and privies often featured multiple seats.) Privy-vaults protect the environment and the groundwater, but the poop in them takes even longer to decompose. When pits were full, landowners relied on night-soil men to cart the putrid poop away; sometimes farmers bought it for fertilizer, but typically it was just dumped somewhere else.

Two forces have driven sanitary evolution: social crises and individual laziness. Usually, the latter causes the former. Whether littering or polluting or pooping, if people can break the rules to cut corners with little or no accountability, they will. It's not necessarily a problem when one person does it, but it is a problem when it becomes standard practice. The chamber pot, for instance, existed originally for urinary convenience, a receptacle for when it was too cold, rainy, or otherwise inconvenient to go to the privy. Kept under the bed to be emptied later, chamber pots are ill-suited for poop because nothing stinks quite like a fresh turd lying uncovered in a bowl. But just as cesspools were built to deal with those who couldn't (or wouldn't) go all the way to the ravine or the river to poop, those who couldn't (or wouldn't) go all the way to the cesspool spurred innovation by turning their lazy asses toward their chamber pots.

Night (Four Times of the Day), by William Hogarth, 1738.

Chamber pot use spurred further innovation in the form of the close-stool, a cabinet for a chamber pot, with a hole in the top so a user could squeeze one out while sitting. With a well-designed lid, a close-stool could ensconce the scent; sprinkling sawdust or ash on the mess helped. With the smell contained, the owner could empty the chamber pot at his convenience. But who has time to lug a brimming chamber pot all the way from the close-stool to the cesspool? Especially when there's a window so close by?

The histories of cities such as Paris, Edinburgh, and Cambridge are redolent with the stench of neighborhood cesspools, of endless rains of poop and urine from upper-story windows, of piles of garbage and dead animals and rotting food in the streets—of an utter lack of sanitation. These histories show the consequences of population growth outpacing crap-cleansing capacity. The Black Plague, for example: twenty to thirty million people across fourteenth-century Europe dead from an illness spread by fleas living on rats that thrived in filth. In contrast with epidemics to come, such as cholera and typhoid, fecal contamination was only an indirect cause of the Black Plague; nevertheless, proper sanitation management could have averted this holocaust. The end of the crisis came, unfortunately, not through improved sanitation, but through the elimination of 25–50% of the continent's poop-producing population.

Many large Western cities built municipal sewer systems, but before the nineteenth century, not for sanitation. Cities from ancient Rome to eighteenth-century London built sewers to combat flooding on poorly-drained streets. They were for rain, and for the poop, garbage, and dead animals the rain washed down, but not for household poop. (The rich and important were exceptions—wealthy neighborhoods and municipal facilities often had the privilege of connecting directly to the sewers, but most households stuck to cesspools.) Still, because they helped keep the streets clean, rain sewers gave a city a tremendous boost in its crap-cleansing capacity; had fourteenth-century European cities built sewers, the plague would have been much less severe.

This was the situation in America and England in the early eighteenth century: wastewater sewers helped keep streets clean in only the biggest cities, and people everywhere pooped in chamber pots, close-stools, or privies. Aside from the conveniences of the extremely wealthy, sanitary management hadn't progressed much between ancient Rome and the seventeenth century. But the Industrial Revolution changed cities and everything else. Rural workers inundated the cities. From 1750 to 1800, London grew by 300,000 people to nearly a million—and that million produced 500,000 pounds of poop a day. The accumulation of waste spiraled out of control as cesspools were overwhelmed. Cities like London became ideal breeding grounds for diseases like cholera, which is spread by fecal contamination of water. By 1854, London's population was well over 2.3 million, but a number of cholera epidemics had killed thousands at a time. Unlike during the Black Plague, however, this time sanitary innovation would save the masses—by subjugating them to the flush toilet.

The Flush Toilet: See No Evil, Smell No Evil

The Industrial Revolution changed the basis of the class structure from heredity to economics. Power had thitherto been concentrated among the gentry and royalty, whose ranks were nearly impenetrable to the low-born. The royalty maintained their power by convincing the masses that it was God-given; the rest kept it through economic might and brute force. But under capitalism, for the first time, the system that made one person rich could just as easily elevate another. And with opportunity achievable through sweat instead of just blood, the threat of God or the King's wrath could no longer keep the masses in check. The elite now had to differentiate themselves in other ways than money.

Thus the rise of capitalism begat meritocracy and a new form of the Protestant work ethic. Both concepts posit wealth as a reward for hard work—that if you wanted to enjoy life as those with money did, you had to work hard, as they had. The promise of social ascent through work oppressed as much as it seemed to empower, because it was the rich for whom the workers worked so hard.

But as the middle class grew, so did the worries of the elite. In late eighteenth- and early nineteenth-century England, so many were attaining comforts previously unknown in the slums that it was diluting the elitist advantage of wealth. More worrisome: if

Water closet design by Joseph Bramah.

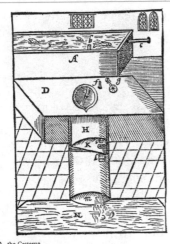

A. the Cesterne.
B. the little washer.
C. the wast pipe.
D. the seate boord.
E. the pipe that comes from the Cesterne.
F. the Screw.
G. the Scallop shell to cover it when it is shut downe.[53]
H. the stoole pot.
I. the stopple.
K. the current.
L. the sluce.[54]
M. N. the vault into which it falles: alwayes remember that (   )[55]
at noone and at night, emptie it and leave it halfe a foote deepe in
fayre water. And this being well done, and orderly kept, your worst
privie may be as sweet as your best chamber.

A design for John Harington's Ajax.

the pleasures of life were available to the masses, the masses might grow complacent and not work as hard for their bosses.

The elite realized it was in their best interest to make the gulf between the classes as wide and visible as possible—visible so the masses couldn't be happy with a mere middle-class existence, and wide so they'd never exceed one.

Cleanliness is next to godliness, and everyone wants to be next to God, something money makes easier. The elite in every culture have always tried to differentiate themselves from the rabble through the trappings of wealth—fancy clothes, fine perfumes, cultivated table manners, affected speech. But in the late eighteenth and early nineteenth centuries, as capitalism spread wealth wider than ever before, fears of the surging middle class forced the elite to continuously raise the bar. Their dress, food, and houses grew increasingly opulent and unattainable. When that wasn't enough, they developed exacting etiquette to pretend that more than money elevated them above others.

This Victorian ideal—known as such today because its heyday coincided with Queen Victoria's reign, from 1837–1901—could only be achieved by adhering to customs, morality, and etiquette that mandated the total denial of the sights, sounds, smells, and desires of the human body. The elite perfumed their bodies because the masses reeked of sweat. They powdered their faces white (or, after Queen Victoria declared makeup vulgar, ate chalk or drank vinegar or iodine) because the masses were tan from working in the sun. The masses pooped in communal outdoor privies, so the rich embraced the opposite extreme: private indoor rooms. The stench of shit permeated poor neighborhoods, so the rich filled their chamber pots with water to eliminate open-air logs. To sweat, to have bad breath, to burp, to show sexual desire or other strong emotion—all these were taboo because the Victorian elite identified them with the brute masses.

But the Victorians made a mistake: they believed their own propaganda. Soon it wasn't enough for masses to believe the elite didn't poop—the other elites had to believe the same thing. Before ceremonial balls, for instance, Victorian ladies took medicines to clean themselves out, because there were no toilets at the balls to contradict the Victorian worldview. To answer nature's call, a woman had to make excuses and take her carriage home. It was a problem of decorum outpacing technology: Victorian men and women could poop in odorless privacy in a water-filled close-stool, but standing up nevertheless revealed a floater just as repellent as those dropped by the servants who would be coming in shortly to collect it. Victorian etiquette taxed even its authors. Thus, as Dan Inglis points out in *A Sociological History of Excretory Experience*, the desire for an apparatus to hide feces existed well before the apparatus itself. But desire spurs demand. And fortunately for the Victorians, demand spurs innovation.

In the sixteenth century, a member of the court of Queen Elizabeth I named Sir John Harington had invented the Ajax, the first flushing toilet that used moving parts to remove the poop and refill the water tank. His invention didn't take off. Although some of the elite between the sixteenth and eighteenth centuries had systems that used water from cisterns to flush their chamber pots, those primitive water closets were prohibitively laborious to install and maintain. But in 1775, Alexander Cummings, an English watchmaker, recognized the economic potential for a functional flush toilet. Cummings drastically simplified Harington's design with a single sliding valve that emptied the bowl, released water from a cistern to clean it, and then refilled the cistern. This new toilet clearly had great potential, so other inventors jumped on the bandwagon. In 1778, Joseph Bramah converted the sliding valve to a hinge flap, simplifying the mechanism even further. By the turn of the century, Bramah's company had sold and installed over six thousand toilets across England.

Early toilets were cast-iron contraptions that flushed inadequately (leaving smears and clogs), and early plumbing couldn't keep smelly sewer gasses from creeping the wrong way through the pipes. Significant improvements came seventy-five years after Bramah, during the heart of Queen Victoria's reign. George Adamson incorporated siphonic flush-down, George Jennings improved on it, Thomas Crapper devised the pull-chain method for flushing, and Thomas Twyford encapsulated the whole system into porcelain for easy cleaning and sanitizing. While early toilets were by today's measures loud, inefficient, and hard to clean, they sufficed for those who wanted to poop and leave no evidence.

In England, the spread of flush toilets coincided with the modernization of the water infrastructure. In the past, water came through communal wells and pumps; now, for the first time, it was piped directly into the home. Water consumption skyrocketed as people enjoyed the benefits of washing, bathing, and flushing. Surprisingly, fresh-water infrastructures were usually installed before wastewater infrastructures. Early engineers usually tried to direct wastewater into cesspools, but flooding was the inevitable result. Engineers eventually realized that the water and waste had to go somewhere. This flooding and fears of "miasma" (disease-causing air emanating from stagnant water) eventually spurred wealthy households to connect their wastewater outputs to municipal drain systems.

Water went in, poop went into water, and water and poop went out. By the last third of the nineteenth century, the gilded throne of feudal monarchy had given way to the porcelain throne of Victorian morality. The Victorian demand for a seemingly impossible degree of fecal denial had engendered an infrastructure that could provide it. Now the affluent could emerge from their bathroom with no evidence left behind, as though they didn't poop at all. Social strivers now had one more thing to strive for. The rest, enveloped by the stench of their privies, close-stools, and chamber pots, could only stare in envy at the flush toilets they could never afford.

The Throne for the Common Man

Just as the poor and middle classes coveted the food, housing, and clothing of those who had better, so did they covet their fecal fastidiousness. But even to afford a toilet was not yet to afford the plumbing it required, and the lower classes had to continue squatting over communal facilities. And so the reek of their homes and clothes and asses served as a constant reminder of their place in the economic system. The toilet not only allowed the wealthy to realize their impossible fecal denial, but also served as yet another marker of class stratification.

Across the Western world, the Industrial Revolution was uprooting traditional population distribution. People from the countryside streamed into the cities in search of jobs at the new factories, and overcrowding followed. The slums were packed with people, industries, cow-sheds, slaughterhouses, and grease-boiling dens, all discharging their waste willy-nilly. The streets were toilets for horses; the sidewalk was a cesspool for upper-story chamber pots. Some neighborhoods had sewers, but these were often poorly built, leaching contaminants into wells and other water sources.

In the nineteenth century, the crap-cleansing capacity of the cities grew ever more strained as population densities skyrocketed. Tenements grew taller, and the poop-productivity of the slums soared with them. A number of great cholera outbreaks—including ones in 1831, 1849, 1854, and 1866—ravaged the west. The 1849 outbreak killed 35,000 in England and Wales beyond 15,000 dead in London alone. All over the Western world, as endless waves of migrants flocked to the cities for jobs, cholera followed. 2,200 people died in Quebec City in 1832, 8,000 in Havana in 1833, 5,000 in New York City in 1848–49, and 1,000 in Sacramento in 1850.

During London's 1854 epidemic, a doctor named John Snow proved the correlation between cholera and contaminated water by observing the death rate among Londoners around the Broad Street pump in Soho. As chronicled in Steven Johnson's 2006 book *The Ghost Map*, Snow painstakingly investigated the afflicted neighborhood during the very height of the epidemic, going door to door to learn where the sick and the dead in each house got their water. Working later with a local reverend named Henry Whitehead, Snow was even able to trace the contamination to its source: a woman named Sarah Lewis who had dumped the wash water from her sick daughter's soiled clothes into a cesspool in front of her house. That cesspool drained into the Broad Street pump's water supply.

In a perfectly equal society, poop threatens each member equally. But cities during the Industrial Revolution were far from equal. The wealthier neighborhoods, with much lower population densities, were clean and relatively sanitary. Most migrants settled in the poor neighborhoods, and the poor bore the punishment of the Industrial Revolution's poop. But tens of thousands of working men and women dying year after year does affect the high classes in one way: it's the workers toiling in the factories that earn profits for the owners. Thanks to Snow, Whitehead, and a number of other scientists and sanitary reformers, the upper classes now knew how to fix a major threat to their labor pool: replacing cesspools with modern, watertight sewer systems to separate poop from people and water supplies.

By the end of the nineteenth century, reforming the sanitary conditions of the poor became a pet cause of the English bourgeoisie. Led by people such as Edwin Chadwick and Octavia Hill, a movement grew to transfer the responsibility for clean water and sewage disposal from individuals to societies and governments. These sanitary reformers were probably genuinely concerned for the well-being of their less fortunate neighbors; the enthusiasm of the lawmakers and business and social leaders who joined them may have been motivated more by an understanding of the influence of sanitation on the unskilled labor force's numbers, and on the capitalist's bottom line.

Chief among the sanitary reformers' proposals was eliminating the dangers of leaching cesspools, open street-level gutters, leaky sewer pipes, and flying feces dumped from chamber pots, by instituting a system for the simple and efficient removal of feces: flush toilets in all homes, and the water and sewage system they necessitated. To save the population from the dangers of poop, the elite's fecal habits had to be disseminated across society. The English launched massive public works campaigns toward that end—there, the state engineered the spread of the toilet. Between 1859 and 1865, London city engineers led by Joseph Bazalgette built 100 miles of main sewers, 450 miles of interceptory sewers, and 13,000 miles of local sewers, using 318 million bricks and excavating 3.5 million tons of Earth in the process. And in the decades following London's last great cholera outbreak in 1866, the state legislated a number of provisions mandating the same kind of amenities for the working class that the middle and upper classes had long since embraced. By World War I, England was a toilet-based society.

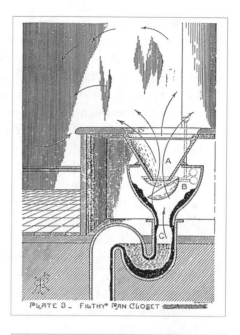

In the late 19th century, American scientists discovered the dangers of a weak sewage infrastructure. Images from Cyrenus Wheeler, Jr. "Sewers: Ancient and Modern; with an Appendix," a paper read before the Cayuga County Historical Society on December 14, 1886. From the Collections of the Cayuga County Historical Society.

In America, the fecal infrastructure was equalized across classes through a different process. According to Maureen Ogle in *All the Modern Conveniences*, the state wasn't initially involved. The vibrant sanitary reform movement in America, led by men such as John Griscom and Jacob Riis, concentrated mostly on the plight of the urban poor. More important in introducing the toilet across American society were the trends of optimism, faith in industry, and belief in family that swept the country in the mid-1800s. Improving domestic life was a cornerstone of these trends, and modern conveniences such as running water, dumbwaiters, and speaking tubes were eagerly adopted by the middle class as well as the rich. Soon they turned their attention to the backyard privy, built over cesspools that were, for obvious reasons, some distance from the house. To take advantage of running water and to save people the embarrassment of being seen walking to and from, Americans were soon feverishly constructing bathrooms adjacent to and even inside the house. Toilets and technology were imported from England at first, but American inventors provided an endless rush of innovation, resulting in a confusion of techniques and designs as more and more variations were rushed to market. The technology was faulty and inefficient, but Americans were caught up in the spirit of sanitizing their domestic experience. Across the country, flush toilets flourished.

Then came the Civil War. American optimism crashed, and faith in cold, hard science took its place. By the 1870s, scientists had started to look at the conveniences that had been installed in the previous decades, and they were horrified. Cheap pipes, defective faucets, faulty drainage, leaky gas traps, leaching cesspools: this was plumbing without science. The nation was soon awash in hysteria over the dangers of poor plumbing, the potential for disease built into everyone's homes. People began to realize that the problems earlier thought confined to the poor actually threatened the middle and upper classes, too. The laws of science, they realized, did not discriminate. Nor should the laws of man. The solution was public responsibility. Municipal governments received the mandate to enact plumbing laws and public health codes, and they did. By the end of the century, the water going into the house and the water and poop coming out were under stringent government regulation. The fecal infrastructure across America was standardized: rich or poor, urban or rural, no household was complete without a private bathroom and a flush toilet.

The flush toilet emerged to meet the ideological demands of the elite Victorians. In England, the state spread it to all classes to protect the labor supply. Although America took a different route—America's interest was in protecting the middle and upper classes from the dangers of bad plumbing—it reached the same place. In both countries, pooping practices were no longer the individual's private choice; they were in the government's purview. Private bathrooms and flush toilets were the will of the state.

And their will was done; today it's nearly impossible for us to imagine doing it any other way.

Sewers: Not in My Backyard

If the half-pound-per-day average is accurate, then Americans grunt out about 150 million pounds of poop every twenty-four hours. According to the EPA, 72% of the population is served by the 16,000 publicly-owned multi-million dollar wastewater treatment facilities around the county. So every day roughly 108 million pounds of poop are dumped into 32 billion gallons of pure drinking water and sent through 600,000 miles of publicly-owned sanitary sewage pipes to sewage plants that return the drinking water to circulation by separating out the original 108 million pounds of poop. It would be much easier and cheaper if the poop didn't have to be separated; and for a half-century of widespread water-sluiced sewage disposal, deciding that it did not was exactly how cities solved the problem.

Until the 1870s in America, household wastewater disposal was wholly the household's responsibility. Some houses used cesspools, some diverted their waste into nearby streams, and some built private sewer systems. Upon recognition of the noxiousness of America's abysmal plumbing infrastructure, the government instituted standards requiring urban household wastes to be channeled into municipal sewers.

In both England and America, sewer design assumed the then-predominant filth theory of disease. This theory, espoused by the great scientists and reformers of the first two thirds of the eighteenth century, held that the smells generated by rotting organic material—called "miasma"—were the cause of disease. But by the mid-nineteenth century, researchers such as Louis Pasteur were advocating germ theory, hypothesizing that microscopic filth-loving organisms caused disease. Though germ theory had firm experimental support by the 1870s, it didn't gain widespread acceptance until the 1890s. By that time, the damage was done: most municipal sewage systems had been engineered in accordance with filth theory, which held that it was enough to just channel sewage into moving water. The maxim of sanitary engineers: "The solution to pollution is dilution." To them, "dilution" meant municipal sewage systems that emptied directly into rivers, lakes, and oceans.

Some people saw folly in channeling a city's filth into its waterways, and many techniques arose to deal with the raw waste pouring through the city's sewers. The motivation, however, was almost always economic—the search for a profitable method for the conversion of rivers of poop into fertilizer. Attempts to mine this brown gold included chemical precipitation (introducing chemicals that combined with dissolved poop to form particles that could be strained from the water) and sewage farms (pumping uncomposted sewage directly onto farmlands to irrigate and fertilize them). But no one ever made it profitable. And since science hadn't yet repudiated sanitary engineers' maxim about dilution, downstream pollution ensued. This was, of course, a problem for cities downstream. Cities dutifully invested in water purification plants, which saved their drinking water, but beaches and waterways became cesspools, and the smell of sewage wafted along the streets once again.

By the early twentieth century, as germ theory took hold, the danger of dumping unprocessed sewage into waterways finally became clear: fecal contamination threatened the users of downstream water supplies with disease. Algae thrived on the nitrogen in poop, blocking sunlight from aquatic plants and consuming the oxygen other water creatures needed to live.

Supposed solutions to local sanitation crises had created regional ones, merely smearing the threat around instead of wiping it out.

Encouraged by environmentalists and sanitary reformers, state and national governments realized that it would be cheaper to treat sewage as it left a city than to suffer the environmental damage, disruption of the aquatic food chain, and poisoning of drinking water downstream. Cities slowly began putting treatment plants at the outflows of their sewer systems—a difficult and inefficient process, of course, because sewage treatment plants are an afterthought, not an integral part of the system. But they did their best, with impressive results. Most modern sewage treatment plants are multi-billion-dollar poop-processing behemoths. The North River wastewater treatment plant in New York City, for instance, processes 125 million gallons of wastewater every day during dry weather. Serving westside poopers from Greenwich Village to the tip of Manhattan, North River is built on a 28-acre reinforced concrete platform over the Hudson River. It opened in 1986, eliminating discharge of raw sewage into the Hudson for the first time in New York City's history. The roof of the structure is a state park, with three swimming pools, sports fields, an athletic center, a skating rink, and an amphitheater. Like most modern sewage treatment plants, North River processes sewage in a few stages: primary treatment that settles the water, secondary treatment by organic digestion, and finally, sterilization. Disinfected water is released into the Hudson, and leftover solids, after further organic digestion and dewatering, become concentrated sludge used as fertilizer.

Getting Water from Grime: Modern Sewage Treatment

Preliminary treatment uses screens or grinders to capture or macerate solids such as wood, Q-Tips, and dead alligators so that they don't muck up the works further down the line.

Primary treatment, the simplest, involves letting suspended solids settle. This treatment removes up to 70% of suspended solids, but leaves high levels of pathogens.

Water then flows to secondary treatment tanks for digestion by the organisms introduced here along with oxygen to help them thrive. Byproducts of this process (for example, methane) sometimes help power the plant. Leftover solids, in a concentrated form called sludge, are sequestered for further processing.

After secondary treatment, sewage water is still rich in concentrates of nitrates, phosphates, and other pollutants. Sadly, many plants say "good enough" and discharge such water into the environment. Other plants employ tertiary or advanced wastewater treatment, from ultraviolet light to sand filters, to finish the job.

Of the incredible volume of solids and liquids that enter sewage treatment plants each year nationwide, several billion gallons pass straight through, untreated, back into the water cycle. In some cases this neglect is by design; in others, it's unavoidable. To save money while building capital-intensive municipal sewage systems, many cities elected to combine their wastewater sewers with their drainage sewers. Consequently, rainfall channeled into the treatment plant is much more than it can handle. Rather than overload the system, cities divert the confluence of rain and sewage, untreated, into the water. New York City's fourteen treatment plants process 1.4 billion gallons of wastewater per day. An inch of rain falling on the 120,000 acres of city property served by combined sewers yields an additional 3.14 billion gallons. That's much more than the system can handle, which is why city officials advise against going to the beach the day after a heavy rain.

A sewage treatment plant removes solid contaminants from water, meaning that a lot of solids remain. This sludge is pumped into anaerobic digestion tanks that accelerate decomposition. First, raising the temperature creates a stimulating environment for bacteria to ingest the organic matter, and then raising it further kills the bacteria off. The process is similar to composting, and responsible municipalities dewater the sludge and sell it as fertilizer or apply it to depleted land. Less responsible municipalities bury it in landfills or burn it. In 1998, Congress wisely voted to ban dumping sludge at sea.

Sewage treatment is an expensive and impressive solution to a social crisis, and it's seemingly effective. City, state, and federal governments assure us that the treated water is pure and the sludge safely disposed of or recycled. This may tempt one to think that humanity has solved the problems of poop accumulation. After all, our cities no longer smell like poop, cholera epidemics are past, and the population poops compliantly, sanitarily.

But there's still a problem: sludge is dangerous.

If it were only poop, pee, and water flowing into sewage treatment plants, then we'd have a perfect waste disposal system. After all, it's easy to separate water from organic matter and convert the leftover sludge into fertilizer. But poop and pee can contain residual antibiotics, hormones, and other pharmaceutical chemicals. Household wastewater often includes paper products, blood, soapy water, bleach, Drano, paint, motor oil, and pharmaceutical compounds that have passed through the body. Worst of all, industrial waste regularly flows into the sewers—sometimes illegally, but sometimes with the municipality's blessing. Consequently, inorganic contaminants pass through the sewage treatment plant, discharged into waterways—or, worse, concentrated in the sludge.

What happens to those contaminants when the sludge is applied to the land? We don't know. Sludge fertilization concentrates a large amount of contaminants in a very small space. Farmers can use lime to maintain a pH balance that binds the toxins in the ground, keeping them from moving up to accumulate in plants and the animals that eat them, or down to accumulate in groundwater. Ensuring the right pH balance, however, requires work and oversight, and we've already seen how people tend to respond to situations requiring effort when accountability is negligible or nonexistent. One farmer's negligence might not cause an epidemic. But how long will isolated lapses take to add up to big problems? And what happens if a farmer moves on and no one maintains the pH balance on his land?

Our current system might be infusing concentrated contaminants into the food chain and water cycle at a rate of 108 million pounds of poop per day.

FIVE THOUSAND YEARS of history records the struggle of people and governments against ever-higher mountains of poop. As settlements grew into cities, and as food and water became more plentiful, social customs standardizing waste disposal begat laws regulating it; waste disposal technology advanced, and investment in infrastructure grew larger and larger. For the good of society, the urges of the individual came under the authority of the state. Today's infrastructure of private bathrooms, flush toilets, and sewers is the culmination of humanity's struggle against the personal and social ramifications of the urge to poop.

Our current system of sewage treatment indubitably is a drastic improvement over dumping untreated sewage into the water. That system indubitably was a huge improvement over neighborhood cesspools. And toilets indubitably are an improvement over close-stools and chamber pots. But the dissemination of modern sanitary practices isn't without some major disadvantages. The potential environmental impact is just one.

The psychological and sociological impact of the toilet is another. The toilet was designed to implement the Victorian mandate for fecal denial. Disseminated as a convenience and aid to hygiene, it is still an apparatus of ideology. The toilet and the bathroom conceal the sight, sounds, and smells of poop, making them everyone's dirty secret. Consequently, contemporary culture is a culture of fecal confusion. Everyone knows that everyone poops, but everyone poops using apparatuses designed to create the appearance that no one does. Our infrastructure makes invisible what our bodies make universal. A tremendous social contradiction is the result.

CHAPTER 2

THE SHAMING OF THE POO

"...AND STAY OUT!"

The heavy iron gate crashed shut. A deadbolt turned, footsteps faded; silence fell. Eve looked at Adam, shrugged, and picked up her suitcase. Adam lingered a wistful moment, then followed.

The rocky land beyond the Garden hurt their bare feet, and their new loincloths chafed. Exhausted after hours of wandering, they decided to stop—they'd only eaten a few bites of fruit that morning, and their hunger was unfamiliar and frightening. They gathered a meal of grass and weeds, set up their tent, and went to sleep.

Hours later, Eve woke with humanity's first stomachache. Exiting the tent, she looked at the stars, now seeming much more distant than they had in Eden. For the rest of time, humanity would be punished for the couple's surrender to temptation, knowing pain, hunger and thirst, and shame about our bodies.

Eve's stomach twisted. Still looking up, she squatted and brought forth from her fundament the foul of man. This brown serpent stank terrifically, and with all that roughage, it was tremendous. In the Garden, she and Adam had pooped, but they hadn't really paid much attention to it; it certainly had never been preceded by such pain nor pursued by such odor. This was embarrassing. In the Garden, it had never been embarrassing.

Eve listened to her breath, harsh and ragged in the back of her throat. A tardy fart squeaked out. Her mouth tasted like weeds. In the Garden, she hadn't noticed how repulsive her body could be. Now she crossed her arms self-consciously, wishing she'd sewn a few more leaves on her loincloth.

Eve slunk back into the tent. The smell followed. Adam, already jolted from sleep by those strange splutterings, gagged. Eve was mortified.

The next morning, Adam suffered his own ordeal with a malevolent serpent. But, wanting to avoid creating in Eve the kind of revulsion she'd caused in him, he excused himself on the pretext of stretching his legs and conducted his business over a rise, behind a bush, hoping she wouldn't see, hear, or smell that his poop was as shocking as hers was. Twenty-four hours out of the Garden, Adam and Eve were humanity's first shameful shitters.

A shameful shitter will choose the discomfort of postponing the answer to nature's call over the humiliation of being known to heed it. Taking no consolation from the knowledge that everyone poops, a shameful shitter thinks people will judge him or her because of the sounds and smells emanating from his or her butt, and will go to absurd lengths to prevent others hearing or smelling them. If you're not a shameful shitter, you've certainly encountered them: a pair of feet hiding in a stall, a figure at the urinal with no sounds of splashing, a pair of hands washing at the sink for far too long. On the toilet, a shameful shitter coughs or flushes to mask the sounds of shitting. Upon encountering a coworker in the office bathroom, a shameful shitter pretends she just came in to check her makeup. A shameful shitter waits in the stall silent and still, long after the business is done, until the bathroom clears out so she can exit unseen. A shameful shitter will refuse a stall next to an occupied one, for fear the person next door might recognize his shoes.

It seems reasonable to blame the behavior of shameful shitters on the toilet infrastructure and norms created to enable the Victorian denial of bowel function. But if infrastructure were the only influence, then everyone raised on Toto or Kohler or American Standard would be a shameful shitter. That's not the case. For all the shitters squirming in their cubicles, trying to hold it to the end of the day, just as many stride unabashedly across the office, entering bathrooms with newspapers and smiles. For every shameful shitter, there's a shameless shitter, responding to the nature's call in the most natural way.

POOP IN AMBIGUITY: THE RISE OF SHAMEFUL SHITTING

Consider a booger: in your nose, or on a Kleenex in the trashcan, benign. But on your lip, less than a centimeter from where it is benign, a booger gains the power to permanently contaminate you in the eyes of anyone who sees it. Pretend you're on a blind date. A booger on your lip, whether you put it there intentionally or not, makes you disgusting; no matter how fascinating or hilarious you've been, all your date will remember about you is the booger.

The anthropologist Mary Douglas wrote in her seminal 1966 book *Purity and Danger* that every culture categorizes things so that its members know to perceive them as in place or out of place. A leaf, a shoe, a hamburger—if it's in a place that your culture deems appropriate (on a tree, on a foot, on a plate), you might not even notice it. But when something is out of place—a hamburger strapped to someone's foot, or a shoe between two pieces of bread—you notice, and you don't like it. "Matter out of its place" has the power to contaminate, physically and symbolically, you wouldn't eat bread that came in contact with a shoe, and you would think a man wearing a hamburger on his foot is insane. Douglas rightly says that we see matter out of place as a threat (because if you get contaminated by it, other people might recategorize you).

Norms both reflect and reinforce a culture's categorizations of matter. One who throws away shoe-contaminated bread follows and expresses acceptance of the norm. The totality of one's responses to norms communicates one's place in, and attitude toward, society. Choosing to tuck or untuck one's button-down shirt, for example, communicates whether one is uptight or laid-back, and is a message that is understood by tuckers and untuckers alike. Getting multiple piercings in one's nose works the same way—a punk rocker and a society matron will disagree as to whether it's chic or disgusting, but both agree on the rebellion it represents.

For Douglas, the most basic classification of matter is the distinction between "self" and "not-self." That's why stimuli straddling that border, such as poop, urine, semen, gas, spit, mucus, hair, and fingernails, possess great power to contaminate—because they are so intimate. Only among intimates is one person's semen allowed to touch another; in any other circumstances, it would be an unforgivable breach of cultural etiquette or humiliating accident, and provoke an emotional response. That's why a little green booger placed gently on your steak would not only render the meat inedible (a physical contamination), but also elicit visceral anger and disgust toward the person who put it there (a symbolic contamination).

Everything has its culturally-determined place, pooping included. In contemporary American society, pooping's place is in private, on a toilet. If you poop in public, on the table, you'd be irreversibly contaminated in the eyes of others. Both of those examples are clear-cut. Problems arise from ambiguity—when a stimulus is not easily recognizable as in or out of place. What if you poop in your bathroom at home, in private, on the toilet, but your family in the other room can hear the flush, or your fart, or the plops? Or what if you poop in a public bathroom but with no door on the stall keeping passers-by from seeing you?

There's no ambiguity in the rule that pooping must take place in private, out of the sight, smell, and hearing of others. And if all toilets fulfilled this condition, there would be no problems. But a significant portion of the 350 million toilets in America are in schools, offices, churches, theaters, and other places of public accommodation, where the boundary between public and private is blurred and pooping occurs in a room appropriately sequestered from public space, but nevertheless within the sight, smell, and hearing of others. Because of the contradiction of these public bathrooms, people observing the behavior of poopers in public bathrooms are unsure about whether they are reinforcing social norms or violating them. From this uncertainty shameful and shameless shitting arise.

Ideology from Infrastructure

Eating from the Tree of Knowledge made Adam and Eve aware of their nakedness. With that knowledge, they grew ashamed of their bodies—not just their nakedness, but their whole flabby, smelly, farty, burpy, poopy bodies. In exile from the Garden, they instilled that shame in their children, and their children instilled it in theirs. No matter how historically reliable you find the Bible, the point remains that shame is so ingrained in the human psyche that its story is one of the first the Bible tells.

Sources of shame vary from era to era and culture to culture. In some cultures it's a source of shame that one's nipples show through one's shirt; for others, it's just as shameful for one's ankles to show under one's robe. While there are no universal sources, shame exists in all cultures.

Shame in our culture occurs when the body defies the will of the soul in violation of a norm—when a manifestation of one's animal nature is out of place. A verbal gaffe, an escaped fart, an inopportune erection— these uncontrollable actions are the triumph of animal nature over civilized will. Shame is the awareness of others' awareness of a contaminating and disgusting act.

To a shameful shitter, the sights, smells, and sounds of pooping are contaminating. A shameful shitter believes that someone seeing, smelling, or hearing them would disgustedly categorize the person who created them as contaminated. So the shameful shitter strives to avoid pooping in places where others might see, hear, or smell it. There are degrees of shameful shitting: while some might only

Automatic disinfecting closet.

Close-stool disguised as a pile of books.

avoid office bathrooms, others will feel too humiliated to buy toilet paper or talk to the doctor about rectal health problems. God forbid that an extreme shameful shitter should get a hemorrhoid!

At the height of the Victorian era, pooping was less ambiguous: since the sounds and smells of the human body belonged solely to the lower classes, creating them was a contaminating act. This norm long preceded the flush toilet. Until the flush toilet, even for the most pretentiously wigged and powdered nobleman on the most lavishly gilded and jeweled close-stool, standing up after bearing down would inevitably reveal a stinking log, a reminder that he was no less animal than the filthy servant boy who must clean it up.

Before the flush toilet arrived in the late eighteenth century, the English pooped in chamber pots, close-stools, or privies. While chamber pots and close-stools were used inside the house, and the privy was typically separate from the house, none of these necessarily afforded total privacy. Pooping was almost communal. The poor could little afford to waste precious living space for periodic acts of excretion, so chamber pots or close-stools were used in the presence of parents, spouses, and children. A privy was shared between multiple families, and usually featured more than one seat. Even for a rich person with a private room for defecation, the product was still there when he or she stood up, and somebody was going to have to do something about it. Before the toilet, for all classes, shit was a stinky, inescapable fact of life.

Because of the unprecedented class mobility in Victorian England, the elite embraced hygiene as a class differentiator with new enthusiasm. The rich were clean and fresh-scented and above their animal proclivities. The poor were filthy, smelly, and ruled by their bodies' desires. The bourgeoisie associated the disgusting body with the lower classes, and anyone fancying himself upwardly mobile had to comply. But in England, the importance of a healthy labor supply made correcting the noxiously unsanitary conditions of the poor more important than retaining poop as a marker of class stratification. To bring the rabble up to their moral and hygienic standards, the Victorians instilled their values along with their sanitary technology. Pooping, peeing, sex, spitting, cursing, table manners, body odor—whereas once the upper classes used these to distance themselves from the masses, they now used them to distance the masses from their former selves. Consequently, where Victorian morals, etiquette, and taboos were once unique to the elite, they were now aspirations for all of society.

In America, in contrast, the potentially catastrophic sanitary conditions of the middle and upper classes forced the state to instill bathroom standards. But just as in England, novel etiquette and morality accompanied the new infrastructure. In *All the Modern Conveniences*, Maureen Ogle writes that Americans "produced etiquette, grooming, and deportment books by the dozens during the nineteenth century." Some of this American etiquette mimicked Victorian etiquette, including the decorum surrounding poop—fecal denial grew just as prevalent in American society as in English. Despite the centrality in the national dialogue of toilets and plumbing, as Ogle says, "[The etiquette books] had little, in fact almost nothing, to say on the subject of plumbing etiquette."

So in both countries, moral reform accompanied sanitary reform, and Victorian fecal denial formed the basis of the pooping infrastructure. The state and other ideological apparatuses (churches, schools, etiquette guides, magazines, etc.) encouraged people to accept flush toilets by vilifying those who didn't. To poop in a close-stool, a chamber pot, a privy, or any other outmoded plumbing was to be savage; to refuse the flush toilet was to hang back with the brutes and slow society's progress toward a new era. Re-education worked. By World War II, flush toilets and private bathrooms were nearly ubiquitous, and the ideology behind them was almost universal.

It's hard to recognize the toilet as an ideological tool because it seems like such a natural part of our lives. But it is. It is because of the toilet and the bathroom being the way they are that we view pooping as private. That's not to say that pooping *shouldn't* be private; it's just to say that understanding the role of poop in society requires recognition of the huge influence of the toilet on that role. The flush toilet, with its roots in fecal denial, is one of the main causes of the confusion about pooping in our society. Some people think its purpose is sanitary, and others think its purpose is to facilitate fecal denial.

What exactly is the ideology of fecal denial? Fecal denial associates pooping with savagery. It doesn't mean that poop doesn't exist;

far from it. Fecal denial is predicated on the fact that *other* people poop—the filthy poor, the filthy animals, the filthy foreigners. Rather, it is denial that the person in denial poops. Because he associates pooping with savagery, he doesn't want anyone to know that he poops. Fecal denial means so vilifying the poop of others as to preclude acceptance of one's own. Fecal denial is not shameful shitting. Fecal denial is an extreme ideology; shameful shitting is a worldview influenced by fecal denial, among other things. Fecal denial condemns anyone who poops, while a shameful shitter might wish he could poop like everyone else (but is simply too embarrassed to do so). There are degrees of shameful shitting, and fecal denial is just one of the influences working on the mind of the shameful shitter.

It is ambiguity about poop that makes some people shameful and some shameless—and it remains such because fecal denial makes clarifying the ambiguities surrounding poop as taboo a subject as poop itself.

IN THE 1950S, Lucy and Ricky Ricardo slept in separate beds. In 1952, Lucy got pregnant, but television censors wouldn't let them use that word. In 1960, Jack Paar briefly quit *The Tonight Show* because NBC censors cut a joke featuring the words "water closet." During this era, sex and other bodily functions were hidden, unsuitable for public discourse. Then came the '70s. Archie Bunker shocked the country, first with his bigotry and then with the first broadcast of the sound of a flushing toilet. In 1972, the title character of *All in the Family*'s spinoff *Maude* had an abortion. In 1977, viewers saw the first openly gay recurring character, on *Soap*. 1986 featured the first mention of a condom. The '90s brought us lesbian kisses, bare asses, and babies out of wedlock. By the turn of the millennium, no topics were too private to discuss on television— menstruation, masturbation, fetishes, to name a few. Shows such as *South Park* seemed to exist just to see how far they could push the envelope.

This timeline illustrates the changing boundaries between public and private. In the '50s, to imply a sexual relationship even between married characters was inappropriate; today, sexual details are part of the public dialogue, from sitcoms to presidential politics. The repression of the body in public that peaked during the Victorian era has relaxed considerably. Poop, however, has been mostly exempt from this new candor. Television cameras will follow their subjects into the bedroom eagerly, but a closed bathroom door tends to stay closed. To watch two beautiful people steam up the bedroom on *The Real World* is titillating but no longer shocking; to join either of the same two people as they steam up the bathroom, on the other hand, would be scandalous.

To be sure, poop does appear regularly in contemporary culture. The wit in *Seinfeld* often revolved around the toilet. But most manifestations of poop in culture are highly sensationalized, used for humor, satire, or shock value. Realistically quotidian representations of pooping are rare—poop and pooping are almost always shown symbolically. Friends and family do broach the topic with relative ease among themselves, but the laughter that typically accompanies such discussions shows the unfamiliarity of frankness about this topic. While sexuality has come out, the everyday act of pooping is still in the (water) closet, benighting attempts to resolve the ambiguities that encourage shameful shitting.

WHAT MAKES A SHITTER SHAMEFUL?

It's 10:30 a.m. and the two cups of coffee you drank have reached your colon. Caffeine is a laxative; gravity and peristaltic action have sent it crashing into the poop in your colon to work its magic. Your bowel loosens and your stomach begins to cramp, and what was formerly the dormant remnant of last night's hamburger is now a churning, fibrous mess that demands immediate exit.

But the unrelenting muck in your bowels can't overcome the unmovable block in your psyche. You're a shameful shitter. To reach the bathroom, you'd have to walk past the receptionist's desk; and then twenty minutes later, with sweat on your brow, you'd have to walk by her again. She'd know what you had been doing in there. You can't stomach that kind of humiliation, so you're going to hold it until you get home—eight hours from now.

For so many Americans to routinely endure such discomfort, the forces at work in the shameful shitter's psyche must be powerful indeed. Just as every person's poop is made unique by different diets, metabolisms, and environmental influences, and yet still can be immediately identified as poop, so too vary the causes and manifestations of shameful shitting. But the shame has two main influences. The first is the Victorian infrastructure designed to deny that poop exists—a task today's shameful shitter identifies as its principal purpose.

The second influence is the widespread misinterpretation of instinctive fecal aversion.

Stink and Instinct

It wasn't a good night for Eve. As if suffering Montezuma's revenge five thousand years before he was born were not traumatic enough, she faced the humiliation of having totally grossed out fifty percent of Earth's human population. As Adam pretended to sleep, his eyes still wide in shocked disgust, Eve pretended to believe he was sleeping while she wondered what was wrong with her and what Adam must think of her. But as they lay there, the stench hanging over them both and Eve whimpering because toilet paper hadn't been invented yet, Adam's stomach began to churn and boil, just as hers had moments before. He didn't let on, though; he recognized her humiliation, and it was an experience he wished to avoid. So he bit his lip and endured the pain that night, and pooped in secret the next morning; and the next time Eve had to go, she hid her pooping, too. And so it went. Each believed the other's disgust was accompanied with condemnation. Eventually they came to know that each was pooping as repugnantly as the other; but instead of realizing that they were both normal, they both felt like aberrations.

Why should such an egalitarian act be so revolting? All people poop—so shouldn't we view pooping as neutral, a shared human experience, unremarkable because universal? No, because poop is disgusting—not by any cultural standard, but by instinct. While it's unnatural to feel like a social aberration because you poop, it is natural to find poop disgusting. Fecal aversion is the belief that poop is malodorous, gross, and untouchable. Studies of cultures at all levels of development have found this to be a universal human view. To understand why, one must first understand the basics of disgust.

The science of disgust starts with the reflex of distaste. When something tastes bad, our tongues extend, our noses wrinkle, our upper lips curl, we feel nausea, and we're compelled to get that taste out of our body, whether by spitting, gagging, coughing, or barfing. This set of responses is instinctive and independent of culture. Babies exhibit distaste, which shows that it's nature, not nurture. Distaste is a reflex based strictly on sensation.

Disgust is more than a reflexive response to sensation. It is based on the stimulus' position as matter out of place, so it requires knowledge of the culture's classifications of matter. A good example is discovering that a cook spat in your hamburger. You may not have tasted it, or it might even have tasted good; but once you know you've eaten it, your body will immediately go through all the motions of distaste in order to purge your palate, as though it had tasted bad. This appropriation of one bodily process by another is called exaptation. (Another example of exaptation is speech. The human tongue and mouth evolved as eating and breathing organ structures; their shape and form happened to be able to make articulated and repeatable noises as well. As the human brain advanced, the noises the mouth could make were "exapted" for use in spoken communication.) Disgust, then, exapted the body's instinctive response to something that tastes bad to condemn something that *means* bad.

Things that *mean* bad are usually culturally determined. While Americans might retch at the idea of eating duck tongue, many Chinese would salivate. According to psychologist Paul Rozin, one of the leading scientists of disgust, only a small set of stimuli are universally disgusting—that is, universally found to *mean* bad even if they don't taste bad. Included in "core disgust" are bodily secretions out of place, but also diseased people, certain creatures such as rats and maggots, and rotting flesh. Degrees of the strength of core disgust vary by individual (if you drop your wedding ring in the toilet, for instance, you're probably going to overcome your aversion to poop water) and by culture (poop fresh and steaming on the dinner table is going to bother an elderly Victorian duchess much more than it will a macho construction worker), but Rozin has confirmed that the core disgust stimuli evoke disgust across all cultures. Neither the Victorian matron nor the construction worker, for example, would take a fork and knife to that poop.

Disgust evolved to protect us from dangers that didn't necessarily offend the senses. A spitburger may taste just fine, but since another person's spit is contaminating, we want to purge it the same way we'd purge something that tastes bad. Stimuli within core disgust may not even trigger distaste. Freud noted that babies and toddlers don't find the smell of poop repulsive, and will even play with and eat it. Rozin can explain this: babies don't find stimuli within core disgust repulsive because they have not learned their culture's order and classifications of matter.

Rozin has identified a commonality among core disgust stimuli: they're all edible, organic, and contaminating substances. Disgusting stimuli that don't meet those three criteria have been socially contrived to be disgusting, even though they evoke an equally visceral response. Piercing your nose and marrying your first cousin are not reviled universally across all cultures, only some. Cultures instill this kind of disgust not to protect your body, but to protect your soul. In other words, society appropriates core disgust to inculcate morality. A nose ring represents rebellion; to those who believe that rebellion violates norms, a nose ring is disgusting.

Parents, teachers, church, and other ideological apparatuses instill socialized disgust to get us to reject stimuli that threaten the values of their culture. Socialized disgust can be outgrown by rejecting the values of one culture (say, cheerleader culture) in favor of another (punk, for instance).

Fecal aversion is part of core disgust. Shameful shitting may arise from mistaking fecal aversion for socialized disgust: the belief that poop is a moral as well as physical threat. If it is, then poop is at odds with your culture. Therefore, you don't want others who share your culture to find out that you poop.

Socialized disgust protects us from moral threats. Core disgust protects us from physical threats. If poop is an object of core disgust, it must be a physical threat. But how could something that comes out of your own body be a physical threat to you? Why would your body create something that could hurt it?

The answer is that it doesn't. Your own poop can't hurt you, but everyone else's can. Poop harbors bacteria and viruses that thrive in it and pass on to other hosts through fecal contamination. Poop attracts insects and vermin. Poop represents the presence of another person, and one of the most basic human instincts is to see other people as a threat—not only because they might attack you, but because they also may have diseases to which you haven't been exposed.

But your own poop can't hurt you. You can't catch any disease from your poop that you don't already have. Your own poop doesn't represent the danger of another person or tribe—it only represents you. You feel this every day. Knowing that a poop in the toilet is yours tempers the disgust you would feel if it were a stranger's. That's why few of us are as repulsed by the smell of our own farts and the sight of our own poop as we would be by those of others'.

Your own poop, to your instincts, is not disgusting. Your poop, your sweat, your spit, your semen, your tears—any revulsion you feel toward these is socialized, not instinctive. We aren't much repulsed by the smell of our own farts or the sight of our own poop because we know instinctively that it's not a threat. Disgust requires knowledge; knowing the poop is our own, we aren't disgusted. Those who say they are disgusted by their own have been socially conditioned to feel that way. They have learned to condemn poop as a moral and not merely physical threat—which is why they try to hide the signs of their own need to do it.

In *Civilization and Its Discontents*, Freud wrote, "in spite of all man's developmental advances, he scarcely finds the smell of his own excreta repulsive, but only that of other people's." Freud, too, seemed to think that disgust at one's own poop is learned, and that lack of disgust at one's own is an inner rebellion against society. Unless someone worries that his lack of disgust at his own poop might indicate an antisocial pathology—that's another path to becoming a shameful shitter.

Other Sources of Shame

The ideological design of the bathroom and the toilet, coupled with misinterpretation of fecal aversion, account for much of the influence on a shitter's status as shameful or shameless. But just as each poop is a unique snowflake, so too is each person's attitude toward pooping an amalgamation of countless conscious and unconscious influences. It's impossible to name all that might influence a person's psychological outlook toward pooping, but here are a few of the more common ones.

Toilet training. As Freud teaches us, the actions and attitudes of the parents during toilet training resonate throughout the child's life. A shameful parent may consciously or unconsciously instill his or her outlook in the child during this time, but a rebellious child may gravitate toward shamelessness precisely to defy her parents. Toilet training's influence on shameful or shameless shitting is tempered by all the other stimuli influencing the child's psyche and his relationship with his parents; the subject will be discussed in greater detail in Chapter 5.

Fears of vulnerability. You know that the office bathroom is perfectly safe, but your instincts may abandon only with difficulty the feeling that you are squatting behind a bush on the savanna with hungry lions and other enemies prowling around. Feelings of vulnerability during elimination are adaptive, because once you start, it's extremely hard to stop. While no one really thinks a saber-toothed tiger is lurking in an adjacent stall, the instinctive awareness of vulnerability still makes it difficult to relax—for some people, it's easier to just wait and drop their dook in the psychological safety of home.

Mysophobia. It may be gleaming white porcelain, but there's still no telling what germs are growing on a public toilet. For some people, it's just not worth the risk. Technically, mysophobia—fear of germs—isn't shameful shitting, but its symptoms are often indistinguishable.

Psychological trauma. Perhaps you pooped your pants in front of your kindergarten, and everyone laughed at you. Such gaffes can scar you for life. If you associate poop with humiliation, you're going to do all you can to avoid a repeat performance—no pooping at the office for you.

School bathrooms. It's an academic no-man's land. There are no prying eyes to see who's smoking, who's skipping class, and who's getting beaten up. From doorless stalls to bullies gone wild, the school bathroom is a major source of trauma that easily mutates into a fear of public bathrooms going far beyond grade school.

An Unhealthy Way to Live

Whatever the causes, a shameful shitter values mind over splatter. For him or her, it's more important to poop in the right place than to poop at the right time. Thus shameful shitters lead their lives holding it in. Psychologically, shameful shitting can cause stress, alienation, and (should things go wrong) more humiliation than is avoided by shamefully slinking around. Should the dam break, ridicule and ruined underwear ensue. Even worse, extreme shameful shitters can suffer permanent physical damage.

The human body is, of course, designed to hold it in. The rectum is built with kinks that buttress the impatient poop, keeping the full pressure of an impending load off the sphincter. But when the body wants to poop, it has good reason—it's time to expel. The longer the load stays in the body, the more water may be drawn out. The drier it gets, the harder it is to pass. Soon psychological constipation has become physical.

Constipation can lead to a vicious circle of health problems. Many Americans suffer hemorrhoids, which can result from straining so hard to poop as to cause a vein in the anus or lower rectum to bulge out. Hemorrhoids can be excruciating, and severe ones can take the form of prolapsed cauliflowers of flesh protruding from the anus.

Many Americans treat their constipation with laxative drugs or enemas. Both help soften the stool to move it along. But idle peristaltic muscles grow weak, necessitating more laxatives, exacerbating the muscle weakness. Too often, laxative and enema abuse allow peristaltic muscles to atrophy, leading to severe bowel impairment and nasty surgeries.

Even when not enduring the pain of ignoring increasingly frantic calls from the colon, getting constipated, or ruining their shorts and reputations, shameful shitters are worrying that they're one bean burrito away from any of these. It's a stressful life.

UNTIL THE PRIVATE TOILET spread across Western civilization, pooping was often a semi-public experience. People did it in neighborhood privies or on the side of the road, sitting or squatting, knowing that at any moment a neighbor or stranger might walk in and say "hi" and complain about how much taxpayer money was spent on that damned Louisiana Purchase. On cold nights people would roll out of bed and squat over the bedroom chamber pot, in full view of spouses and children, who wouldn't care, because pooping was unremarkable. The shared privy and the unhidden chamber pot were culturally approved. The mandate of fecal aversion is aversion to poop out of place, not to poop per se.

The Victorians went far beyond fecal aversion to put themselves in a straitjacket of etiquette. The flush toilet specifically served their unattainable standards—the influence of Victorian etiquette is inseparable from the infrastructure. Although recent years have seen the private body grow more public, the bonds constraining poop are as tight as before, leaving its role ambiguous. Vestiges of Victorian etiquette suffice to make discussing the problem as taboo as the act itself. We all agree on pooping's place, but we're forced to determine for ourselves the acceptability of the sights, sounds, and smells that accompany it. When the conflict between the shameful and the shameless is finally resolved, pooping will be unworthy of angst, meriting as little ceremony as eating or drinking. That's what it means to be a shameless shitter. You aren't an exhibitionist or a pervert—you simply feel the urge to poop, and you do it, and you feel better. If it sounds easy to you, then you're not a shameful shitter—because for the shameful shitter, this simple act is fraught with psychological trauma.

Can our society clarify the role of poop and create Pootopia, a society of shameless shitters? It can, but only by clarifying the norms about pooping in public toilets. Only when we understand the toilet as a sanitary, not ideological, apparatus, and poop as a physical, not moral, threat, will society be freed from the tyranny of the bowel. Rise up and join the Brown Revolution!

CHAPTER 3

RITES OF PASSAGE: TECHNIQUES AND TOOLS

IT BEGINS AS A DISTANT SENSATION, a mere slight pressure among the many stimuli your brain is processing, firmly but unobtrusively present in your subconscious. It grows, first hinting, then nagging, and finally demanding attention. Steadily, inexorably, the hierarchy of your body's needs, wants, and desires upends as this sensation works its way to the top of your consciousness. Lying on the couch, watching your favorite show? Not important. Sitting in the boardroom, presenting to the CEO? That can wait. Standing at the altar, exchanging your vows? There will be another chance. The longer you wait to answer nature's call, the more it will usurp your priorities, appropriating mental resources and processes one after another until your ass commands your brain's exclusive focus. The longer you wait, the less you care about such things as work, the law, and the safety of others. Ultimately, it becomes impossible to think. All you can do is doo. Right now, dear reader, I'm asking you to do something different. Get up and go to the bathroom. Right now. But don't doo. Instead, this time, think.

There are nearly 300 million Americans, and there are 1,440 minutes in a day. Assuming for the moment that each American poops once a day at times evenly distributed over the twenty-four-hour period, then as you head to the bathroom right now, so do 208,000 of your countrymen and—women. All across America, people have stood up and grabbed books or magazines or handheld gaming devices. 208,000 belts unbuckle and 208,000 asses swivel.

Here is when unity in action dissolves. The vast collective soul that entered the bathroom in unison undergoes one schism after the next. The trunk of parallel experience splinters into branches of techniques, and each branch splits further as individuals position themselves for the function, execute it, and clean up after it. 208,000 Americans answer the same urge every second, but not in the same way. The unsuspecting are shocked to discover that other techniques exist—first, that people do things differently at all; and second, that the differences are so big.

Before the state mandated the private bathroom and flush toilet, children grew up with people pooping all around them. Potty training was much more informal. Kids didn't need to be taught that grown-ups pooped in the grown-up chamber pot—they'd been seeing their family do it all their lives. They'd seen their neighbors and total strangers in the communal privies. They didn't have to be taught what to do behind closed doors, because the doors had never been closed to them. But once the act moved into the private bathroom, children could no longer just pick it up; parents had to teach them.

But that teaching, too, took place behind closed doors, so that, through the generations, variations in bathroom techniques evolved without meaningful points of comparison or convergence.

Once the bathroom door closes, the behavioral similarities end. One person's pooping technique, from posture to cleanup, may completely befuddle another. As bathroom technology has evolved, minor variations in techniques have led to wild dissimilarities in behavior. Today, we all use the same equipment—but within regions, neighborhoods, and even families, with amazing variance.

So enter the bathroom and go through the motions. Sit as you would normally sit, wipe as you would normally wipe. Think about what you do, and why. Then read on. While you're not the only one who does it that way, you'll be surprised at how many other ways others are doing it.

SIT DOWN AND OPEN UP

You're in the bathroom. Your butt is bared. And there is the object of your mire, gaping like a baby bird waiting for its mother to feed it. Your belt is open, your pants are down, and your ass is

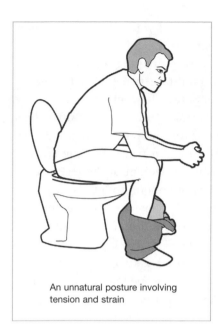

An unnatural posture involving tension and strain

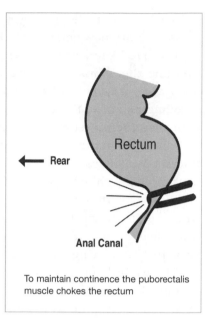

To maintain continence the puborectalis muscle chokes the rectum

The relaxed, natural squatting posture

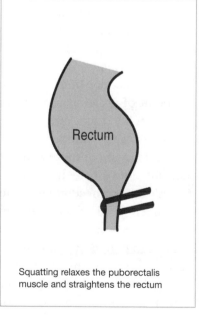

Squatting relaxes the puborectalis muscle and straightens the rectum

Sitting Versus Squatting. Illustrations by Gregg Einhorn.

swiveled. All that's left is for you to aim. If you're like most Americans, you are now going to sit down on the toilet.

If you're like most Americans, you're pooping wrong. The rectum and the sphincter evolved to facilitate two tasks: to release poop when it's appropriate, and to retain it when it's not. In the standing position, the rectal cavity folds into three baffles that help keep the pressure of an impending poop off your sphincter. Only in the squatting position do these baffles withdraw so that the rectal cavity earns its name. The full weight of the feces bears down on the sphincter, which obligingly opens to let it out.

When you're standing, the rectal baffles are fully extended; when you're squatting, they're fully retracted. When you're sitting, they're open about halfway. Feces can pass through, but impeded. That's why pooping can be such a struggle.

There's little mainstream science on proper pooping position. Among the alternative health communities, however, there is little doubt: pooping while sitting is a scourge on Western civilization. They point to the sitting toilet as a cause of ailments including appendicitis, hemorrhoids, irritable bowel syndrome, diverticulosis, colorectal cancer, bladder incontinence, and prostate cancer—all, they claim, rare in cultures that use squat toilets. Their reasoning: feces that isn't completely evacuated in the sitting position can grow stagnant in the colon; straining during defecation increases blood pressure in the anal veins to the point of prolapse; and straining during defecation causes the perineum to bulge out, stretching and damaging pelvic nerves that control the bladder, the prostate, and other organs.

While many of these ailments have also been attributed to the high-fat, low-fiber, junk-rich American diet (which certainly doesn't help), anecdotal evidence suggests that squatting leads to full, timely, and stress-free elimination, and helps relieve hemorrhoids. But squatting takes a strong pair of legs, sitting is more comfortable, and our infrastructure is clearly biased—even if you wanted to squat, the toilets we've got don't make it easy.

Unlike most of the problems with our contemporary toilet infrastructure, this one isn't completely on the Victorians' hands. Examples of close-stools and privies designed for sitting have been found as far back as the Roman and Sumerian civilizations.

To have a sitter, all you need is the money to build one and a place to put it; still, since real estate has always been precious and holes have always been cheaper than chairs with holes, sitting facilities were historically more of a luxury than a standard convenience. What we can blame the Victorians for is creating a social requirement that all households dedicate both the space and money to a sitting-based pooping infrastructure.

Until the beginning of the twenty-first century, the western shores of England were the last frontier of proper pooping. The further east of that line one traveled, the greater the likelihood of coming across squatting-based facilities grew. But the ratio of squatters to sitters has dramatically declined as globalization has spread Western facilities wherever tourists and businessmen travel. Consequently, Americans are much less likely to return from Eastern countries with horror stories of primitive toilets; Easterners are, however, much more likely now to tell horror stories of colon disease.

Of all the variations in pooping procedure, defecation posture is the most consistent in America; unlike other bathroom behaviors, it is less likely to vary by family than by culture. The stereotype of the Western sitter finds him leaning slightly forward on the seat, poised to read the morning paper. So unless you were potty trained by foreign-born parents or new-age hippies, that's probably how you've ended up. There are only a few minor variations:

Flat Footed. This is standard practice: two cheeks on the seat, two feet on the floor.

Raised Feet. To make the angle between torso and thighs more acute, mimicking the squat to unkink the rectum, some sitters raise their legs on their toes, or even place their feet on a stool.

Seat Squatting. Even in a nation of sitters, some pay more attention to their bodies' design than to their bathrooms'. Some modern toilet squatters perch precariously with two feet on the seat, and others build or buy special platforms to convert their sitter.

WAYS OF WIPING

And so you've swiveled, you've pointed, you've unclenched some muscles and clenched tightly on others, and the focal point of your entire awareness is poking out of your anus. It's like a baby leaving the womb, and its cries of pain are filling your nose. And so it dangles, caught in limbo between colon and water, a battle between gravity and structural integrity. And then gravity wins, and the bough breaks, and down tumbles baby—a plop and a splash, and you are unburdened.

All immediate physical urges have passed. But solid waste is not entirely solid. It's 75% water, and coated with mucus secreted by your colon to reduce friction, helping you ease your load through your puckered hole. Both substances tend to leave their mark on the faucet through which your poop just dripped. Experience teaches us that a good wipe now will eliminate discomfort later: that itch more irksome than any wedgie, and those telltale brown streaks, betraying your dirty ways to anyone who sees your dirty laundry. So you reach for the toilet paper.

The duration and intensity of wiping required depend on two factors: pooping posture and poop consistency. When squatting, one's cheeks spread clear, wide enough to avoid any smearing of the sides; with a respectably solid log, wiping is little more than formality. When sitting, however, the cheeks are closer together and pressing on the anus, which puts the starship in danger of bumping the docking bay doors. Poop consistency, the other factor, is a function of diet and environment. Certain foods initiate particular variations in texture: high-fiber diets result in clean, cohesive logs, for instance, while spicy foods induce quite the opposite. Diarrhea and other bowel problems are more prevalent in unsanitary environments, and evidence of contaminated food or water will manifest in your pants. Messy splatters require much sanitary attention, even sometimes for those who squat.

The body predates both toilets and toilet paper, and is intended to function without either. Before toilet paper, many people simply used a hand; others used leaves, discarded sheep's wool, coconut shells, and even snow. Sitting's historical exclusivity implies that the masses usually squatted, and that wiping was more common among the sitting classes. History is littered with the extravagancies of the wealthy wiper: lace, wool and rosewater, and even the downy neck of a goose.

But as sitting became more common, so too did the messes left behind, and so too did the economic reward for providing comfortable, affordable wiping products. A decade before Thomas Twyford made the toilet easier to clean by encasing it in porcelain, the Gayetty firm of New Jersey produced the first modern toilet paper to provide that same ease of cleaning to our beleaguered bungholes. For fifty cents, users purchased five hundred sheets of Gayetty's aloe-soaked "Therapeutic Paper" for their cleaning comfort. In 1890, the Scott Paper Company became the first company to manufacture toilet paper on a roll.

One hundred and fifteen years later, we live in the Golden Age of toilet paper. Perforated, medicated, quilted, scented, colored, multi-ply… Today the perfect brand waits on the shelf to serve any wiping preference or need. For those who value money over comfort, there are brands such as Marcal, which would be a good substitute for sandpaper, if only it didn't fall apart so easily. Such wonders as Charmin Plus and Quilted Northern meet the demand of the affluent for tissue so soft that it will seem as though God himself were gently wiping you with His beard.

Victorian-mandated sitting toilets created much of the demand for toilet paper, but Victorian etiquette in America wouldn't allow anyone to talk about it. With no national ad campaign and no newspaper articles, nothing gave Americans a uniform introduction to the product. Discussions about the new product and techniques for its use took place only among intimates, if at all. As time went on, the brands did begin advertising, but euphemistically and vaguely to avoid directly confronting the taboos. One ingenious marketer coined the slogan, "Ask for a roll of Hakle and then you don't have to mention toilet paper!" Not much is different today: teddy bears and fluffy clouds abound, but straightforward discussion of the product's functionality is still conspicuously absent.

So toilet paper entered our society with no instructions included. Individuals and families had to improvise techniques, while taboos prohibited widespread comparison or standardization. Parents taught their techniques to their children, not as one way but as *the* way. The result is today's myriad methods and eternal debates about correct technique.

ORIENTATION OF HANG

Ever since Scott introduced toilet paper on a roll, people have argued about the orientation of the hang. This argument is less about overhand vs. underhand than overhand vs. indifference—many religiously advocate overhand, and while a few are fanatic about underhand, the remainder don't care.

For an objective reason to choose one over the other, there is really only this: the distance one must reach to grasp a sheet is reduced by a few inches with an overhand hang. The overhand hang is more energy-efficient, and thus, for no other reason, superior.

NUMBER OF SQUARES

Grasping the leading sheet, you unroll the desired amount. Per-wipe paper quantity is contingent on ensuing wiping method, but there is a commonality: one square is never enough. Toilet paper is designed to disintegrate in water to pass safely through sewage systems and septic tanks, so a single square inevitably lacks the structural integrity to do the job. Any attempt to wipe with insufficient buffer risks tearing through the paper, touching contaminated skin, and perhaps embedding cling-ons under the fingernails. The wise will err on the side of thickness.

STRUCTURE: SCRUNCH VS. FOLD

To ameliorate the fragility of the paper, users fractalize the surface, folding or scrunching to add a dimension of thickness and create an adequate buffer between one's fingers and one's filth. Scrunchers bunch the toilet paper to create a thick surface; folders take their time to neatly achieve the same effect.

While wadding creates a thicker buffer, folding gives more grasping surface. A wadder thus requires more paper than a folder to achieve the same effective wiping surface area, assuming the folder creates a suitably thick parcel.

Thus a wadder requires more paper than a folder, and can expect higher lifetime toilet paper expenditure. Then again, the extra seconds per poop it takes to fold the paper add up as well. The basic question for the wiper is one of time against money—when wiping, which is worth more?

ACCESS POSTURE

With your toilet paper folded or scrunched, you now reach for your anus. But, framed on three sides by porcelain, the anus is inaccessible to the wiping hand. To enter ground zero, one must spread the legs and reach through, or lean forward and reach around, or stand.

Standing causes the cheeks to clench tightly around their juicy center, smearing anything stuck on one cheek to the other. Further, one has to force one's way in and potentially smear one's way out. Standing wipers know that the only way to make their technique completely safe is to lean forward, opening the cheeks like a pair of French doors.

ANGLE OF APPROACH

Standing or sitting, with your toilet paper folded or scrunched, you've readied yourself by spreading, leaning, or standing to reach for your anus. The anus is located in the butt; to access it, you have to either reach around your waist or between your legs. Reaching around requires a somewhat ungainly contortion of the body; reaching between runs the risk of contaminating your thighs with the used paper on the way out. Both problems, however, pose little risk to the experienced pooper.

For reasons of symmetry, reaching between is probably the more aesthetically pleasing choice. (For whatever that's worth—in the bathroom, aesthetics are rarely the primary consideration.)

DIRECTION OF WIPE

Standing or sitting, with your toilet paper folded or scrunched, you reach between or behind for your initial wipe. Centering the paper on the taint, you press and wipe up, scrubbing and collating and snowplowing all filth onto the paper, exiting the area via the valley of the ass cheeks.

Or perhaps not. It's similarly popular to go sphincter spelunking, starting at daylight and moving downward, beginning at the pole and working your way south.

Most women choose to start down and move up and out, for obvious reasons. Among men, up vs. down is usually contingent on between vs. behind, vector of wipe following from angle of approach. Practically speaking, behind-and-up is the same as between-and-down: both are pulling the mess into a collection point. The converse is pushing, which is harder to control. Although pushing methods are not without adherents, they're also not without peril.

APPRAISAL

Standing or sitting, with your toilet paper folded or scrunched, you've reached between or behind and completed your initial wipe. Having left the anal vicinity, your toilet paper is moments from assuming the same value as the poop itself, a transformation accomplished simply by increasing the space between your fingers and thumb until the tissue tumbles from hand into water. But to some, this tainted piece of paper serves one last function.

The blind have no choice but to judge a wipe's efficacy by feel; following their example, some of us just wipe until we feel clean. Others, wanting to entrust the job to a more reliable sense, look at the paper to ensure they've nabbed everything; and, perhaps, to admire the color, consistency, and even the smell of their work. If the paper is white, the anus is clean. If it is not, the ritual is repeated, until sanitary conditions are adequate.

REFOLDING

Standing or sitting, with your toilet paper folded or scrunched, you've reached between or behind, completed your initial wipe, and may or may not have inspected the paper. But one pass is never sufficient—even if it seems so, the prudent go in for another.

During the economic boom of the 1990s, young dot-com millionaires wiped like princes, squandering toilet paper with no thought for the dark days ahead. Today we live in more frugal times and are thriftier with nonrenewable resources. Accordingly, many people refold their used toilet paper to stretch the roll.

For the amateur, it's a dangerous technique, but once mastered, it's efficient. Deftly manipulating the fresh brown stain into the center of the bunch or fold, the user carefully regrasps the wad, born again as a pristine surface, freshly white on all exposed sides, ready for reuse, with the fingers and anus free from the dangers of (re)contamination.

LOOK AT WHAT YOU'VE DONE

With your anus clean, your poop is over. If you're not standing already, physiology dictates that you now do so. Society dictates that you flush. But for many, psychology intercedes, encouraging a look back.

Some look at their poop for signs of colonic dysfunction: blood in the stool, for instance, is an unambiguous tip to call the doctor. Others look out of guilty curiosity, to see what horror their body has wrought. But for many, perhaps even most, the look is to take pride in their creation. In the afterglow of a successful movement, these proud poopers turn and face their demon—once their tormentor, now their vanquished foe. If it's abnormally big, they feel pride; if it's unusually small, they feel disappointment; if it's terribly messy, they feel artistic. Whatever the case, seeing the poop is closure. The struggle has ended.

It seems contradictory that waste, which is by definition something the body used up or rejected, should engender pride. Poop is an amalgamation of the substances most useless to us. While we've already established that it possesses no threat to the person who created it, and thus should not be viewed negatively, why view it positively? Why should one not view it as a neutral fact of life, no more worthy of comment than breathing?

Pooping: a struggle, a creation, a surge of pride. The obvious parallel is to a mother's first glimpse of her baby after labor. Freud pointed out that children, before they are taught better, assume that babies exit Mommy's tummy the same way poop exits their own; thus, the act of defecation is subconsciously associated with childbirth. Does pride in poop stem from that same instinct, to love one's newborn child?

But Freud has more to say. Each of us harbors, he says, an innate coprophilia—"the instinctual drive to be at one with, to touch and to smell, and even to ingest one's own faecal products." Observations of the behavior of small children and the severely mentally ill (two groups assumed to be unaware of, or unconcerned with, rules and taboos) provide evidence for instinctive coprophilia; observations of how authority figures react to their fecal behavior provides evidence of institutional repression. Perhaps we look at our poop to appease our unconscious—indulging the id when the superego knows we're hidden from judgmental eyes.

Child psychologists have a simpler explanation. During toilet training, our parents encouraged us to poop in toilets like grown-ups, and lavished us with praise when we did so. The suggestion is that our pride comes from unconscious memories of positive reinforcement. And, as Freud points out, all young children instinctively see the world in terms of 'bigger is better,' so the bigger the poop, the more love we feel our parents giving us.

As Mary Douglas puts it, "If anal eroticism [in the Freudian sense] is expressed at the cultural level we are not entitled to expect a population of anal erotics. We must look around for whatever it is that has made appropriate any cultural analogy to anal eroticism." So we must seek out whatever it is that has made poop a symbol of something in which we take pride. One such analogy might stem from class and economics. In their essay "Toiletry Time: Defecation, Temporal Strategies and the Dilemmas of Modernity," David Inglis and Mary Holmes observe that mass production changed the relationship between worker and manager so that a worker's time was now measured in minutes, each of which translated directly into profit. To take full advantage of the worker, owners created strict constraints on every aspect of that time, including bathroom time. Under strict time constraints, a worker might grow to view pooping as a moment of freedom on the company's payroll—the only workday activity that didn't directly make someone else rich. Even today, to take pride in poop at work is to directly rebel against the goals of the company.

The simplest explanation of why people like to look at poop, however, stems from the first duality of poop, as described in chapter one: the more it hurt to hold it in, the better it feels to let it out. To those for whom this feeling is positive, it's only natural to learn to associate the sight of the poop with the euphoria.

WHERE MANY HAVE GONE BEFORE: TECHNIQUES FOR PUBLIC RESTROOMS

Somewhere in the world, there is a toilet that you trust (because you know who uses it and what sanitary situation awaits you). This toilet may not always be pristine. Diarrhea happens, and men urinating are lazy, but you know that a few swipes of toilet paper will get it clean enough to suit you. If you're lucky, you've got multiple toilets that you trust—at home, at your friends' or family's, or even at the office (if you're particularly blessed). But no matter how many ports of call you've got, leaving them creates the risk of having to poop in a public toilet.

Life for the public pooper has gotten much easier in the last decade. The frequent carping about the proliferation of chain stores and restaurants tends to ignore their estimable tendency to provide clean facilities to their customers. The mallification of America means you're never too far from a nominally clean bathroom. Still, bathrooms aren't sanitized and restocked after every user, and outside the chains, an inquiry into the facilities may elicit a key attached to an oversized wooden spoon and directions to a cold metal door in the back of the building. Public pooping always runs this risk: a bathroom where flies buzz and faucets drip and a strange yellow film coats the floor.

The incidence of such crimes against humanity decline as chain stores replicate like cancer, but people almost invariably still poop differently when they're using a public toilet. That's because of the users who preceded you, of course, but also because of concern about users of adjacent receptacles—and concern for them.

The Courtesy Flush

During a prolonged session in a multi-stall bathroom, many users show their concern for their fellows by flushing immediately after each deposit, ostensibly to reduce the fragrance of their poop. The premise of the courtesy flush is this: the less time one's log lingers in the outside world, the less it will smell. The courtesy flush saves others from the full assault of last night's Buffalo wings. But does it work? Or, once the bullet hits the bowl, has the damage already been done?

For you to smell a solid, molecules have to float off of its surface and make their way to your nose. One reason that the Victorians embraced the water closet is that water keeps the smell molecules from spreading. Water is much denser than air; molecules from a piece of immersed poop find it difficult to break free and float away.

When it comes to poop, the bulk of olfactory damage actually occurs the moment the turd makes its entrance. A turd in the open air is shockingly pungent, but the time between the turtle-head poking and the tail submerging is short. Assuming you flush in a timely manner, the smell from the solid turd is not going to permeate the room any more than it already has—once it's underwater, its smell is contained. And while your farts may asphyxiate the entire room, flushing can't do anything about that.

Fiber-laden turds, however, float, and diarrhea has a tendency to spread along the surface of the water. If you do deposit a floater, the exposed tip of the turdberg will release unfettered smell molecules. Only in those instances will a courtesy flush prevent further stink from permeating the bathroom. For the shameful shitter, there is one other benefit: a well-timed flush can drown out the sound of a sputtering ass.

The Urinal Rules

Most public bathrooms in America sequester each toilet behind three walls and a door, ensuring the privacy and anonymity of the pooper. But since men prefer urinating standing up, most men's restrooms dedicate considerable real estate to a wall of urinals. At a urinal a man is neither private nor anonymous, and so an elaborate system of rules governs which urinal he uses.

Unlike many of the norms of excretion, the urinal rules are clear. When confronted by multiple available urinals, a man relies on them to minimize the probability of standing next to another man. He picks a spot that maximizes the number of empty urinals between him and anyone already there. If standing next to someone is unavoidable, a man chooses the urinal that minimizes the probability of someone standing on the other side. The worst thing that can happen in a public bathroom is to pee between two other men.

The urinal rules are easy to learn. Although there are sub-rules and corollaries and advanced techniques, the general premise is easy to grasp. Perhaps more difficult to grasp is their rationale. Hypotheses include penis envy, homophobia, and latent homosexuality. A 1970 study in *the Journal of Personality and Social Psychology* went so far as to note that urination duration increases with personal proximity; since urination is known to slow with male physical arousal, the authors concluded that men are aroused by the presence of other men, and that the urinal rules aim to hide the awful truth that all men are gay.

Perhaps, but there's a much more probable cause: territorialism. Once an excretory act has commenced, it requires Herculean effort to stop; during the act, the man is helpless and vulnerable to attack. The urinal rules minimize the advantage potential adversaries have against a man during his moment of weakness, because the further away a man is from potential enemies, the more likely he'll be able to react to their approach.

The urinal rules also apply when men choose a toilet from a row of stalls. But if the doors are closed and extend down far enough to hide the area where a user's feet might be seen, it's hard to tell which contain active users. In such circumstances, violations in choosing a toilet are forgivable.

The Public Toilet Seat

Most of us don't mind porcelain-mediated ass-to-ass contact with our family or our roommates. But few of us tolerate similar intimacy with strangers. To combat the invisible fecal phantoms lurking on public toilet seats, we've devised a variety of methods to make the seat seem safe or remove it from the equation entirely.

Wiping the seat. A perfectly logical exercise both at home and in public, the wipe is performed to remove water, urine splatters and any other evils that may lurk.

Seat covers. Many public bathrooms provide disposable paper toilet seat covers. Too thin to keep moisture from seeping through, these covers provide little more than a placebo effect; even the slightest shift of the rear will expose one to bare germ-ridden porcelain. But seat covers are useful in revealing moisture on the seat: moisture seeping through the paper means more layers are necessary.

Buffering. In the absence of (or in addition to) seat covers, some fastidious poopers create a makeshift barrier of strips of toilet paper, gingerly covering every bare inch of porcelain. Many layers are required to be effective, and the structure is as tenuous as paper seat covers.

Stoop 'n' Poop. Poop waits for no one. But in many places, the public toilet is unfit for human use—so disgusting that no toilet paper construction could create a buffer thick enough. Here most people will bend as low as they can without touching; the fire in the sphincter is then matched by burning in the thigh muscles, but neither as bad as actually touching the thing.

Bus stations aside, the danger of a public toilet seat rarely outweighs the threat of a wet ass. Butt skin is probably cleaner than other parts of the body. Hands, for instance, touch a lot more than do butts, yet we shake hands blithely. The same person who lays down an inch of toilet paper may have no qualms about handling stall locks or sink faucets, which are usually much dirtier than the toilet seat, being cleaned much less often. Our efforts to maintain a hygienic rear are usually successful—not so with the rest of us.

THINKING OUTSIDE THE BOWL: ACCESSORIES AND INNOVATIONS

The basics of popular bathroom technology have remained mostly the same for the last hundred years. We poop in flush toilets, and we wipe with toilet paper. But there have been a few technological breakthroughs in that time—not enough to alter the basics of the excretory experience, but enough to make quite a few fortunes. We've seen toilets grow smaller and more efficient with improvements in manufacturing and in household plumbing. We've seen toilet paper grow less like sandpaper as manufacturers discovered plies and quiltings and rediscovered aloe. We've seen the introductions of hands-free technologies such as automatic flushers and even automatic toilet-seat-covers.

Many more technological breakthroughs are to come. A trip to Japan reveals a toilet that may portend the future of pooping: toilet seats that heat up automatically; nozzles that push out, spray you with warm water, and retract; and toilets with speakers to mimic the sound of flushing water to hide the sound of your splatters in a more environmentally sound way. On the drawing board are plumbing that recycles water from sinks and showers into the toilet tank, toilet seats that glow in the dark, lids that lift after an infrared sensor detects an approaching user, and a toilet that can measure weight, body fat, blood pressure, and urine and stool content, and email the results to your doctor.

These technological wonders come with a high price, and it's hard to conceive of them as anything less than extravagancies. But then again, the same might have been said about bathroom accessories now standard.

The Seat

This toilet accessory, one of the first, proved so popular that today it's impossible to imagine a toilet without it. Toilets have always had lids. Lids were crucial when the toilet was first introduced, because the primitive plumbing did not yet have traps and vents to keep gasses and smells from climbing up the sewers into the bathroom. Seats, however, weren't always hinged as they are today. The first toilets were one-piece—the seat, whether raised above the lip of the bowl or at its level, was part of the bowl. The hinged seat was introduced to address a major sanitary weakness in the system: lazy, splattering men. "The reckless abuse of water closets by men and boys," engineer Edward Philbrick said in 1878, produced "one of the most disgusting items encountered in the proper management of the household."

Strangely, however, custom has evolved so that the seat must be kept down at all times for the convenience of the sitter. A standing urinator is supposed to lift the seat before peeing, and lower it afterwards. Yet, if the seat aims to make up for the laziness of men, why put the onus of lifting on them? Conventional wisdom burdens the man with both lifting and lowering. The lazy man quickly discovers that, if he shirks both tasks, the unsuspecting female may think he has accomplished both—which puts the toilet seat in constant danger of being peed on. Thus, if the woman's goal is confidence that the seat is dry, why not insist that the man keep the seat up at all times? This strategy ensures that a man too lazy to wipe his splatters won't have to exert the effort to lift the seat, which is safe at all times. The only requirement is for the man to lift the seat when he's done pooping—just one task, much more likely to be completed than two. Furthermore, if the woman discovers the seat down, she is immediately on her guard for splatters. The strategy promotes clean seats and provides warnings of unclean ones.

The only major drawback: it might get poop on your toothbrush. Your stomach hosts billions of bacteria that help you break digest food. When your feces comes out, a host of bacteria often accompany it. Ideally the bacteria will go down with the ship. But bacteria love nothing more than water; they'll grow on any surface where moisture clings. Bacteria that escape flushing will hang out in the bowl, multiplying and thriving. Flushing will clean them out, but even the twelve hours between your morning poo and your bedtime pee is enough for them to colonize your toilet well.

Environmental microbiologist Dr. Charles Gerba has spent the last thirty years studying home contamination. One of his discoveries is that the swirling water of a flushing toilet creates a cloud of aerosolized water that will spread up and out, settling on every surface within a six-foot radius: the seat, the sink, the walls, the ceiling, the doorknob, your toothbrush. For some people, it doesn't seem to matter that these bacteria probably won't cause you any harm—just knowing is enough. Closing the lid when flushing contains this bacterial miasma. If women were to require the toilet seat to remain raised at all times as suggested above, the lid would likely remain open for the flush. The seat would be safe from splatters, but at what cost? The most logical and sanitary solution is to require that the seat and lid be kept lowered when not in use, leaving the onus again squarely on the man. Sorry, fellas. I tried.

The Low-Flow Toilet

The most dramatic and far-reaching toilet innovation in recent years happened in 1992 when Congress passed the Energy Policy Act, establishing water-use restrictions for new toilets, showerheads, and faucets. The EPAct set the national manufacturing standard for most toilets at 1.6 gallons per flush, beginning January 1, 1994.

Toilets manufactured in the 1980s typically used 3.5 gallons per flush; older toilets relied on five or even seven gallons of water to wash down everything from a pound of poop to a dead goldfish to a few sprinkles of urine. These toilets wasted incredible amounts of water. A 1999 study by the American Water Works Research Association found that people typically flush a toilet five times a day; for a family of four, a low-flow toilet saves almost 14,000 gallons a year over the 3.5 gallon standard. The EPAct standard was enacted in large part to conserve water, but also to save municipalities from the costly expansion of water supply and wastewater treatment infrastructures that such heavy water use necessitated.

Although low-flow toilets had been marketed in the U.S. since the 1980s, and although seventeen states had established a 1.6-gallon standard by 1992, the low-flow toilet law met visceral and rabid opposition matched only by the floods of brown water so many consumers were shocked to find spreading across their tiled bathroom floors. The 1.6 gallon standard may have saved the infrastructure, but at the cost of the flush-and-forget-it bathroom American lifestyle.

The reason for this flushing inadequacy was that big toilet manufacturers either didn't have enough time to meet the new standards or were simply unwilling to do so. Many toilet manufacturers marketed low-flow toilets that were really just 3.5 gallon designs modified with dams or early-close flush valve flappers that only allowed 1.6 gallons of water to fill the tank. Predictably, toilets designed to flush with 3.5 gallons of water failed with less than half that volume. Blockages and outrage followed. Politicians and pundits denounced the intrusion of the government into the bathroom (as though this were the first time bathroom technology had been changed by the government for the good of society). Michigan Republican Joe

Knollenberg sponsored a bill to repeal the standard, although he claimed pro-free-market, not anti-water-conservation, reasons.

But in the face of new requirements, the marketplace did eventually respond. Toilet manufacturers learned how to optimize their products for the stringent requirements, increasing the size of the trapways and the surface area of the water covering the bowl between flushes, and adjusting the size and placement of water jets in the rims of the bowl. Many manufacturers experimented with pressurized water and vacuum pressure to boost flush capacity. Today's low-flow toilets can operate on par with or even better than their thirstier predecessors. The government intervention of 1992, so reviled during its early years, forced toilet manufacturers to innovate and improve efficiency in ways they may never have otherwise opted to explore. New York City estimated that low-flow toilets saved it $605 million from a twenty-year deferral of water supply and wastewater treatment expansion projects. Taxpayers and water drinkers across the country should be glad that Congressman Knollenberg's short-sighted opposition to low-flow toilets failed.

The Bidet

The anger that greeted low-flow toilets (and helped Dave Barry find his niche) wasn't an anomaly. People grow ornery at challenges to their comfort zone and will vehemently embrace the status quo, however flawed, in response. A striking example of this stubborn adherence to tradition is Americans' continued reliance upon toilet paper.

In theory, regular toilet paper clears your crack of poop residue. The by-the-book user wipes and wipes, checking the toilet paper each time until it comes up as white as it went down. But in practice, this technique is flawed—because with every pass, the user is smearing poop flecks into the folds and crevices of the area around the anus. While it's only a thin layer that remains, it is still liable to itch or streak. Furthermore, the pain of a sensitive anus, whether from the irritation of dry skin or the fire of undigested Tabasco, is exacerbated by toilet paper. To avoid the pain, one might try to wipe with wetted toilet paper, but it'll just break up on contact, leaving a crack full of dingleberries. But few Americans will consider any alternative to this inefficient and unsanitary tradition.

Many Europeans, of course, have a different way. They may lag behind us in per-capita greenhouse-gas production, but they're well ahead of us in bathroom sanitation technology, thanks to bidets. Imagine a soothing geyser of warm water washing over your quivering sphincter, providing hygiene and comfort beyond wiping's reach. With a simple twist of a knob to adjust temperature, and a mere flip of a lever to determine pressure, a jet of water surges blissfully over your most sensitive parts. If you've never tried it, you are missing out.

People in most other parts of the world use water to clean their asses after pooping. In many Eastern cultures, a bathroom is incomplete without a hose and a sprayer. But for optimizing comfort, sanitation, and pleasure, you can't beat the bidet.

There are two different kinds of bidets, vertical and horizontal. The vertical bidet creates a small fountain in the middle of the bowl; the horizontal shoots water across it. In either case, the user, while facing the appliance, sits or squats to maneuver the contaminated area into the stream. Drying with toilet paper or a towel follows, and you're on your way.

Given an American obsession with cleanliness that far exceeds most European standards, it's odd that we haven't embraced bidets wholeheartedly. It is inconsistent with general practice: if you got poop on your arm, you'd wash it off, not smear it off. And yet, for the butt, we're content to smear. Probably "bidet" sounds too much like "ballet"—too effeminate (or too French) for Americans to latch on. Market it as a "buttsink" and watch bidet sales soar.

Wet Wipes

Its name and foreign derivation are clearly some of the reasons for the bidet's unpopularity in the States. But no story better illustrates the American resistance to bathroom change than the story of wet wipes: an indigenous product, clearly functionally superior, nevertheless utterly rejected by the American public.

Americans do recognize the benefits of wet wipes, having used them on babies' sensitive bumpers for decades. Until recently, however, wet wipes were not marketed for adult use, mostly because they don't dissolve—baby wet wipes retain their structural integrity in water, much to the chagrin of anyone who has ever flushed a handful of them and watched the toilet back up and spill over.

That changed in summer 2001 when, with great fanfare and after months of promotion, Kimberly-Clark launched Cottonelle Fresh Rollwipes. The result of three years and $100 million of research and development, Rollwipes were heralded as a major breakthrough, functionally superior to their dry predecessor and expected to exceed $150 million in sales in the first year.

In developing Rollwipes, Kimberly-Clark met two challenges: to make moist wipes "dispersible," so that they were strong enough to survive the rigors of the wipe but would still disintegrate in water; and second, to make them as convenient as toilet paper. The company's engineers developed a sturdy but water-degradable material and designed a refillable dispenser that held both wet and dry toilet paper rolls and fit snugly on top of the standard bathroom dispenser.

2001 was to be Year of the Wet Wipes. The economy was still relatively strong, and the country still felt relatively safe, so the toilet paper companies felt that the time was right for a great wipe forward. Wet wipes' success seemed so assured that Procter & Gamble jumped on the bandwagon, buying a similar moist-wipes-on-a-roll product from a Boston inventor and rushing them to the same test markets at the same time; their advertising even started on the same day.

This kind of overzealous capitalism causes some to suspect conspiracy and collusion. But regardless of the duopolistic implications, and despite millions of marketing dollars, both manufacturers failed to achieve sales anywhere close to what they'd hoped for. Less than a year after the launch, sales were a fiasco; *The Wall Street Journal* reported that the product was confined to regional markets in the South, and sales were "so small they aren't financially material."

Perhaps the attacks of September 11 reminded Americans that there are things more important than the comfort of their asses.

More likely, though, the story of wet wipes is the same as the bidet: Americans are bathroom Luddites. With all our worries, some extra bathroom comfort would be welcome, and yet, despite the superiority of wet wipes and the incomparable satisfaction of the bidet, we cling stubbornly to our inferior ways. Our sphincters suffer needlessly.

It may take nothing less than another act of Congress to raise American pooping standards to where they should be. The No Pile Left Behind Act will propose tax breaks to bidet manufacturers, mandate wet wipes in every public stall, and subsidize functional low-flow toilets. Until then, what begins with a sit and ends with a flush will be subject to endless variations stemming from nurture, economics, and cosmopolitanism or lack thereof. Assuming taboos remain as they are, the future is likely to see little convenience consensus convergence. It seems that all we'll all ever agree on is this: poop goes in the toilet.

The toilet was created to solve eighteenth-century problems of decorum, and was spread across society to solve nineteenth- century problems of sanitation. Now, two hundred years after the flush toilet took Victorian England by storm, we have a few twenty-first-century problems: the cost of the sewage infrastructure and its environmental impact. The flush toilet can't solve the problems this time, because this time, the flush toilet *is* the problem.

If the turd is not smiling, dispose of it.

CHAPTER 4

GROSS NATIONAL PRODUCT: THE COSTS OF POOP

"DO YOU REMEMBER THE STINK YEARS, MISTER STRONG?"

At the poorest, filthiest urinal in town, the townspeople have revolted. They have taken over the amenities and are peeing at will—for free! Two decades after the government outlawed private toilets in the face of catastrophic drought and amenities owned by the Urine Good Company became the only legal place to answer nature's call, the Company's greed has finally pushed the towns-people too far. They know that the penalty for peeing anywhere but in officially sanctioned public toilets is exile to Urinetown—but to the city's poorest, even exile is preferable to the sacrifices they are forced to make every time they have to pee.

"We'll not return to the Stink Years, Mister Strong." Bobby Strong, leader of the proletariat rebellion, has come to the gleaming tower on the hill to negotiate with Caldwell B. Clad-well, the Urine Good Company's president and owner. Cladwell understands why the poor are angry. But he also knows the price of liberty. The Urine Good Company was chartered in a time of crisis, and Cladwell understands the threat today's rebellion represents.

The Stink Years

"The first years," Cladwell reminds Bobby, "when the water table started to drop and then just kept on dropping." When private toilets were outlawed to curb water usage, people took to doing their business wherever the urge struck. "No one thought they had much time then, and many of us did ... questionable things, much like the things that are happening right now." And the environment suffered. The city was practically uninhabitable. It was only the ruthlessness of the Company and the brutality of the police that made the town fit for human beings again. Sanitation returned, water usage was reined in, life went on, and the crisis was over. The only price was urinary liberty.

Urinetown The Musical tells the story of just how far individual sacrifice can be pushed in the name of the public good, and what happens when the cost of the public good grows too high for the individual to accept. The play ran on Broadway for more than two years, garnering three Tony awards and ten nominations along the way. Theatergoers left the auditorium after each show chuckling at the imagination of the playwrights as they went to urinate—for free! God bless America!—in the many bathrooms situated off the lobby for the ticketholder's convenience. *Urinetown* was a hilariously terrifying universe in which peeing and pooping cost money. It made you glad to live in a society where the most important things in life are free.

But they're not. Glistening in the stark bathroom light, bobbing gently in the toilet bowl, framed by a chocolate halo on the water's surface, your poop is unneeded by your body and unwanted by society. You need only flush to remove it from the consciousness of both. But the simplicity of that mechanism belies the intricacy of the infrastructure and the magnitude of the capital invested in the sanitary-industrial complex that makes it so easy. The effortlessness of pressing a little lever to remove a fresh poop from any bathroom anywhere in the country at any time of the day may be the birthright of every single American, but it is not free.

Many members of our society have interpreted the bathroom infrastructure passed down to us from the Victorians as an imperative of fecal denial—that poop should not be seen, heard, smelled, or touched (or tasted, for that matter). Even among the shameless shitters, having all five senses cut off from our poop has engendered a sense of fecal invisibility. We're ignorant of the cultural forces that sculpt the common turd into an object of almost occult dread, and ignorant of its economic ramifications. We don't know where it goes or what happens to it, or appreciate how the answers to those mysteries affect us.

Our physical and psychological urges have made billion-dollar industries out of plumbing, toilet manufacturing, building sewers, and treating sewage, not to mention fortunes in complementary industries such as toilet paper, plungers, air freshener, and even books about poop in contemporary culture (hopefully!). The financial cost of all this is staggering; just as shocking is the general ignorance of the cost. Pooping isn't free. If our government, as in *Urinetown*, started charging for each flush, the only difference would be in awareness of cost. When poop comes out your ass, you're already paying through the nose.

PAY PER PHEW: THE PRICE OF A FLUSH

The two most obvious costs of poop are those that touch your butt: the toilet and the toilet paper. A toilet costs anywhere from a hundred to a few thousand dollars, depending on efficiency, comfort, durability, opulence of materials, and the presence or absence of heated seats and automatic water and air nozzles to wash and dry you. Toilet paper costs a few dollars per week. (The average American, according to Charmin, uses fifty-seven squares a day. With 176 sheets on a regular fifty-cent roll of Charmin, that comes out to $59 a year.)

Now consider the water you poop in. Where did it come from? How did it get there? Where does it go when you flush? One homebuilder interviewed for this book finds that a new home's plumbing makes up 7% of the "hard cost" of construction (which excludes land, fees, and permits). A home that costs $200,000 to build therefore has about $14,000 in plumbing. Beyond that 7% are water and sewer "tap fees" for connecting the house to the municipal systems. These fees depend on local scarcity of water, the particulars of a city's infrastructure, and other variables. Federal Heights, Colorado, for instance, is "landlocked," meaning that it possesses no undeveloped land and can therefore accommodate new development without building new infrastructure. There the water and sewer tap fees for a single-family home in 2006 were $8,055 and $1,967. But the city of Arvada, just eight miles away, has plenty of free land to develop, so its tap fees for single-family homes reflect the cost of extending the sewer and water infrastructure: $10,165 for water, and $1,120 for sewers. Those costs, of course, are passed to the buyer in the price of the home.

If you live in Arvada, your new home's $34,000 plumbing infrastructure has operating costs. Your monthly water bill pays for the water you flush with and the sewers it flows through, and your taxes pay for the billion-dollar sewage plant that lies at the other end. The cost of water also varies by municipality, and calculating it can be complicated. For instance, Arvada's 2006 bimonthly sewer charge was $2.21 plus $2.41 per 1,000 gallons; water was $5.45 bimonthly plus $2.38 per 1,000 gallons.

Spreading fixed and variable costs over the 8.2 years the Census Bureau says the typical American homeowner lives in a house before moving, the conclusion is that pooping is far from free. For a home-owning family of four living in Arvada in 2006, it cost around 41 cents every time the toilet flushes.

And that's just the monetary cost.

The True Cost of Water

While two dollars per thousand gallons may sound modest, water and sewage infrastructures are heavily subsidized by the local, state, and federal governments, which means that you pay for them, too. The true cost of water is subject to much debate, but when you consider the price tag for capturing, treating, distributing, and reclaiming it, operating water and sewage utilities, and accommodating the ever-expanding demand for water as suburbs sprawl and more people drink and poop in areas with finite rainfall and river flow, most experts agree it's much more than the fraction of a cent most Americans pay per gallon. Furthermore, with supply dwindling and population growing, shortages and rising costs are inevitable.

SUNK COSTS	
Water tap fee	$10,165.00
Sewage tap fee	$1,120.00
Materials cost, $200k home	$14,000.00
	$25,285.00
VARIABLE COSTS	
Flushes per day per person*	5.46
Flushes per year, family of four	7,971.60
Gallons per flush	1.60
Gallons per year, family of 4	12,754.56
Water cost per 1,000 gallons	$2.38
Water usage cost per year (12,754.56 gal)	$30.36
Water fixed costs per year ($5.45 bi-monthly)	$32.70
Water total cost per year	$63.06
Sewage cost per 1000 gallons	$2.41
Sewage usage cost per year (12,754.56 gal)	$30.74
Sewage fixed costs per year ($2.21 bi-monthly)	$13.26
Sewage total cost per year	$44.00
Toilet paper cost per year	$59.00
Total variable cost per year	$166.05
Total variable cost, 8.2 years	$1,361.65
Total cost over 8.2 years	$26,646.65
Total cost per flush	$0.41

* Mayer et al., *Seattle Home Water Conservation Study*

WHAT COMES WITH POOP, STAYS WITH POOP

Poop doesn't simply disappear down the toilet; it travels through municipal sewage systems into one of thousands of multi-million-dollar municipal sewage plants that remove it from the water you flush it with. Once the plant has processed and released the water—often mixed with tons of chlorine to kill any bacteria—it still has tanks full of sludge to deal with. Some of it goes into landfills, some into incinerators, and some onto farmland. If it were wholly organic, applying sludge to land would be environmentally sound. But sludge is contaminated by inorganic chemicals and metals from industrial and household byproducts dumped into the sewers by businesses and individuals who believe that out of sight is out of mind.

American industry uses 70,000 different chemicals in commercial quantities. While much of the waste it creates is separated at the source and treated appropriately, some certainly flows both legally and illegally into the sewers and is eventually captured in sludge, creating impossible-to-predict compounds with unknown staying power in soil. The EPA addresses this variously, in part by restricting sludge fertilization to non-food crops and telling farmers who apply sludge to their land to add lime to the soil. Toxic metals move slower in alkaline soil than in acidic soil, so lime helps keep the contaminants suspended. But the regulations are underprotective, especially considering that normal (not acid) rain can be acidic enough to magnify any imbalance in the pH level of the soil enough to let the dangerous metals move. More significantly, unless the pH stays in the safe range for all eternity, contaminants will eventually return to circulation, either by sinking down into the water table or up into plants rooted in the contaminated soil.

This is the true cost of pooping: forty-one cents per flush for our Arvada family today, and the inevitable contamination of land, water, plants and animals sometime in the future.

If sewers could be restricted exclusively to poop and pee, then our current sewage treatment system would suffice. But doing that would force the industries and individuals dumping waste into the sewers to internalize the costs of waste disposal, and increasing costs to protect the environment is as politically feasible as telling people that environmental salvation lies in giving up their toilets for five-gallon buckets.

ENVIRONMENTAL SALVATION IN A FIVE-GALLON BUCKET

Your poop would make a fine meal. Hundreds of species of bacteria, insects, and scavengers look at the poop you flush, smack their microscopic lips and think, "Mmm, I'd love a piece of that." A fly seeking a nice food source in which to lay its eggs watches you flush your poop with the same kind of horror you'd feel watching that fly lay its eggs on your pork chop. For these organisms at the bottom of the food chain, and for all the creatures that feed on them, human customs of poop disposal are catastrophic violations of the natural order. Fecal aversion represents poop as waste. But our poop actually marks humanity's position in the circle of life—our feces and our urine are only "waste" when we waste them.

In nature, the end of one creature's digestive process is the beginning of another's. A deer eats a plant, the plant becomes energy and poop, the poop becomes food for bacteria, and waste from the bacteria becomes food for another generation of plants that another generation of deer will eat.

Americans flush 108 million pounds of plant food down the toilet every day.

At the same time, according to lobbying group The Fertilizer Institute, the U.S. uses 12 billion tons of nitrogen fertilizer alone every year-65 million pounds a day. 55% of it is imported.

Our poop is being wasted. That which isn't incinerated or buried in a landfill is applied to the land contaminated with industrial chemicals. Inorganic fertilizers are introduced into the food cycle as a substitute for the poop that should be used instead. The circle of life has a gaping hole—it ends with a toilet flushing, and begins again with chemical fertilizer used on farms.

Some environmentalists point to many Eastern cultures' poop disposal practices as more sanitary and holistic than Western models. While most Western cultures have historically viewed poop as waste and disposed of it accordingly, many Eastern cultures saw it as a resource, collecting it for agricultural use. This was most common in Asia, where for thousands of years they've irrigated their fields with raw sewage from the villages and cities. But while we might admire their recovery of the resource, we now know that this practice is trouble. Raw poop reeks horrifically, creates a breeding ground for vermin, and allows bacteria and viruses to move down into the groundwater, up into the food chain, or get tracked home on the farmer's shoes to where baby innocently sleeps. Eastern traditions of land application provide no better a model for sanitary poop disposal than Western traditions of privy vaults and cesspools or sewer pipes and sewage treatment plants.

The solution is somewhere in between: composting. Composting is the process through which bacteria and heat break down organic materials into humus, a rich, brownish-black product that looks like dirt, smells like the forest floor, and makes great fertilizer. Food scraps, lawn clippings, leaves, sawdust, and cow manure can all be composted, and so can human poop. Because of its potential to carry pathogens, poop composting requires a bit more care than other forms of composting, but properly executed, poop composting is clean, safe, and completely free of smell.

Composting your poop is simple. Gather it in a pile, cover it with straw, hay, or sawdust to contain the smell, and let bacteria run wild. Their frantic digestion will heat the pile to 150°F, hot enough to drive away any insects, kill any pathogens, and convert the biological matter into nitrates. After collecting a year's worth of household poop in your pile, start a second pile, leaving the first to digest for another year or two. And then, dig in! Breaching the surface with your shovel will release the surprisingly pleasant scent of fresh humus, rich in nutrients and ready to grow prize-winning tomatoes.

Successful composting, easy as it sounds, does present two challenges. The first, by far the tougher, is to ignore society's exhortations to view poop as waste and see it as a resource, not to be squandered. While similar cognitive shifts have occurred in the last few decades (about aluminum cans, glass, paper, and plastic, which most Americans now see as "recyclables" rather than as "trash"), to tap your ass' brown gold is a much larger cognitive leap. But the threats of rising water and sewage treatment costs, dwindling water supply, and land and water contamination all necessitate thinking differently about our poop.

The second challenge is collection. Easiest would be to redirect household plumbing to deposit the poop right onto a compost pile. Unfortunately, that won't work: composting requires a proper balance between water and organic material. If there's too much water—and 1.6 gallons per flush is far too much—then the pile will rot and breed pathogens instead of becoming wholesome and sanitary compost. The challenge, then, is to get your poop from your butt to the compost pile without using water. Here is the biggest stumbling block on the road to household composting: breaking the addiction to the flush toilet.

In that case, the most obvious solution is to poop directly into the compost pile. This is different from pooping into a cesspool or a privy-vault—the dark, damp conditions of pits promote rot and stench, not organic digestion, as the odor of any Forest Service latrine attests. (Healthy composting is completely odorless.) A few companies build composting toilets of which the collectors, enclosed in furnace-sized bins, are built into the house, directly under the toilet. It's not just a pit for poop, but a watertight, well-ventilated structure, often with electrical heating to promote growth or evaporate moisture. Composting toilets cost a few thousand dollars, are laborious to install, and take up a lot of space below the bathroom. Fortunately, there are self-contained models with built-in collection devices starting at around $1,000. With capacity for two to six adults, these save much of the trouble of installation (although they still need to be vented) and don't use much more space than a regular toilet. But they're much smaller than built-in composting toilets, so they need to be emptied more frequently.

The biggest limitation of composting toilets is that your butt must be situated directly above the poop pile. You cannot poop indirectly onto the pile, as through a network of pipes, because poop is too viscous to travel through pipes without a liquid to lubricate its passage. Solid poop would leave smears on any part of the pipe it touched, and diarrhea would be even messier. Without something to flush it out, such a pipe would soon become a horror. But pooping directly onto the pile requires direct exposure of the pile to your butt, and a few minutes is enough for smell to get out and insects to get in. A system of pans or other receptacles to transfer the poop from the bowl to the pile is conceivable, but then cleaning becomes a chore.

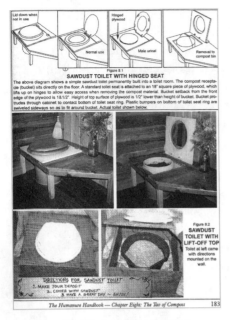

A humanure toilet. Photo from *The Humanure Handbook* by Joseph C. Jenkins.

A humanure toilet. Photo courtesy Joe Jenkins.

For those with the money, knowledge, and space, composting toilets are great. But there's a much cheaper and easier method for those without.

Joseph Jenkins, author of *The Humanure Handbook*, coined "humanure" as a benign alternative to coarser words for what comes out of one's butt. Jenkins and his family have been composting humanure at their Pennsylvania home for nearly three decades, and they've got the prize-winning tomatoes growing in their humanure-fertilized garden to prove it. Not only is Jenkins an expert in building and maintaining backyard compost piles, but he's developed an alternative to the flush toilet that's as simple as it is ingenious: five-gallon buckets, wooden cabinets, and sawdust.

Jenkins has modernized the eighteenth-century close-stool, the wooden cabinets that ensconced chamber pots so that people could sit and poop. Jenkins' cabinets, tall enough to hold a five-gallon plastic bucket, are fitted with a standard toilet seat for comfort. Next to each cabinet is a second bucket full of sawdust. The user poops onto a few inches of sawdust already laid in the bucket, then covers his deposit with another scoop of

Joe Jenkins' family spreads composted humanure in their garden. Photo courtesy Joe Jenkins.

sawdust, containing the smell completely. Each bucket is enough to hold one adult's poop and urine for a week. When a bucket is full, Jenkins takes it to his backyard compost pile and pours it on, adding cover material such as straw, weeds, or hay to prevent the escape of odor. After about a year, he starts a new pile and leaves the old to sit for another year, plenty of time to turn into humus.

His system works flawlessly, and he has letters of thanks from thousands of practitioners around the world to prove it. His toilets are as comfortable and odorless as flush toilets, and the only extra effort they require is taking an odorless bucket to the garden once a week. For the environmentally conscious person able to lift a twenty-pound bucket and the outdoor space to build a compost pile, Jenkins' system is ideal.

But the foresightful and industrious few cannot avert the coming crisis. To drastically reduce our water usage and to stop contaminating our farmlands, we need a poop composting system that every American will use. It must accommodate city dwellers without backyards, the elderly and those who can't lift twenty-pound buckets, the lazy who would empty their bucket out the window to save a trip to the pile, and the indoctrinated—the vast majority, loyal to the institutions of fecal denial who would fight like hell in their refusal to deviate from it. It's conceivable that society can be persuaded to accept a neighbor's poop compost pile if it doesn't smell or attract vermin, but it's hard to imagine most Americans giving up their beloved porcelain thrones for sawdust-filled, manually-emptied five-gallon buckets.

THE FUTURE OF FLUSH

For universal composting to be feasible, it has to rely on a disposal infrastructure that doesn't force people to see, smell, or touch their poop any more than they do with today's toilets. But 1.6-gallon-per-flush toilets are out. Sewers are out, cesspools are out, composting toilets are out, and sawdust-filled five-gallon buckets are out. So what's left?

The solution still involves pooping into water, but much less of it. Boat and RV owners are familiar with microflush toilets. Microflush toilets rely on air pressure to increase the velocity of the water moving into the bowl or vacuum power to increase the velocity of the water and waste flowing out. Using only sixteen ounces of water per flush, these toilets send water through the bowl faster than low-flow toilets do, which makes them more efficient. Microflush toilets can discharge into a collection device similar to composting toilets, but because there's still enough water to carry the poop through the pipes, the collector can be anywhere, making installation simpler and cheaper. These toilets use just enough water to move the poop along, and not enough to overwhelm the composting process.

Sixteen ounces of water per flush is pretty good; three is better. Clivus Multrum, founded in 1973 to develop composting toilets, is one of a few companies working on foam-flush toilets. Mixing a biocompatible alcohol with three ounces of water, these toilets generate a foam blanket that lubricates the bowl and the pipes below, so that poop slides easily into the collection receptacle. Like microflush and 1.6 gallon-per-flush toilets, foam-flush toilets clean the bowl while emptying it. But they do so using 81% less water than microflush toilets, 98.5% less than 1.6-gallon toilets, and an astounding 99.66% less water than the 3.5-gallon toilets of the 1980s.

Foam-flush toilets are the most promising alternative yet. Clivus toilets are being installed and tested not only in homes and small buildings but also in high-volume venues such as rest stops and public beaches. Like sawdust-filled buckets, these technologies at first seem feasible only for those with the money and the space to devote to them. Unlike sawdust-filled buckets, however, these technologies have the potential to be applicable on a large scale—in office and apartment buildings, for instance.

Current foam-flush toilets don't have much carrying capacity. The foam lubricates the pipes instead of carrying the waste, relying on steeply-angled pipes and gravity to do most of the work. That's fine for new constructions, but older buildings' plumbing would need extensive (and expensive) remodeling to accommodate these commodes. But Clivus toilets' real potential lies in increasing the foam's carrying power—making a little water go much further. If carrying capacity can be boosted, then foam-flush toilets will be much cheaper to install, and hence viable for widespread and large-scale adoption.

A foam flush toilet from Clivus Multrum. Photo courtesy Clivus Multrum, Inc.

A 500,000-use capacity Clivus composter in the basement of the Wawayanda State Park Bathhouse in Hewitt, New Jersey. Photo courtesy Clivus Multrum, Inc.

Microflush and foam-flush toilets suggest that the dreams of minimizing water usage, keeping poop out of sewers and separate from contaminants, and composting poop into natural fertilizer are tantalizingly within reach. But aside from carrying capacity of the water or foam, there's another major challenge: reducing the space the receptacles require. Current residential or commercial microflush and foam-flush toilets are designed for on-site composting on a timeline of years or even decades. That means that their collection receptacles would take up tremendous amounts of space in large-scale installations—imagine rows of tanks, each 62 x 82 x 82. Compare that to a sump pump in an average twenty-six-story Manhattan building, which needs only a six-foot-diameter, twelve-foot-deep footprint in the building's foundation to pump the building's waste into the sewer pipes. Building owners are likely to resist any system that requires them to sacrifice much more space than that. The need for space could be alleviated by designing receptacles for more frequent emptying, so the contents could be periodically transferred off-site for long-term composting, but that creates new problems of infrastructure and logistics.

These technical problems, though considerable, are not insurmountable. But just as daunting as the technological hurdles is the problem of bureaucratic inertia. Current sanitary systems are subject to intense regulation, from the number of toilets per floor and the size of the pipes to backflow protection and pumping specifications. Nontraditional toilets and composting disposal methods, which deviate from accepted standards in all aspects, often require special permits from city, county, or state officials who may be unfamiliar with—or suspicious of—zero-discharge systems. Some states support composting, but nevertheless require conventional wastewater systems installed as an expensive backup alongside any composting systems.

But while government is always wary of new technology and slow to adapt, demand for alternatives to today's wasteful and harmful poop infrastructure is sure to grow. And with it will grow the profit potential of the next generation's infrastructure. Profit potential will beget industries, and industries will beget lobbying groups, and when that happens, these things seem to almost magically work themselves out.

One thing's for sure: if we cannot keep absolutely all household and industrial contaminants out of the sewers (and we can't), then we cannot keep putting poop into them. It will take millions of dollars of investment to create the solutions and billions more to implement them. But those expenditures are justified, because the potential for environmental catastrophe and water shortages give us no other choice.

Power from the People

With microflush and foam-flush toilets, it's possible to get the best of all worlds. Comfortable, odorless toilets. Waste disposal with a simple pull of a lever. Environmentally sound poop collection and disposal. The savings will be astounding: billions of gallons of water per day, billions of dollars that would otherwise extend and maintain the sewers and sewage treatment plants, and tons of contaminants kept from being concentrated and spread in sludge. But this system still invites the question: what do we do with all that poop? Relatively few of us are gardeners, so it's unrealistic to expect that a system that collects poop in on-site receptacles will result in it being applied to the land by those who pooped it. History teaches us that people are too busy, too lazy, or otherwise unwilling or unable to dispose of their own poop. While some will reap the benefits of local composting, most will rely on the municipality to do it for them.

Cities already have curbside garbage pickups; curbside poop collection would operate similarly. It would probably prove cheaper—and certainly simpler—than today's sewers and sewage treatment plants. Basement poop collection devices could empty into buckets light enough to take to the curb but sturdy enough to prevent spills, raccoon breaches, or pranks by mischievous kids. Trucks could exchange full buckets for empty ones, taking them to plants for automated emptying, composting, and bucket-washing. Whether the cost and pollution caused by trucks and buckets is less than the cost and pollution of sewers and sludge remains to be studied, but in the decades it would take to wean ourselves from our sewage infrastructure, we can hope garbage trucks powered by non-polluting fuel will have emerged as well.

Experimental poop fuel cell systems. Photo courtesy Dr. Bruce E. Logan, Penn State University.

The specifics of such a system are beyond the scope of this book. Waste management systems are incredibly complex, and great minds have worked for years to build systems that work. A radical new system cannot be planned in one paragraph. Municipal poop collection needs just as much investment of thought and money as the systems we have today. The point is that alternatives to flush toilets and sewage treatment plants are feasible and sustainable; flush toilets and sewage treatment plants are not.

If poop were kept separate from water, it would be much cheaper and simpler for municipal waste treatment plants to process. If it were kept free of pollutants, the resulting sludge would be much safer to compost. Cities might find themselves in the fertilizer business, selling a practical alternative to inorganic fertilizer. Even if they still chose to ship their sludge all the way to West Texas to be applied to the land (as New York City does with some of its sludge today), the environmental impact would be greatly reduced.

But in between the collection of poop and recycling of it as compost, it may have another value: as a source of power. The secondary treatment stage at sewage plants introduces bacteria to digest the poop that produce byproducts including methane. Most treatment plants just burn the methane off, but a few are starting to collect this "biogas" to turn turbines that generate electricity. The King County Wastewater Treatment plant in Seattle has pioneered an innovation in exploiting methane by sending it into a fuel cell system. Their system breaks down methane into hydrogen and carbon dioxide; the carbon dioxide is then transformed into carbonate, which is recombined with the hydrogen to produce electricity. Not only are fuel cells more efficient at generating electricity than turbines, but their byproducts—water, carbon dioxide, and heat—are relatively innocuous. Burning methane doesn't produce much pollution, but the King County system produces none.

The King County experiment isn't yet cost-effective, but the technology is in its infancy. This is a good step toward maximizing the value of poop as a resource. Even better, a group of researchers at Penn State University are working on their own fuel cell system to generate electricity from poop at the household level. This experimental system involves dropping poop into a container of bacteria. A microbial fuel cell captures electrons that bacteria release as they digest and converts them into electrical current. Poop goes in, electricity and sludge come out—the electricity to power the homes of the people who pooped, and the sludge ready for composting. Household plumbing that generates electricity and fertilizer: it's like a utopian vision of the future. Instead of wasting our poop, we could be using it to power our homes and fertilize our crops. And while it seems farfetched that poop could be so rich an energy source, doesn't it seem equally improbable that a 200-pound body can be powered for fourteen hours a day on a bowl of Corn Flakes, a tuna sandwich, and a sensible dinner? Our most advanced technology is still decades, if not centuries, away from generating the kind of power from organic matter that our bodies do every day. Perhaps poop has just as much potential as food. Perhaps poop is the next great energy frontier waiting to be tapped, a renewable resource that grows ever more abundant as our population does.

But as sanitary management technology and philosophy advance, we must remember the flush toilet's significance in human history. It's been said that the toilet has saved more lives than any other invention. Without it, waterborne disease would have continued to decimate urban areas. Unquestionably, the toilet's benefits have far outweighed its costs. The task now is to eliminate those costs without sacrificing the benefits—to make toilets as efficient as they are effective.

Accomplishing this requires perfecting microflush and foam-flush toilets for high-use environments and creating municipal collection and composting infrastructures. Plumbing and sanitation systems are the complicated and intricate result of tremendous investments of time, money, and thought; the next generation of toilets will require at least as much investment as the previous. Besides technological advances, we will have to make psychological ones, learning to view poop not as waste but as a resource. It will be socially acceptable for poop to fertilize our vegetables and power our homes only when we realize to use it thus is to take our rightful place in the circle of life.

The day that you come to view your ass as a power plant will not herald an era defined by the stench of feces billowing out of backyards and basements. Any use of poop as a resource will still accord with the fact that poop stinks and no one wants to see it, smell it, or touch it. We'll view poop holistically, and use it fully, but we won't live in the Stink Years. Without the environmental crises this holistic attitude toward poop will avert, the future will be quite the opposite.

CHAPTER 5

HEADS AND TAILS: POOP & PSYCHOLOGY

WE FIRST MEET Reuben Feffer, played by Ben Stiller in 2004's *Along Came Polly*, on his wedding day. Feffer is an anxious, uptight, and neurotic risk-analysis expert who micromanages even his wedding, reminding the cook to be careful with the fish ("Harry Bird at table seven is violently allergic to seafood") and worrying about the slipperiness of the dance floor (because 23% of his guests are over seventy).

Naturally, Feffer's new wife leaves him (for a carefree scuba instructor, on the first day of his honeymoon). Feffer slinks back to New York broken, but soon meets an old acquaintance, Polly Prince, played by Jennifer Aniston. Polly is a free spirit, as laid-back as Feffer is buttoned-up. Opposites attract, and soon Polly is taking Feffer to her favorite ethnic restaurant, where they sit on the floor and eat with their hands and enjoy exotic spices of which Feffer has never dreamed.

Feffer has irritable bowel syndrome, of course. The kind of guy who blots pizza with a napkin to get the grease off, he's used to bland foods. He tries to play it cool, even though the sweat is dripping off his face and his churning stomach almost drowns out their conversation. The bathroom at the restaurant is occupied.

Polly invites Feffer in for a nightcap. His stomach is grunting like a corn-fed hog, but he's too ashamed to say anything. Implying that he needs to pee, he goes to the toilet in her apartment, sits on it, and turns on the shower to mask the noises he makes. But he's too embarrassed to ask Polly for toilet paper or a plunger, and in the ensuing catastrophe he pays the price: he destroys a hand-embroidered towel and a $200 Scandinavian loofah, over-flows the toilet, and leaves her apartment humiliated.

Reuben Feffer is a shameful shitter. He has other problems too, such as his worries about his ".013% chance of getting hit by a car" and "1-in-46,000 chance of falling through a subway grate": his horror when his boss touches his shoulders with unwashed hands after using a urinal, and his need to methodically arrange sixteen throw pillows on his bed every morning and just as methodically take them off every night.

We call people like this "anal."

This book has already explored our own poop's external influences on our relations with others and our environment. But poop exerts strong internal influences, too, on the formation of our personalities.

We get the term "anal" from Sigmund Freud's pioneering psychological theories. Freud founded the psychoanalytic school of psychology on his theory that neurotic, hysterical, and aggressive behaviors are caused by conflicts arising from repressed desires—that is, from the unconscious. By identifying and confronting these unconscious desires through psychoanalysis, Freud believed, patients could engage and conquer their problems. The stereotype of psychoanalysis, not wholly inaccurate, is a doctor asking about your childhood and your mother. Freud's work rests on the belief that childhood experience shapes adult character.

ANAL FIXATION: STUCK IN THE MIDDLE OF POO

Freud theorized that we all pass through five stages from infancy to adulthood: oral, anal, phallic, latency, and genital. The name of each stage refers to the object of the child's gratification—the mouth (in suckling and eating), the anus (in retaining and expelling poop), the genitals (in manipulation of them, though not necessarily masturbation), and finally the genitals as the focal point of sexual gratification. (The latency stage is one of general psychological calm that doesn't seem to figure as strongly into personality development.) The first stage typically occurs from birth until the child is eighteen months old, the second from then until the child is three, the third from three through six years, the fourth from six until puberty, and the fifth from puberty through adulthood. Someone who successfully completes all five stages grows into a healthy adult, confident, stable, and able to have normal sexual and non-sexual relationships. But certain kinds of psychological trauma can interrupt development, causing a child to become fixated in a particular stage instead of passing through it. And that fixation, Freud thought, can affect how that child behaves as an adult.

Perhaps you've heard the term "oral fixation." This refers to someone fixated in the oral stage of development. In the oral stage, the child's pleasure is derived from sucking such things as its mother's breast or baby bottles, usually while being held in a parent's warm embrace. Fixation at this stage can occur if the baby's need to suckle is frustrated. Perhaps mother refuses to nurse, or cuts nursing short before the child is full, or perhaps the child is abruptly weaned. The orally fixated unconsciously want the pleasure denied in their infancy, and they seek to satisfy it through certain behaviors, such as demanding or dependent attitudes, gluttony, and excessive drinking and smoking.

The anal stage, which usually coincides with potty training in Western societies, can take two forms. In each, the child experiences both pleasure and conflict centered in the anal area. The difference lies in how the pleasure and conflict occur: whether through pooping out, or through holding in. The former is more likely if the parents are supportive of the child during potty training, encouraging her as she learns to save her poop for the toilet and cheering her when she does. The latter is more likely if difficult potty training turns the bathroom into a site of conflict with her parents. Then the child is more likely to hold in her poop as long as she can, to avoid the bathroom as much as possible.

Fixations in the anal stage tend to occur at either extreme of the potty-training spectrum. If the parents excessively mollycoddle and extravagantly reward the child during toilet training, she may grow to think of herself as queen of the house, and of her parents as loyal subjects who adore even her poop. Fixation for this child means expecting nothing but this kind of treatment. As an adult, she'll exhibit what Freud called an "anal-expulsive" character—assertive, demanding, rebellious, and temperamental.

At the opposite extreme is the child whose parents pressure, punish, or humiliate her in their efforts to teach bowel control.

Perhaps they believe that early potty training is a sign of intelligence, and want their kid to reach that that milestone before their friends' kids; or perhaps they are just sick of dirty diapers. But the nerves that allow a child to control her sphincter don't fully develop until around the twentieth month. If the child is not ready, then potty training isn't going to work. This might turn the bathroom into a site of yelling, crying, and frustration in a child physically unable to do what her parents ask. As the child's sphincter nerves do develop, she might find that holding in her poop is a way to avoid the bathroom. In addition to chronic constipation that might develop to further compound the problems, the child will retain the expectation that holding things in can avoid confrontation. As an adult, she'll exhibit an "anal-retentive" character—constricted, introverted, perfectionist, obsessive, neurotic.

Shameful shitting: don't blame fixation... necessarily.
While Reuben Feffer is obviously a shameful shitter, being a shameful shitter has no correlation with being anal-retentive. As is described in Chapter Two, many influences throughout life might encourage shameful shitting. Anal fixation is just one of them.

Reuben Feffer is anal-retentive: obsessed with rules and order, rigid and obstinate, overly meticulous in every aspect of life. If Feffer were real, we wouldn't be so quick to judge, because it takes years for a psychoanalyst to identify the repressed desires underlying a patient's behavior. Freud knew that everyone internalizes and builds on childhood experiences in his unique way. His broad theories don't apply to all; rather, he was able to identify certain recurring patterns. But Feffer is a Hollywood stereotype written to conform to the anal-retentive character as laid out by Freud. From the tension in his scenes with his parents we can infer that potty training is to blame. Reuben Feffer is who he is because of how he was taught how to poop. But so is everyone. Toilet training has an enormous influence on character, even for those who don't grow up anally fixated.

POTTY TRAINING: YOUR BUTT VS. THE WORLD

A baby has it good. She eats, drinks, sleeps, and poops. Mommy and Daddy cuddle her, play with her, clean her, and keep her warm. It's a sweet life, just responding to the whims of the body as they come. Tired? Sleep. Hungry? Cry and get food. Need to poop? Go ahead. It doesn't get any better than that.

Until the day it all changes. Suddenly Mommy and Daddy are telling the baby that she's not supposed to do what her body asks. She can't just poop when her body wants. Instead, now she has to go to a special room and sit on a special chair to poop. If she does this, she'll be a big girl and Mommy and Daddy will love her. But if she doesn't, Mommy and Daddy will be unhappy, and she'll be a baby forever.

Typically beginning between eighteen and twenty-four months of age in the United States, potty training is the process by which the child is weaned from ad lib defecation and taught to confine it to a particular time and place as a requirement for graduation from infancy. But in the child's view, potty training is about more than a time and a place—it forces the child to grasp life-changing ideas.

The narrow lesson of potty training is simply that poop is bad except when it's in a toilet. And even when it's in a toilet, even though poop comes from you and you're good, your poop is bad; and if you do anything other than flush it, people will think you're bad, too.

But the broad lesson of potty training is more crucial. Potty training teaches the child that things have meanings. Some things are good, and some are bad, and the meaning can change with time and place.

Toilet training practices in America used to be much different from—and much stricter than—today's. Before the 1950s, most people believed that children should be potty trained by a particular age. Consequently, most parents adhered to rigorous and structured regimens designed to force the child to achieve particular milestones at particular ages. The conventional wisdom at the time advocated a variety of draconian measures supposed to regulate infantile defecation, including holding kids over or strapping them to toilets, chamber pots, or privies for extended periods of time, and even sticking soap sticks or glass rods into a child's rectum to stimulate the need to poop and associate the urge with the location. Parents whose children weren't potty trained by a particular age were considered failures. Add to that the mother's having to wash the baby's soiled swaddling clothes by hand, and the eagerness of parents for expeditious potty training is easy to understand.

Things began to change in the 1940s. In 1946, Dr. Benjamin Spock released *Baby and Child Care*, the most popular parenting book of all time. He was the first pediatrician to apply psycho-analysis to childrearing, and his advice rejected traditional practices designed to build discipline and hurry development. He advocated potty training that let the child learn at her own pace instead of on an arbitrary schedule, and he advised parents to be compassionate instead of strict. At the same time, automated washing machines were spreading across society, which greatly facilitated cleaning up after the baby. The disposable diaper soon followed, making things even easier.

Thanks to changes in technology and custom, potty training is much more relaxed now than ever before. Nevertheless, it's still a difficult stage, and relaxed or not, it still introduces the child to the adult idea of responsibility. Potty training teaches the child how to categorize things, including herself, and makes her aware that the desires of the body are sometimes in opposition to the rules of society. This is the most far-reaching lesson of potty training: if you don't adhere to the rules of clean and dirty, good and bad, right and wrong, time and place, then society will reject you.

Defense Mechanisms: Poop Becomes Symbolic

None of this means that potty training is unethical or unnatural.

In 1891, the ethnographer John G. Bourke published *Scatologic Rites of All Nations*, the 500-page product of ten years spent researching scatological folklore and customs across the world. He details myriad rituals involving bodily fluids, from the urine-drinking ceremony of New Mexico's Zuñi Indians to the way the followers of the Dalai Lama in Tibet would collect the holy one's excrements, dry them, powder them, and sell them as everything from medicine to condiments. Bourke extensively catalogs pooping practices past and present, but nowhere in his book does he describe any tribe or culture in which adults poop like babies, whenever and wherever the urge hits. Every adult he talks about can hold it for the appropriate time or place.

The lack of contradictory evidence from Bourke or any other source suggests that controlling the bowels is a natural part of human development, which means that every culture has some form of potty training. So potty training itself should not be demonized. But it's imperative to understand that it involves more than just poop. Potty training associates a physical action with an ideology.

As potty training progresses and the child begins to understand that physical objects have symbolic meanings, she learns that she can manipulate these symbols for her own purposes. But poop is the only symbol over which she has control, the one thing wholly hers. So the child learns to reward and punish others by controlling her poop. She can deposit it in the toilet and make her parents happy, or she can withhold it and make them upset. She can turn poop into a gift, or a punishment. Or, by forcing people to confront poop in particular circumstances, she can even use it as a weapon. As Norman O. Brown said in his landmark 1959 interpretation of Freud, *Life Against Death: The Psychoanalytic Meaning of History*: "Thus some of the most important categories of social behavior (play, gift, property, weapon) originate in the anal stage of infantile sexuality."

How do children make a leap to something so broad from something so narrow as poop? They make the leap because the conflict between the body and society forces the child to repudiate her instincts about poop. During the anal stage, the child must reject the desires of her body to gain acceptance into society. Freud believed that those desires don't just disappear. Instead, they are denied, displaced, intellectualized, projected, rationalized, regressed, repressed, or sublimated—that is, they meet the defense mechanisms the mind uses to protect itself from anxiety. In many cases, defense mechanisms help people face challenges; in the case of poop, they help us reconcile our body with social rules. Ineffectual or inappropriate use of defense mechanisms, however, can cause neurosis, in which the repressed reappears as the unconscious root of problematic behavior.

One fairly common example in Freudian theory involves the sublimation of poop into money. It's not easy in Western society to say so, but pooping feels good. The longer you hold it in, the better it feels when you let it out. But because potty training discourages sensual appreciation of poop, the child must deny the pleasures of retaining and releasing it. The yearning for this pleasure doesn't go away, however. While some people may rediscover it as they grow older, others will sublimate it—that is, channel it from an impulse condemned by society into an acceptable one. In his 1914 essay *The Ontogenesis of the Interest in Money*, psychoanalyst Sandor Ferenczi traced the sublimation of poop into money.

According to Ferenczi, mud comes first. Brown, sticky mud can approximate poop in the child's mind, and playing in mud might seem like the next best thing. But as the child grows older, she must learn to avoid things that make her dirty. When that happens, sand makes a good substitute. But further development forces further sublimation. Sand is replaced first by pebbles and stones, and then by marbles or buttons—hard, dry, odorless collectables that please the child to retain or expel at will. (Ferenczi's premises here may be a bit dated, insofar as kids don't play with buttons or marbles any more. Baseball cards are a more up-to-date example.) Finally, as development progresses even further, even innocuous pursuits such as collecting things are no longer appropriate. And so, according to Ferenczi, the child turns to the one collectable everyone approves of: coins. Bills. Money.

By Freudian logic, Ferenczi's connection between poop and money explains why so many people with loveless lives turn to money and material objects—because they made the choice during potty training to choose the love of their parents over the pleasures of poop. In the absence of affection, they turn to their sublimated anal desires in hopes of recovering the gratification they traded for parental approval.

Psychoanalysts rely on such associations to understand patients' behaviors. Another helpful association is the one between poop, babies, and penises. Children know that babies come from Mommy's stomach, and they know that poop comes from their own. By their infantile logic, there's only one way the baby can come out of Mommy: the same way poop comes out of them. This equivalence makes them tend to view poop as their own special creation—just as Mommy loves the baby she pooped out, so too does the child love her own ass-baby. At the same time, poop is symbolic of the penis, not just because of the phallic shape, but also because it dangles from the groin area and then drops off. Following the progression of penis-poop-baby, Freud even suggests that a woman's desire for a baby is really an extension of her penis envy, with poop inter-mediate term in the equivalence.

Fecal Attraction

Despite the psychic twists and turns poop can cause, most people are able to successfully cope with their unconscious anal desires and function as normal adults. Even anal-retentive and anal-expulsive personalities can, in all but the extreme cases, still function in society. But there are some whose unconscious impulses motivate behaviors wholly at odds with the rules of society—people whose repressed anal desires manifest in the realm of the genitals. Poop fetishists, in other words.

Poop fetishism, or scat, comes in many degrees and has many nuances. Some scat aficionados are content simply to observe people on the toilet. Some just want to smell it. Some want to actually see it coming out, or see the end product in the toilet, or even reach in and grab it and touch it and, in the extreme cases, eat it. Some want to poop on others; some, vice versa. Some people want to rub their poop all over their bodies; others enjoy pooping in diapers and walking around with it squishing in their pants all day. Like its manifestations, the unconscious roots of the scat fetish also vary from person to person. While psychoan-alysts can probably trace each variation on the scat theme to one or another particular childhood event, there is a unifying theme. We're taught that poop is the ultimate negative; at the same time, the experience of pooping is a pleasurable sensa-tion, in proximity to the sexual organs. Scat fetishes come from the contradictions between the positive and the negative, between the repressed and the accepted. It may occur from anal fixation or because of some psychological trauma during potty training, but it may also originate in the phallic or genital stages.

Like any other fetishist, a scat-lover will argue that he's not alone in his desires, only in his candor and freedom about them. And like other fetishists, scat-lovers are likely to confine their activities to the bedrooms (and bathrooms) of consenting adults. The creepy guy in the gas station bathroom might be a scat fetishist, but so might the well-dressed banker filling up his BMW at the pump. And like other fetishists, their affinity is not a danger to society or even to themselves—one's own poop can't hurt you, and others' poop is only dangerous if they have a fecally-transmitted disease. If the participants are clean and consenting, the only real danger in scat fetishes lie in society's reaction if they're found out.

BROWN'S BROWN UTOPIA

Not everyone becomes a fetishist. Not everyone becomes anally fixated. But everyone who goes through potty training has to endure the trauma of giving up bodily pleasures for social acceptance. If the millions of people in our society are coping with their own unconscious desires in one way or another, these desires probably have influence beyond each individual's behavior.

So Norman O. Brown realized. The aggregate of millions of individuals is society. And society has a psyche, fixated (Brown thought) firmly in the anal phase.

Writing in the late 1950s, Brown saw certain American ways of life, including capitalism, as anally-fixated behaviors. Society's obsession with categorization, its relentless desire to subdue nature, and its lust for luxury goods worthless in all but the status they confer on the owner are evidence of anal repression, both expulsive (in society's frantic desire for more) and retentive (in its need to categorize everything). Brown saw these as signs of sublimation of desire by a society in denial of its bodies. And just as Freud believed that psychological problems can be overcome by confronting unconscious desires, so did Brown believe that a society that could learn to accept the body instead of denying it would be able to cure its problems. Instead of refusing our stinky, absurd, ridiculous-looking bodies as flawed and mortal, he said that we should accept them for what they are: stinky, absurd, ridiculous-looking, flawed, and mortal. With this acceptance, the problems rooted in society's unconscious conflicts—such as lust for money, power, and status—would disappear. In this utopia, science would seek to harmonize with nature, not subdue it. Technology would pursue freedom and health. People would work not for money, but for happiness.

Brown may be right; but as with any utopia, the problem is getting there from here, especially when people here are so hostile to poop. What Brown described as a denial of the body we discussed in Chapter Two: fecal denial, the ideology that deems any acknowledgement of poop as uncivilized, causes shameful shitting, and is entwined with the Victorian roots of the flush toilet. Fecal denial is, of course, an impossible standard, because poop cannot be denied. When you shop for groceries, you see toilet paper. When you watch the news, you may learn that a sewer main has broken. When you go to the theater, you see the line for the restrooms. Ideology can't change reality. But it can influence how we interpret it.

Shrek Outhouse.

CHAPTER 6

SIGNS OF THE HIND:
THE SYMBOLIC MEANINGS OF POOP

IN THE BOWELS OF Benjamin Franklin Jr. High School, an awkward young girl creeps into the bathroom. "Awkward" is perhaps too kind—she's skinny, squinty, with big glasses and big teeth, lips agape in a desperate cry for orthodontic work, a broken spirit yearning for popularity even as she strives for invisibility to help her through the daily horrors of the eighth grade. The bathroom is a dangerous place for her, a no-man's land where teachers can't see in, where troublemakers feel safe to sneak a smoke, and where bullies terrorize at will. But a neurotic mind can't always convince an insistent body that it's best to hold it until you get home.

Dawn Wiener needs only to make it from the bathroom entrance into an empty stall, where she can trust the anonymity of her footwear to keep danger at bay until she has to leave. She aims for the third stall of four. But before she can get there, the first stall opens, and out steps Lolita.

Don't confuse Lolita with her literary namesake. This Lolita is a bitter, angry rebel with a defiant scowl on her face and a history of hostility toward Dawn. Seeing her, Dawn changes direction, heading toward the sink with the unnatural gait of someone trying to look natural. Lolita, radiating hate, intercepts Dawn at the paper towel dispenser, slamming it with her hand and making Dawn jump.

> Lolita: "You didn't come in here to wash your hands."
> Dawn: "Y-y-yes I did."
> Lolita: "You came in here to take a shit."
> Dawn: "N-n-no, really. I don't have to go." Dawn holds up her hands. "My hands were just dirty, that's all."
> Lolita: "Liar. I can smell you from here."

Dawn tries to run for the door. Lolita heads her off at the second stall.

> Dawn: "Please let me go."
> Lolita: "First... take a shit."
> Dawn: "But I'll be late for science."
> Lolita: "Well, you're not leaving until you do."

Dawn protests. Remembering the old axiom that all bullies really want are friends, Dawn offers Lolita the vice presidency of a new club she's starting. That doesn't work. Dawn babbles objections, anything to get Lolita to stop being so mean. "But—"

"But shit. Now..." Lolita pushes Dawn to the third stall. "Go." Dawn tries to close the stall door—one is supposed to have privacy when one poops!—but Lolita shoves it back open. "Leave it. I want to make sure you shit. I want to see it with my own eyes." The scene cuts there, mercifully.

This is one of the more excruciating moments in the wonder years of the protagonist of Todd Solondz's film *Welcome to the Dollhouse*, and it is such because it viscerally exploits the specific symbolic meanings the taboo of poop has created around both the product and the act.

The cultural confusion about poo is centered on the act of pooping in a public setting. About poop itself, all agree: outside of the toilet, it is matter out of place. The lesson of potty training—that poop is the ultimate symbol of negativity, and that worthless, nasty poop must be made to disappear forever in the toilet—lasts a lifetime.

As such, we rarely have physical encounters with other humans' poop or their private rituals surrounding the act. But symbolic encounters—such as seeing it in a movie or hearing about it in a joke—are common. And since fecal aversion and denial make it hard to acknowledge poop seriously, poop is almost always invoked for its shock value, to make us laugh or to disgust us. We find it invoked in sources from *Dumb and Dumber* to *Kiss of the Spider Woman*; from Jonathan Swift to Stephen King; from the Bible to Freud; from *South Park* to *Seinfeld*; from Van Gogh to *Cloaca*. We invoke it in conversation, our jokes, our pranks, our insults, and our day-to-day relationships.

Everyone interprets the invocation of poop in his own way, based on his own personal experience. But on the aggregate, a few associations with poop seem to resonate across the board. That's why writers, directors, musicians, poets, and artists in both high culture and low turn to poop to make their point. Unanimity in dislike of poop makes its symbolic meanings easy to understand.

1) POOP EXPOSES THE LOWNESS OF THE HIGH

Of all the troubles facing our boys in blue in *Police Academy IV: Citizens on Patrol*, Lieutenant Proctor is the most infuriating. The bumbling sidekick of the despicable Captain Harris, Proctor has authority in direct proportion to the quantity of ass over which his lips have grazed. A sycophant and an idiot, he kowtows before those who appreciate a good kowtowing, and is rewarded with the authority to be a jerk in the name of his superiors.

Nothing better illustrates Proctor's arbitrary cruelty than his attitude toward the Academy grads' efforts at community outreach. Finding Mahoney and his comrades bonding with neighborhood youths over a game of basketball, he accuses them of goofing off and smugly promises to tell the captain. Driving off, he stops short to dash into a portable toilet on a nearby construction site. His longsuffering subordinates seize this opportunity to humble their tormentor. While Proctor contentedly reads *Archie's Pals n' Gals* as he goes about his business, Mahoney and gang commandeer a crane, lift the porta-potty off the site, deposit it in the middle of a crowded football stadium, and lift off the walls.

And then the national anthem begins. Pants around his ankles, Proctor is still a man in uniform; with the crowd staring, he stands and salutes.

An authority figure is expected to be perfect. His position implies that he's a human being his lessers should strive to emulate. That's why nothing gives an authority figure his comeuppance better than exposing him while he's pooping. Shamefaced with his pants down, what's revealed is the one thing that can undo him: his fundamental similarity to everybody else.

The fear he inspired evaporates into scorn, and his rank, stature, and powerful friends become irrelevant.

It's not just authority figures who have to worry about poop; any façade of dignity is vulnerable. In Neil Simon's *Brighton Beach Memoirs*, a teenaged Eugene Morris Jerome lusts after his beautiful cousin Nora. He struggles to create an aura of sophistication as would befit a beau suitable for the lovely lady, and it's all shattered when Nora walks in on him in the bathroom. He screams at her to shut the door. "She saw me on the crapper!" he laments. "Nora saw me on the crapper! I might as well be dead!" It's not that Nora doesn't herself poop, or that Eugene believed Nora didn't think he pooped, but that poop, the ultimate low, easily brings down the edifice of high.

When we're pooping, we have to drop our mask. When someone sees what's behind the mask, the impression the mask had created is gone. Eugene worries that Nora now sees him as just another stinky teenager. The whole football crowd sees Lieutenant Proctor not as a distinguished officer but as a guy with skinny legs who reads *Archie* on the pot. And while the stigma both Eugene and Proctor suffered comes partly from taboos against showing private parts, pooping makes it much worse. Proctor would certainly pick being merely naked in front of 50,000 people over pooping in front of them. Eugene would much rather Nora had seen him in the shower than on the toilet. As William Plank writes in his essay "The Psychosocial Bases of Scatological Humor," poop "removes the props by which the self attempts to create and control its image: clothing, privacy, secrecy, composition of the face, and self-control."

Reaction, of course, is everything. Exposing somebody only works if it reveals a truth the person wants to hide. Nerds may conspire to kick open the stall door while the bully who torments them is pooping, but if the bully just stares defiantly at them without embarrassment, then their plan backfires. Someone's only cut down to size if he's forced to admit he's not a complete man after all—which is exactly what Eugene was admitting when he was covering his genitals and screaming. When the stall door is thrown open and the authority figure shrinks back, the curtain is parted. The person once respected will be forever associated with that moment cowering on the toilet, powerless and ridiculous, desperately trying to hide the one thing that makes him like everyone else.

Milan Kundera relates an example in *The Unbearable Lightness of Being*. After World War II, Josef Stalin's son Yakov was captured by the Germans and held in a prison camp along with a group of British soldiers. Yakov, Kundera tells, had a habit of leaving a mess in the prisoners' shared latrine. The British officers were naturally upset, even if this was the poop of the son of one of the most powerful men in the world. The English soldiers tried to talk to him about it, but he refused. They tried to make him clean the latrine, but he refused. Finally the conflict grew so trying that Yakov demanded a hearing with the camp arbiter. But the arbiter would not demean himself by discussing a topic so low. Yakov Stalin was humiliated. Cursing wildly to hide his shame, he ran and jumped and impaled himself upon the electrified fence, and died.

Stalin's son, we are told, believed that his social position made even his poop exceptional. When the German arbiter refused to discuss it, Yakov had to confront the contrary. Yakov was being judged, not for his role in the dramas of war, politics, power, or family, but for his poop. The high of being the son of Stalin was destroyed by the lowness of poop. Yakov could not live without that façade.

2) POOP UNDERSCORES THE LOWNESS OF THE LOW.

The tyrannosaurus should have been satisfied after eating a whole live goat. But it turns out that a T-rex will always make room for a tasty human. A goat haunch drops from the sky, landing on the hood of a jeep carrying a slimeball lawyer and two adorable little kids. The T-rex comes down for a closer look. The adorable little kids scream. The slimeball lawyer panics. For Donald Gennaro, attorney for Jurassic Park and all-around sleaze, dinosaurs are interesting only as liability potential. Abandoning the two adorable little kids, Gennaro sprints into a nearby outhouse for park visitors, safe and hidden until the dinosaur accidentally demolishes the bathroom and spies the bar-certified morsel perched on the now-open-air toilet.

You know it's a bad day when first you reveal your cowardice and then get eaten by a dinosaur. What makes it worse is when the dinosaur gobbles you up while you're sitting on a toilet. Even though Gennaro wasn't pooping (at least, not in the toilet), the reference to poop in this scene from *Jurassic Park* makes Gennaro's downfall that much more complete. It adds insult to injury. It's bad to be cowardly dinosaur food, but worse to be cowardly dinosaur food gobbled off a toilet.

Poop's lowness contaminates anything with which it associates. In the film *Chattahoochee*, a Korean War hero named Emmett Foley ends up in a mental hospital where doctors seem more interested in humiliating their patients than in treating them. He rebels and is punished by being forced to sit on a hard bench for hours, until merely sitting is itself torture. The only thing that could make his agony of boredom and pain worse finally happens: he wets himself, and then he soils himself.

In Foley's case, the doctors were teaching him the hard way that they had full control over his physical and mental well-being. That their power extended to bodily functions made the low even lower. That's more explicit than the symbolic affront *Jurassic Park*'s Donald Gennaro experienced. In Gennaro's case, the suggestion of poop intensified his disgrace. In both cases, however, poop furthered the character's development in the same way: a low made lower. This is why *Welcome to the Dollhouse* included an encounter between Dawn and Lolita in the bathroom. It was the case in *Bulletproof*, when the cop handcuffed Adam Sandler to an unflushed toilet; instead of protesting his arrest, Sandler protested his proximity to poop. And it was also the case in *The Air Up There* when a warthog humiliated Kevin Bacon in front of a pretty nun—being chased out of the woods by a warthog is low enough, but being chased with pants around ankles after a warthog found him pooping makes it far lower.

3) POOP MAKES A POTENT INSULT

In *The Wars of the Jews*, Flavius Josephus describes an event that took place when five hundred Roman soldiers came to

Jerusalem for the Passover feast. Standing over the cloisters of the temple, "one of the soldiers pulled back his garment, and cowering down after an indecent manner, turned his breech to the Jews, and spake such words as you might expect upon such a posture." The Jews were enraged, and 10,000 people were killed in the ensuing riots.

The paradigm of waste, poop is the most unambiguous negative in our culture. Literally, it looks, smells, and (presumably) tastes bad. Figuratively, it represents the *worst* of anything—the *worst* smell, appearance, or taste. It's therefore not surprising

Poop is a timeless insult. Shown here, a 14th-century image depicting a Jew being forced to eat a pig's shit. From Alan Dundes' *Life is Like a Chicken Coop Ladder: A Study of German National Character Through Folklore.*

that one of poop's most common manifestations is in the form of an insult or deprecation. "This tastes like shit." "This smells like shit." "Today you played like shit." In that last case, "shit" refers more to an abstract negative than to the actual fecal product; it probably doesn't mean that someone played basketball in the manner of an inanimate lump of feces. Even if it makes no logical sense, to insult someone or disparage something by comparison to poop is to directly associate them with the most negative thing there is.

Poop has been used as an insult for as long as people have instinctively avoided it. The poet Catullus called the writings of his first-century B.C. contemporary Volusius "*cacata charta*"— shit paper. The first-century A.D. satirist Martial harshly criticized a fellow writer by deeming his work a more appropriate subject for a poor poet "who shall with charcoal, on the privy wall / Immortalize your name for once and all." Perhaps the most poignant use of poop as an insult was that to Jesus just before he died on the cross. The public privies of ancient Rome supplied brine-soaked sponges on sticks for Romans to wipe their butts. In their accounts of the crucifixion of Jesus, Mark, Matthew, and John relate that the mocking crowd pushed a vinegar-soaked sponge into Jesus' face, smearing his face as a final indignity before his death.

According to David Inglis in *Dirt and Denigration: The Fecal Imagery and Rhetorics of Abuse*, poop insults fall into one of two major categories: degrading someone by associating him with the physical properties of poop, or defining someone by the way he poops. The first category of insults is how the Romans insulted Jerusalem (associating the temple with a toilet) and how the crowd at the crucifixion insulted Jesus (associating his face with a butt that needed wiping). The second category of insults implies that the recipient is a member of an inferior social group—inferior specifically because of the uncivilized way in which its members attend to their bodily functions.

This association is less poignant today than in the early days of the flush toilet. By the end of the nineteenth century, state and social reformers in both England and America were working hard to spread the flush toilet across society and alleviate critical sanitary threats. Much of the strategy involved the state extending and maintaining modern sewer and water infrastructures, but reformers still needed to convince skeptics that the new bathroom technology was a boon and not a power-grab by the government. To overcome resistance in people who had been pooping in privies or chamber pots all their lives and were quite content with them, they associated health, happiness, refinement, and civilization with the flush toilet. The corollary of that, of course, was that people who didn't use flush toilets were the opposite. In today's society, with nearly everyone using flush toilets, this kind of insult is usually used against "dirty foreigners"—mocking toilet habits that differ from our own, as if ours are the paragon of civilized behavior, and any others somehow indicate barbarism or diminished intellect.

4) POOP REPRESENTS CONTAMINATION

In *The Book of Nasty Legends*, Paul Smith fictionalizes an age-old nightmare:

> Possibly it was the excitement of going out with Dave, her new boyfriend, for the first time. Alternatively, it could have been something she had eaten. Whatever the reason, Caroline had been stricken for the last hour with a rather bad attack of wind. By the time her date arrived it was all she could do to get from the house and into the car without disgracing herself. As Dave closed the door on her side and walked round to his, in desperation Caroline exploded with a very large and loud fart.
>
> Dave, getting into the driving seat, appeared not to have noticed. However, turning to her and indicating toward the back seat he said, "Let me introduce my two friends, Linda and Brian. I thought they would like to join us tonight!"

Smith's imaginary Caroline was probably a very sweet girl. On the ride over, Dave probably talked up her accomplishments—her beauty, her intelligence, her award-winning talent as a sculptor, and the six months she spent digging irrigation ditches for refugee camps in sub-Saharan Africa. But to Linda and Brian, that single fart outweighs any positive impression they may have formed. Caroline's got her work cut out for her to get Linda and Brian to think otherwise.

The concept of filth is deeply integrated with ideas of class and hierarchy. The gist: the more matter you allow out of its place, the less you belong in civilization. In a society that values purity, a filthy body implies a filthy soul. And no other filth is as filthy as poop. Out of place, it invites immediate and total condemnation. If there were a guy on the subway with poop all over his face, you wouldn't come within ten feet. You'd think he was crazy. You'd hold your nose to avoid an odor that would confirm what your eyes told you. God forbid he should actually touch you! Even if he perceived your scorn and gave a good explanation for his appearance—his toilet at work exploded, and he's on his way home to shower—you probably wouldn't believe it. Such is the contaminating power of poop that it will incite enduring condemnation on the puniest evidence. A spot of poop overwhelms reams of clean record.

Many symbols have this kind of contaminating power in our hierarchy of taboos, but poop is the most potent. Picture this: a swimming pool on a hot summer day, filled with frolicking children, laughing babies, and beaming adults. The water is pure, fresh, invigorating. And then: something brown floating. "Doodie!" screams the first kid to spot it. "Doodie! Doodie!" Bedlam. The pool empties as mothers scramble after children and men shove women out of the way.

This scene from *Caddyshack* is an exaggerated depiction, but real life isn't much different: operators of most public pools will clear out the swimmers and drain the water upon the discovery of feces. Never mind that the pool is still two million parts water to every part poop (or, as it turned out in *Caddyshack*, every part Baby Ruth bar). And never mind that just removing it would be enough to ensure the safety of the swimmers. Pool water is rich in germicidal chlorine. A few particles from a floater won't cause any harm. And yet poop seems to have the near-supernatural ability to contaminate anything it touches—so much so that we'll reject a hundred thousand gallons of water because of six ounces of poop. Overreaction to its contaminating presence is the norm.

On January 31, 2006, Gothamist.com reported that one of New York City's A trains was suddenly taken out of service at the height of the morning rush. The only official explanation was "excessive vandalism," but eyewitnesses reported that a homeless man had pooped in one of the cars. Even though New York City's subways can close a single car while keeping open the rest, they decided to take the whole train out of service and force hundreds of people to de-train (which, as any New Yorker will tell you, introduces chaos into the commute) because of one man's bowel movement.

One night in August 2005, vandals attacked Chattanooga's Red Bank High School, smearing urine and feces on lockers, walls, and floors, in classrooms and on stairwells. Upon discovering the mess the next morning, administrators immediately shut the school down, sequestering arriving students in a gymnasium until they could be sent home. The school brought in the county's health department for a 280-man-hour cleaning. The school was open the next day, but the cafeteria remained closed for a special cleaning, even though there were no reports of any poop in there. Whether or not you believe that is an overreaction even given the school's imperative to protect students, some people ascribed so much magical power to the contamination that they felt it threatened the school's very soul. A few days after the vandalism, *The Chattanoogan* published a column, "Red Bank High School— What Vandalism Can't Erase." The columnist cataloged illustrious graduates of Red Bank, apparently terrified that this act of vandalism would besmirch the school's name forever. His conclusion: "There is not enough waste in the world that can drown out the tens of thousands of accomplishments of the men and women who have walked the blue and white halls of Red Bank High School. Let it be their fragrance that we remember."

5) EMBRACING YOUR OWN POOP UNDERSCORES YOUR CONTEMPT FOR OTHERS

In the fictional Arthurian England of *Monty Python and the Holy Grail,* farting is presumably as taboo there as it was in the 1970s England in which the movie was made—just as in 1970s England and in most of the Western world today, public farting would invite social condemnation. So why is it that when an arrogant Frenchman shrieks at King Arthur and his men, "I fart in your general direction!" it is the crusaders who are insulted? Shouldn't the person who farts in public be the one disgraced? This chapter already established that if you associate someone with poop, you associate him with the ultimate low. Further, one exposed as someone who poops is thereby stripped of dignity and stature. How, then, can farting in someone's general direction strip him of his dignity and yet leave the farter's intact?

This is one of the most fascinating aspects of the poop taboo: breaking it to send a negative message amplifies your message, placing the target beneath your own fundament. Compare saying, "Hey, Joe, you smell like poop," to, "Hey, Joe, you smell like *my* poop!" Though you broke the taboo, the contamination is transferred to Joe.

This logic is universally understood, especially by teenagers, who love to harness it to enforce the laws of teenage hierarchy that demand merciless abuse of the unliked. In their arsenal: a turd in the mailbox, a flaming bag of poo on the doorstep, a bit of ass butter smeared on the underside of a car door handle, or perhaps an upper decker—that is, fecal matter pooped surreptitiously into the tank of a toilet where it will slowly disintegrate, staining the water brown and baffling the toilet's owner until the lid is lifted and the awful truth is discovered.

Normally we would think there's something wrong with a person who poops into a paper bag. But if they're doing it as part of an insult, the taboo evaporates. This loophole has created techniques for being mean with poop that are as clever as they are awful. Unscrew a light switch, stuff the insides with poop, close it up, and laugh as the victim wonders where the smell is coming from. Poop in a plastic Ziploc bag, write "brownie" on it, and put it in someone's freezer. Break into a dorm room and poop in the closet, as Najeh Davenport of the Green Bay Packers did in 2002 (he was charged with a second-degree felony count of burglary and a misdemeanor count of criminal mischief). Or force someone to poop in front of you, as Lolita did to Dawn. Even though the rules of society would normally condemn Lolita as disgusting for watching someone else poop, it was Dawn who suffered the indignity.

Poop is a symbol without ambiguity. A few months after Hurricane Katrina, a string of emails between FEMA director Michael Brown's office and FEMA representatives in the hardest-hit areas were released. Marty Bahamonde, FEMA's regional director for New England, tried repeatedly to warn his superiors about the awful situation in the Superdome. After learning that Sharon Worthy, Brown's press secretary, was sending messages more concerned with such trivial matters as finding a restaurant for Brown to eat in, Bahamonde wrote back, "Just tell her that I just ate an MRE and crapped in the hallway of the Superdome along with 30,000 other close friends so I understand her concern about busy restaurants."

Perhaps the most striking example comes from Lyndon Johnson, the thirty-sixth president of the United States. Johnson was infamous for receiving reporters and junior staffers while on the toilet. According to the rules of society, Johnson's stature should have been tarnished for so flagrantly violating the taboo against pooping visibly. The disgust felt by his audience should have completely undermined his authority. But the effect was the opposite: it was the people in front of whom he pooped who were degraded. Those who tried to maintain decorum when confronted by their pooping president suffered worst of all. In *Lyndon Johnson & the American Dream*, Doris Kearns Goodwin writes of LBJ's delight while telling her of "one of the delicate Kennedyites who came into the bathroom with me and then found it utterly impossible to look at me while I sat there on the toilet. You'd think he had never seen those parts of the body before. For there he was, standing as far away from me as he possibly could, keeping his back toward me the whole time, trying to carry on a conversation. I could barely hear a word he said. I kept straining my ears and then finally I asked him to come a little closer to me. Then began the most ludicrous scene I had ever witnessed. Instead of simply turning around and walking over to me, he kept his face away from me and walked backwards, one rickety step at a time. For a moment there I thought he was going to run right into me. It certainly made me wonder how that man had made it so far in the world."

6) POOP CAN COMMUNICATE PROTEST

At a 1989 exhibition at the Center for the Development of the Visual Arts in Havana, the Cuban artist Angel Delgado formed a circle with animal bones, placed a copy of *Granma* (the official Communist Party newspaper) in the center, pulled down his pants, and pooped on it. Official response was swift. The exhibition was immediately closed. Delgado was fired from his job. The secret police picked him up and sentenced him to six months in prison. Probably none of these consequences came as a surprise to the artist. "It was an act of political desperation," he said. "I wanted to draw attention to the absence of freedom of expression in Cuba. I wanted to express myself against censorship."

Six years later, Gerard Finneran expressed himself in a similar way. On a flight from Buenos Aires to New York, the 58-year-old investment banker was denied a drink after flight attendants decided he had already had more than enough. Arguing and cursing didn't change their minds; the more he begged and pleaded, the more firmly the flight attendants resolved to keep him dry. He stole drinks from the drink cart and shoved a flight attendant. After pouring drinks on himself didn't persuade them, Finneran went into first class and, in the words of the legal complaint filed against him, was observed "with his pants and underwear down defecating on a service cart used by the flight crew." He then wiped his ass with the first class cabin's fine linen napkins.

What does Gerard Finneran have in common with Angel Delgado? In both cases, each of them was desperate to change a situation over which they had no control, and resorted to poop as the only way to communicate their frustration.

They're not alone. In a 1996 survey of hospitals, prisons, and regional secure units, 38 of the 50 respondents reported 2,693 incidents of scatolia (fecal smearing) in the preceding five years. While most were attributed to mental impairment or psychiatric disorders, 159 were determined by the reporting facilities to be a form of protest. 159 instances of fecal smearing by rational, nonpsychotic persons who, though deemed perfectly sane, nevertheless believed that smearing poop would somehow further their cause.

When not associated with mental illness, scatolia is a response to extreme powerlessness and frustration. Someone believes that his rights have been stripped away and that the system is against him. He wants to communicate his frustrations, but he believes that even his protests are assimilated by the system. As pointed out by Tom Mason in *Managing Protest Behavior: From Coercion to Compassion*, the prisoner feels that the only way to communicate the irrationality of his plight is through a medium that's equally irrational. Mason outlines three such scenarios: a perception of unjust imprisonment; an expectation of abuse in the guise of correctional therapy; and a Catch-22, in which the more he fights the system, the more the system uses his actions to justify its own. In all three scenarios, rational means of communication have seemingly failed; and so he throws his poop at the guards, or smears it all over his cell, or eats it, or plays with it, or poops on a drink cart.

From an outsider's perspective, it seems completely unreasonable for the prisoner to expect to communicate effectively through such antisocial behavior. But scatolia—along with other forms of irrational protest, such as property destruction, hostage-taking, or hunger strikes—communicates frustration to a system that won't acknowledge any other form of communication. During potty training, one must reject poop to enter society; as an act of protest, poop symbolizes the fundamental rejection of an oppressive society.

Scatolia isn't restricted to prisons and psychiatric institutions. Office buildings, governmental institutions, gas stations, and Wal-Mart all encounter disgruntled workers, irritated citizens, or angry consumers expressing their dissatisfaction with layoffs, bureaucratic red tape, or poor customer service using the medium of final resort.

Unfortunately, this kind of protest behavior is almost always misdirected. Rarely does it cause the person or system that inspired such anger to suffer. It only hurts future toilet users and the poor employee who has to clean it up. Accepting the innocent bathroom-goer or custodian as collateral damage in the name of ideology: this is turd terrorism.

A public bathroom needs its users' trust. On the border between public and private, pure and impure, the bathroom is precariously perched, needing little to render it unusable. The ethical imperative for the bathroom user is to leave a bathroom in the condition in which he or she would hope to find it. A turd terrorist shits all over that ethical imperative.

Norman O. Brown identified poop as a child's prototype for the concept of a weapon. Turd terrorism is an adult return to that symbolism. A turd terrorist intentionally violates the purity of the bathroom. He will crap on the toilet seat, piss on the toilet paper, smear poop on the walls, floor, toilet handle, and in the urinal. If you've ever encountered a bathroom so befouled with human waste that you wouldn't even set foot inside, you've suffered the aftermath of turd terrorism. Probably you had to back out and hurry away, lest someone think you were the responsible party.

A politically-motivated turd terrorist may justify his actions as poop patriotism. That might be a fair depiction of an exquisitely poetic form of revenge—getting even, for instance, with a restaurant that knowingly served spoiled food and gave you diarrhea. Such justifications, though, are rare. Even when the act can be justified, it is nevertheless the innocent bathroom users who are forced to endure the mire and make the awful choice: either using it and accidentally touching the fallout from this dirty bomb, or taking the risk to find another bathroom—which attempt, if the need is urgent enough, could lead to catastrophe. Beyond that, it's probably not those who aggrieved the terrorist who will have to clean it up, but almost inevitably a low-paid underling, struggling against the same system.

As upsetting as politically-motivated turd terrorists are, even worse are those who terrorize for terror's sake. These evildoers smear their crap all over bathrooms merely for the cruel thrill of making others feel sick. These turd terrorists are also motivated by frustration, but theirs is an unfocused and generalized antagonism. Symbolically, the apolitical turd terrorist is leaving himself in the bathroom. Knowing the effect his smeared poop will have on those who encounter it, he enjoys power over lives he'd otherwise never touch. To the kind of person who reaches into the toilet water, grabs his poop, and squishes it all over a stall, tainting a bathroom and causing misery for others is fulfillment in an otherwise socially impoverished life.

Messy Ethical Dilemmas

Aside from turd terrorists with a point to prove and turd terrorism with no point, any discussion of the phenomenon must address the grey area: an accidental launch of a weapon of ass destruction. When the sphincter loses poise a moment before the butt hits the seat, the result is a spray that goes every which way but in the bowl. To defile a public toilet thus may have been unintended, but the result is the same as if

Hezbowellah had executed the attack: a toilet ruined for subsequent users, and a suffering cleaning staff.

The bathroom user must follow the brown corollary to the Golden Rule—to leave the bathroom as you'd like to find it—but it's the responsibility of the bathroom's management to maintain the facilities. So, intentional or not, since the ends are the same as those of a turd terrorist strike, do the means make a difference? Must the incontinent seek out a mop and rubber gloves, or at least suffer the embarrassment of telling a janitor? Or is it okay to leave the problem for the next pooper?

These are questions that keep a poop ethicist up at night.

7) POOP REPRESENTS THE MUNDANE

In the film *Fight Club*, Ed Norton's character leads so boring a life that he doesn't even have a name—in the credits, he's identified only as "Narrator." Norton's life is his job and his possessions; he works the former to get the latter. He's the American Everyman, dull, complacent, and shallow. One poignant scene has him fantasizing about an apartment full of Ikea furniture. We see him perusing catalogs, then watch him ordering furniture over the phone while sitting on the toilet.

In *American Splendor*, Harvey Pekar is in a similar situation. He, too, leads a boring life—so boring, in fact, that everyone wants to read the comic books he writes about how boring his life is. Finally something exciting happens: one of his fans turns into a pen pal who eventually becomes a love interest. We see him reading letters from his soon-to-be wife Joyce—in bed, in the kitchen, and on the toilet.

Despite its glorification present thus far, not every poop is a mortal insult, or a representation of class struggle, or a desperate protest. When it's not man-versus-dinner or psychosis-versus-physiology, poop is just poop, an unremarkable part of an unremarkable day. Another day passes, another meal is eaten, another poop is plopped, signifying nothing. It's like riding in an elevator—it has the potential to be interesting, sure, but usually it is just minutes spent waiting for it to be over and forgotten. In real life, poop is usually boring. Hence the poop scenes in *Fight Club* and *American Splendor*. These scenes underscore the ordinariness of the protagonists' lives by showing that their time spent pooping is as worthy of valuable screen time as anything else they do. And this is another reason to feel sorry for Dawn Wiener in *Welcome to the Dollhouse*—because if there's any moment more deserving of a truce from the daily struggle, it's one's time in the bathroom.

The everyday act of going to the bathroom is rarely depicted in the media. We usually only see it in fiction when something exciting, funny, or shocking happens while a character is doing it. But people identify more with pooping when it's shown as a mundane process, because that's how most of us experience it. A boring poop scene adds realism.

This symbolic meaning resonates far beyond the movies. Consider this quote from Vincent Van Gogh in defense of his 1885 painting *The Potato Eaters*. A dark, earthy picture of ugly peasants eating, it's wildly different from the pastoral portraits of peasants admired by many of his contemporaries. Those other paintings idealized peasant life; Van Gogh's presents peasants as they were. In a letter to his brother Theo, Vincent explains:

> [I]t would be wrong, I think, to give a peasant picture a certain conventional smoothness. If a peasant picture smells of bacon, smoke, potato steam—all right, that's not unhealthy; if a stable smells of dung—all right, that belongs to a stable; if the field has an odor of ripe corn or potatoes or of guano or manure—that's healthy, especially for city people.
>
> Such pictures may teach them something. But to be perfumed is not what a peasant picture needs.

To Van Gogh, excrement and realism went hand-in-hand. The same can be said for Gustave Courbet, another French realist. Asked what he thought about a tidy, idealized landscape by François-Louis Français, he said, "You cannot shit in it!"

The Potato Eaters. Vincent Van Gogh, 1885.

8) POOP REPRESENTS THE LIMITATIONS OF THE BODY

Has James Bond ever sat on a filthy toilet in a disgusting gas station and had to spread his knees to keep his tuxedo pants from touching the floor? Did Luke Skywalker ever have to battle the dark brown side of the Force? What's Superman's real reason for visiting his Fortress of Solitude?

Most of us know what it's like to endure an impending poop so urgent that one would shove one's mother out of the way to reach the toilet. James Bond, Luke Skywalker, and Superman, though, have transcended human limitations. The absence of pooping protagonists in six Star Wars movies, twenty-one James Bond movies, and thousands of Superman comics shows just how far beyond our limitations these heroes are. Indeed, the moments that bring out their best are the moments that would bring out our poop. You know this from your childhood—sneaking around while playing hide and seek, tension and adrenaline inevitably coalesce into the urge to evacuate the bladder, bowels, or both. This is a well-documented manifestation of the basic responses of the body to extreme stress, what psychologists call "fight, flight, or fright." When your body encounters an extremely stressful situation—be it defusing a time bomb, stalking a Sith Lord through the dark bowels of the Emperor's throne room, or asking someone to the prom—it instinctively alters its internal priorities to focus on emergency short-term survival.

The body uses different tactics based on whether it intends to battle, to run, or to cower (hence "fight, flight, or fright"). It may release hormones including adrenaline, increase your blood pressure, speed up your heart and breathing to prepare your muscles for effort, and reduce or stop blood flow to "nonessential" organs— including your bladder and your bowels. It may also induce vomiting, urinating, or pooping, presumably to make you lighter if you have to run or less appetizing if your attacker wants to eat you.

Butterflies in your stomach and pressure on your orifices are mild manifestations of the fight, flight, or fright instinct. Fortunately for our dignity, the things that normally induce these minor symptoms—giving a speech, performing on stage, or watching a scary movie—don't usually take the body to its excretory extremes. Still, these are the bodily limitations to be overcome in times of stress. (This is why people with stress or panic disorders often also have digestive disorders—each attack diverts blood from the digestive system, gradually degrading its function.)

In the case of Bond, Skywalker, and Superman, poop is meaningful because absent. If James Bond had to hop on one foot to keep from pooping as he stalked a bad guy, he would cease to be the suave, debonair charmer we all wish we were. Instead of portraying the struggle of good against evil, the movie would be about 007's personal journey to overcome his human limitations. That's not what people want from James Bond. In real life, we know that a moment of greatness is subject to the whims of the digestive tract; we watch James Bond not for real-life situations but to see him kill people in clever ways.

You're much more likely to see pooping heroes in movies like *Hellboy* or *Shrek*, in which the character's savage nature is integral to the plot. In movies of ultimate good versus ultimate evil, no one wants to spend $10.50 plus another $5 to learn how the paragon of humanity is just like you or me.

9) POOPING REPRESENTS VULNERABILITY

A big South American spider has hitched a ride in the coffin of a photographer killed by its bite in Venezuela. Arriving in a small American town, the foreign arachnid mates with a local species to create killer spiders that terrorize the townspeople. 1990's *Arachnophobia* milks our fears for all their worth with tension-filled shots of spiders creeping toward unwitting victims. We shriek and squirm at spiders hovering over a group of schoolgirls singing *Itsy Bitsy Spider*, crawling inside a bowl of popcorn cradled by an unsuspecting TV-watching couple, and—most disturbing of all—crawling into a toilet bowl to wait for its prey: a human butt.

The idea of spiders in toilets—along with snakes, rats, and even alligators, if the urban legends are believed—is horrifying because pooping and peeing are moments of extreme vulnerability. Once you start pooping, once you've given your bodily functions priority, rescinding that priority takes an act of incredible will. Stopping your pee in midstream or retracting your poop in mid-breach is nearly impossible, so if someone or something wants to get you, that is the best time. This is why the bathroom scene in *Welcome to the Dollhouse* cut when it did—with Dawn in the stall and Lolita at the door, there was no reason to agonize us with the inevitable. In the 1992 western *Unforgiven*, a wannabe bounty hunter calling himself the Schofield Kid joins a posse in search of some men who brutally murdered a prostitute. In the posse's assault on their hideout, the Kid watches one of the bad guys enter an outhouse. He waits until the guy has settled down and then bursts in to catch him with his pants down. The bad guy raises his hands in surrender. With his ass bared, his pants shackling his ankles so there's no way he could run or kick, his weight resting entirely on his ass so he has no leverage to jump, and walled on three sides, the man's only hope is mercy. The Kid shows none.

Later we learn this was the Kid's first kill. Sobbing, the Kid regrets that he killed a man on the toilet, whose vulnerability there erased any glory in the kill. In a movie about the moral ambiguity of frontier justice, death on the toilet was carefully scripted to create the most ethically uncertain situation: a revenge killing with the victim unable to fight back, utterly helpless in the middle of moving his bowels.

10) POOPING REPRESENTS INTIMACY

In the 1997 romantic comedy *Fools Rush In*, a free spirit (Salma Hayek) and a stuffed-shirt yuppie (Matthew Perry) marry after a one-night stand gets Hayek pregnant. The rest of the movie focuses on how the newlyweds learn to live with each other and ultimately fall in love. Becoming a husband results in some drastic changes for the uptight groom. There are the little things, such as the day Perry returns home to find the house redecorated in fiesta prints and crucifixes, but more jarring is when Hayek strides into the bathroom during a conversation, pulling down her pants and sitting on the toilet. Extremely disturbed, Perry tries to leave, but Hayek grabs his hand and reels him back in to continue the conversation. The rules of bathroom etiquette apply only to strangers and acquaintances, she seems to be saying; husbands and wives share an intimacy that supersedes regular social protocol.

The connection between intimacy and excretory candor predates even the Victorian heyday. Jonathan Swift, well known for his liberal use of scatological verse, discusses the subject in his 1734 poem *Strephon & Chloe.* Chloe is the most beautiful woman in the land: "So beautiful a Nymph appears / But once in Twenty Thousand Years." Of all her suitors, she chooses Strephon. But there are problems on their wedding night: how can Strephon attend to the needs of his body in the presence of such an angel?

> But, still the hardest Part remains.
> Strephon had long perplex'd his Brains,
> How with so high a Nymph he might
> Demean himself the Wedding-Night.

Chloe, it turns out, has similar worries: "Twelve Cups of Tea, (with Grief I speak) / Had now constrain'd the Nymph to leak. /

This Point must needs be settled first; / The Bride must either void or burst." Finally, she can bear it no more. She reaches for a chamber pot, made of material as fair and white as her skin, and brings it into the bed:

> Strephon who heard the fuming Rill
> As from a mossy Cliff distill;
> Cry'd out, ye Gods, what Sound is this?
> Can Chloe, heav'nly Chloe ——?
> But, when he smelt a noysom Steam
> Which oft attends that luke-warm Stream;
> And, though contriv'd, we may suppose
> To slip his Ears, yet struck his Nose:
> He found her, while the Scent increas'd
> As mortal as himself at least.
> But, soon with like Occasions prest,
> He boldly sent his Hand in quest,
> (Inspir'd with Courage from his Bride,)
> To reach the Pot on t'other Side.
> And as he fill'd the reeking Vase,
> Let fly a Rouzer in her Face.

The dashing groom and the beautiful bride, officially married and yet too awkward and uncomfortable to consummate, become intimate by revealing their bodily functions to each other. The poem rejoins the couple shortly after their wedding night, laughing and happy, enjoying their intimate lack of pretense.

> How great a Change! how quickly made!
> They learn to call a Spade, a Spade.
> They soon from all Constraint are freed;
> Can see each other do their Need.
> On Box of Cedar sits the Wife,
> And makes it warm for Dearest Life.
> And, by the beastly way of Thinking,
> Find great Society in Stinking.
> Now Strephon daily entertains
> His Chloe in the homeli'st Strains;

And, Chloe more experienc'd grown,
With Int'rest pays him back his own.
No Maid at Court is less asham'd,
Howe'er for selling Bargains fam'd,
Than she, to name her Parts behind,
Or when a-bed, to let out Wind.

Swift follows up this celebration of the abandonment of pretense with an about-face—an indictment of exactly this kind of intimacy, admonishing men and women to maintain distance and decorum. Given the positive portrait of the lovers' familiarity by the poem until that point, it's likely that Swift is satirizing those who would prefer cold etiquette above Strephon and Chloe's warm, loving relationship (even if it does reek of rotten egg).

11) POOPING REPRESENTS SAVAGERY

Being marooned on a deserted island relaxes concerns about social niceties. Tom Hanks learns this in the film *Cast Away*: with no one around to judge, he let his beard grow shaggy, wore the same clothes every day, and pooped and peed where and when the urge hit. Stuck on his island with no hope for rescue, Hanks was rightly more concerned with food, water, and shelter than with his vanity.

Watching him poop and pee willy-nilly, you might think the castaway's toilet habits symbolic of his regression into barbarism. On the other hand, you might think that he has become what romantics call the "noble savage": one whose uncivilized ways are more in touch with nature than are the refinements of the "civilized". Barbarism or savage nobility—poop can function as symbols of both. Tom Hanks' unbridled excretions show how far he's degenerated from his neurotic former self. At the same time, he may seem to have advanced far beyond those who waste so time and energy trying to hide their human nature. In his condition and with his worries, a castaway would be nuts if he *didn't* answer nature's call just as casually as he enjoyed her bounty.

Whether poop symbolizes barbarism or savage nobility depends entirely on point of reference. In *Demolition Man*, Sylvester Stallone is thawed after thirty-five years of suspended animation to stop Wesley Snipes from destroying the society of the future. It's a future of peace and harmony, regulated through draconian laws, but a paradise for those who obey them willingly. To the people of the future, Stallone is a boor who curses, resists authority, and rejects decorum. They look on in horror as he eschews their futuristic bathroom techniques in favor of wiping his butt with paper. To the people of the future, these practices reveal a barbarian nature. To the audience, though, they express a rejection of the pretentious and overcomplicated trappings of advanced society, when the noble savage knows that the old ways are better.

Countless travelers have come back from trips to the East with stories of the savage bathrooms they encountered. Those in the East, however, see from the opposite perspective. In *The RE/Search Guide to Bodily Fluids*, Paul Spinrad reports that Mao Zedong, founder of the People's Republic of China, equated primitive pooping with nobility of spirit. "For years, Mao preferred going into fields to defecate over using an indoor toilet, explaining that the toilet's odor got in the way of his thinking. He viewed dung as a symbol of purity and peasant virtue, and branded those who didn't want to handle it as intellectuals and parasites."

12) POOP REPRESENTS NEGATIVITY AT ITS EXTREME

Bernardo Bertolucci's 1987 movie *The Last Emperor* follows Pu Yi, China's last dynastic ruler, from his childhood through his death. When he was a child, the monks who raised Pu Yi attended to his every need with the intense reverence befitting such a holy being. One scene depicts the emperor's bowel movement, a great event attended by rapt onlookers. Once the emperor finishes, a monk removes the chamber pot, swirls the contents, and inhales deeply of the poop. The Emperor is so holy that even his poop is divine.

That phrase is the key: "Even his poop." As Freudian theory posits, we learn the concept of negativity during potty training.

This makes poop the foundation of the badness, the worst thing there is. As such, poop is perfect for use in the *argumentum a fortiori* (argument from strength), a form discussed in Aristotle's *Rhetoric*: "If the less likely thing is true, the more likely thing is true also." If the least likely aspect of the Last Emperor to be holy—his poop—is indeed holy, then every other aspect of Pu Yi more likely to be holy must also surely be as such.

Poop's use in an *a fortiori* argument is pervasive. This use resonates in our culture, for it manifests easily and often, and not just in the movies. People and organizations appropriate the extreme negativity of poop to communicate in jokes, in insults, even in the realms of politics and religion. Its unequivocal power to taint anything compared with it is why some of the most poignant art of the last century has invoked the symbolic meanings of poop.

CHAPTER 7

OF MOVEMENTS AND MEN: POOP IN ART

IN APRIL 1917, Woodrow Wilson was president, Northern Tissue was eighteen years from launching "splinter-free" toilet paper, and The Big Show was the talk of New York City's art world.

They weren't calling it The Big Show for nothing. With 2,500 works by 1,200 artists under one roof, it was to be the biggest art exhibition the country had ever seen. Held at the Grand Central Palace by the fledgling Society of Independent Artists, The Big Show centered on a radical conceit: the absence of juries and awards. This was the Society's attempt to end the hegemony of gallery and museum over art and artists. At The Big Show, no stuffed-shirt curator beholden to a faceless board of directors would be deciding what was "art." No cabal of high-society dilettantes would be choosing the next overcompensated artistic vogue to grace their parlors. At The Big Show, any artist paying membership dues and the six-dollar exhibition fee had the right to exhibit his or her work, to be evaluated only by the people standing in front of it.

As the day of the opening drew near, paintings and sculptures of all sizes and styles began to arrive at the exhibition hall. Each work was prepared for display in accordance with the philosophy of the show: in alphabetical order based on the artist's last name, beginning with a randomly chosen letter of the alphabet. Receiving and preparing so many pieces of art was a dull and laborious task—until the morning when a delivery service dropped off *Fountain.*

Fountain was a sculpture submitted by a thitherto-unknown artist named R. Mutt. Mutt's reputation, or lack thereof, didn't matter, of course. *Fountain* was accompanied by precisely the amount of money that the Society required—which, according to

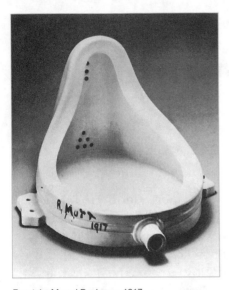

Fountain, Marcel Duchamp, 1917.

Nude Descending a Staircase. Marcel Duchamp, 1912.

the rules of The Big Show, meant it was guaranteed exhibition with no prejudice beyond the luck of the alphabetical draw. Its striking form—flowing white lines, gentle curves, smooth and shiny finish—was irrelevant. To the curators, the six dollars that accompanied it should have made *Fountain* indistinguishable from every other work in the show. But Mr. Mutt's work sure looked exactly like a urinal.

Presented on its back, on a pedestal, it was signed in black paint like any other sculpture. But this was a urinal, created solely as a receptacle for men's urine. Mutt's six dollars be damned—this was different. This was vulgar. And it wasn't even art! It was clearly machine-made, one of a thousand urinals that rolled off an assembly line in some factory down on the Bowery. Mr. Mutt had done nothing more than purchase it, sign it, and send it in. How could this be placed among the other works? It was an insult to the paintings and sculptures upon which so many artists had labored so long and hard. It was an insult to The Big Show.

Word got around. A group of Society decision makers hastily assembled. Among them were the artists Rockwell Kent, George

Bellows, and Beatrice Wood, and collector and patron Walter Arensberg. Bellows, an acclaimed painter of vivid urban scenes still admired to this day, was particularly furious. The ensuing argument is recounted in Wood's 1985 autobiography *I Shock Myself*:

"We cannot exhibit it," Bellows said hotly, taking out a handkerchief and wiping his forehead.

"We cannot refuse it, the entrance fee has been paid," gently answered Walter.

"It is indecent!" roared Bellows.

"That depends upon the point of view," added Walter, suppressing a grin.

"Someone must have sent it as a joke. It is signed R. Mutt: sounds fishy to me," grumbled Bellows with disgust. Walter approached the object in question and touched its glossy surface. With the dignity of a don addressing men at Harvard, he expounded: "A lovely form has been revealed, freed from its functional purpose, therefore a man has clearly made an aesthetic contribution."

Bellows stepped away, then returned in a rage as if he were going to pull it down. "We can't show it; that's all there is to it."

Walter lightly touched his arm, "That's what the whole exhibition is about; an opportunity to allow an artist to send in anything he chooses, for the artist to decide what is art, not someone else."

Bellows shook his arm away, protesting. "You mean to say, if a man sent in horse manure glued to a canvas that we would have to accept it!"

"I'm afraid we would," said Walter, with a touch of undertaker's sadness. "If this is an artist's expression of beauty, we can do nothing but accept his choice." With diplomatic effort he pointed out, "If you can look at this entry objectively, you will see that it has striking, sweeping lines. This Mr. Mutt has taken an ordinary object, placed it so that its useful significance disappears, and thus has created a new approach to the subject."

Two days before The Big Show opened, *Fountain* was removed from display.

A young French artist, Marcel Duchamp, quickly resigned from the Society. Duchamp was the exhibition's Chairman of the Hanging Committee and the celebrated painter whose stunning *Nude Descending a Staircase* had been the centerpiece of the scandalous 1913 Armory Show in New York, the country's largest art exhibition before The Big Show. The 1913 Armory Show had given astonished Americans their first introduction to modern art, and established Duchamp's reputation as a master of Cubism and one of modern art's best talents. It was with this pedigree that Duchamp resigned his prestigious position on the principle that this urinal had just as much artistic merit as any other work in the exhibition. It was Duchamp, after all, who had signed and submitted the urinal in the name of R. Mutt. *Fountain* never appeared at The Big Show. And after brief display at Alfred Stieglitz's gallery, during which time Stieglitz took his famous photograph, it was lost forever (though Duchamp did, decades later, authorize a number of reproductions).

Eighty-seven years after the Society of Independent Artists violated their own vision for The Big Show with their refusal to exhibit *Fountain*, the sponsors of England's renowned Turner Prize surveyed 500 artists, critics, dealers, and curators to determine the twentieth century's most influential work of art. The first choice of 64% of those surveyed was Marcel Duchamp's *Fountain*.

Fountain altered the definition of "art" by giving everyday machine-made objects artistic credence. But that alone does not explain the uproar it caused in 1917, nor does it explain why it continues to influence generations of artists to this day. After all, Duchamp explored the idea before and after creating *Fountain*, classifying a coffee grinder, a bicycle wheel, and a bottle rack all as art, to name a few. He called them "readymades"—mass-produced objects elevated to the level of art by the artist's merely saying so. Readymades force the viewer to consider concepts beyond the aesthetics of the piece, such as the roles of the artist in creating it, the museum in validating it, and the viewer in choosing to trust either or both. *Fountain* was not one-of-a-kind. But what made it so much more famous and influential than, say, *In Advance of the*

Broken Arm, 1915 (a snow shovel), *3 or 4 Drops of Height Have Nothing to do with Savagery*, 1916 (a dog comb), and every one of Duchamp's other readymades was that a urinal, unlike those other readymades, is not a neutral object. As a receptacle for bodily waste, *Fountain* was loaded with the visceral emotion bodily functions tend to invoke. *Fountain* paired the conceptual challenge posed by readymades with the symbolic meanings of poop.

The Symbolic Meanings of Poop: A Quick Refresher

1) Poop exposes the lowness of the high
2) Poop underscores the lowness of the low
3) Poop makes a potent insult
4) Poop represents contamination
5) Embracing your own poop underscores your contempt for others
6) Poop communicates protest
7) Poop represents the mundane
8) Poop represents the limitations of the body
9) Poop represents vulnerability
10) Poop represents intimacy
11) Poop represents savagery
12) Poop represents negativity at its extreme

"You mean to say," Bellows raged, "if a man sent in horse manure glued to a canvas that we would have to accept it!" Bellows wasn't angry because *Fountain* was a readymade. As a member of the Society of Independent Artists, Bellows was surely familiar with Duchamp's oeuvre, although he didn't know at the time that this one was Duchamp's doing. No, Bellows was angry because of *Fountain*'s association with urine, a bodily function polite society demanded be hidden and unmentioned. Bellows saw *Fountain* as an insult to The Big Show (Symbolic Meaning of Poop #3). Never mind that Mr. Mutt was the one who not only touched a urinal but actually put his name on one; that he had gone to all that trouble, Bellows must have thought, only underscored Mutt's

Fountain as photographed in 1917 by Alfred Stieglitz.

Bicycle Wheel. Marcel Duchamp, 1913.

antipathy toward the exhibition (Symbolic Meaning of Poop #5). To Bellows, it would have scarcely been worse if the artist had sent in actual fecal matter. (Duchamp wouldn't have done that, of course; readymades existed to explore ideas concerning mass-production. Poop wasn't in his palette.)

"Someone must have sent it as a joke," Bellows argued. He knew that a show with no judges risked being labeled as a show with no standards, and that critics would seize on the presence of a urinal as tainting all the artwork shown alongside it (Symbolic Meaning of Poop #4). To a critic with a negative bias against The Big Show, *Fountain* would underscore how awful an unjuried show could be (Symbolic Meaning of Poop #2). Even worse, though, an attendee of The Big Show might find his or her enjoyment shattered—he or she would come across *Fountain* and be repulsed, and that revulsion would eclipse whatever positive experience he or she had enjoyed (Symbolic Meaning of Poop #1).

Walter Arensberg interpreted *Fountain* as meaningful and poignant and not, as Bellows thought, negative. Perhaps Arensberg believed that *Fountain* was making a point about human frailty: that for all humanity's aspirations to understand truth and beauty through art—aspirations evidenced by the gathering of 2,500 works under one roof—we are still very much constrained by the limitations of the body (Symbolic Meaning of Poop #8). Perhaps he believed that the artist found beauty in the artifices that tame the savagery of human beings (Symbolic Meaning of Poop #11). Perhaps he even appreciated that *Fountain* underscored the Society's main premise: that art was more than what museums, galleries, and groups of Society decision-makers said it was, but could be found anywhere—even in the bathroom (Symbolic Meaning of Poop #7).

Readymades are honored today as one of the first and purest examples of conceptual art. As artist Sol LeWitt defined it, "In conceptual art the idea or concept is the most important aspect of the work. When an artist uses a conceptual form of art, it means that all of the planning and decisions are made beforehand and the execution is a perfunctory affair. The idea becomes a machine that makes the art." By this definition, it's easy to see why *Fountain* was so influential in 1917 and remains so now—because the invocation of the symbolic meaning of poop takes the concept of readymades to its most visceral extreme (Symbolic Meaning of Poop #12).

If conceptual art lies at an opposite extreme from art created for pure aesthetics, poop is the ultimate tool for conceptual art— because nothing is aesthetically less appealing than poop. If conceptual art is about ideas, poop is just as useful—because few ideas resonate more universally or communicate more unambiguously. *Fountain* had the power to bitterly divide even seasoned art figures. Combining the ideas of readymades with the symbolic intensity of poop, *Fountain* is conceptual art at its purest and most powerful.

MERDA D'ARTISTA

As conceptual art matured and exerted increasing influence on the aesthetics of modern art, it engendered criticism of a certain theme. Many condemned it with a bitterness implying they took it personally, as if conceptual art were a joke perpetrated by artists and museums on everyone outside of their elite circle. It's easy to sympathize with this reaction. To understand this kind of art, it helps to understand its historical and contemporary contexts. If you focus narrowly on the piece without realizing that it is about more than aesthetics or representation, you might be confused about what these art folks could see in something any three-year-old could make, or angry about having paid an admission fee and wasted your afternoon to look at a urinal on a pedestal.

Pablo Picasso provides perfect examples of art that engendered this criticism. Depicting men and women in stark, childlike lines, with features skewed, Picasso was concerned with something other than lifelike representation. His style wasn't due to lack of talent, having proven early in his career his ability to paint in true-to-life detail. His style reflected a belief that abstract human forms communicated his thoughts and feelings better than realistic ones. But to critics unaware of abstraction's role in art, and thus unaware of Picasso's decision to abandon realistic depiction, Picasso's paintings had no more merit than a three-year-old's crayon drawings. To these critics, this kind of thing didn't qualify as art at all, because anyone could create it. Anyone can draw like a child or put a urinal on a pedestal. Would it be any different to smear poop on a canvas and call it art? To someone expecting art to be an expression of technical prowess, this kind of stuff isn't art, it's shit: the one thing everyone can create with equal dexterity.

Criticism like that invites an obvious response, which came in May 1961 when Italian artist Piero Manzoni exhibited ninety cans of his poop in an art gallery in Albisola, Italy. This wasn't shit, it was art. Each can comprising *Merda d'Artista* ("Artist's Shit") was signed, numbered, and wrapped in a label like a can of tuna. On the label, printed in four languages, was: "Artist's Shit / Contents 30 grams net / Freshly preserved / Produced and tinned / in May 1961." Each can was on sale during its exhibition, priced by weight based on the current price of gold. From that base price (around $1.12 a gram in 1960) the value shot up; forty-one years later, the Tate Modern in London paid $34,100 to acquire *Merda* can #004. For what may be poop's first explicit manifestation in the history of art, this worked out to around $1,137 a gram—an appreciation rate well above inflation.

Manzoni spent his brief career (he died in 1963, at the age of 29) exploring the absurdities and contradictions of conceptual art. For 1960's *Scultura Vivente* ("Living Sculpture"), for instance, he signed the torso of a naked woman posing on a pedestal, thus declaring her a work of art (and anointing himself the artist with the Midas touch). He even signed himself, designating himself a work of art. Shortly thereafter he built a pedestal inscribed "*socle du monde*" ("base of the world"). Turning it upside down and placing it on the ground, he presented it as bearing the weight of the world. Manzoni had declared the entire world to be art—his. In this context, *Merda d'Artista* is a logical extension of his oeuvre. But *Merda d'Artista* is Manzoni's best-known work for the same reason that *Fountain* is Duchamp's best-known ready-made: because more than any other work, this one forced the viewer to confront the themes of Manzoni's oeuvre taken to their extreme through association with poop. *Merda* pits the productions society values most—art— against those it values least.

An artist's product, society teaches us, represents truth, beauty, and technical mastery.

A sketch by Picasso.

Merda d'Artista, Piero Manzoni, 1961.

Jackson Pollock in his studio.
Photograph by Hans Namuth.

Piero Manzoni with his finished product.
Photograph by Ole Bagger.

People will come from afar to see it, and many will even pay to own it and show it off. Art is the artist's contribution to humanity's soul. Poop, on the other hand, is the one thing we're all capable of creating with equal skill; neither Duchamp nor Manzoni have any more aesthetic control over the sphincter than you or I. Manzoni's poop did represent a singular intersection of diet and metabolism—unique, it's true, but impossible to pick out of a lineup. So to claim his poop was unique simply because he was an artist was an *a fortiori* argument that pushed conceptual art to its absurd extreme.

Merda invokes the symbolic meanings of poop much as *Fountain* did. But *Merda* goes further by being not just about poop, but about Piero Manzoni's poop. With this added intimacy (Symbolic Meaning of Poop #10), contemplating Manzoni's cans of poop forces the viewer to picture the artist in the process of creation. Did he hold the can under his butt as he pooped into it? Did he carefully remove his poop from the toilet, cut off a measured section, weigh it, trim the excess, and then put it in the can? Or did he save his poop over a week to complete his work in one marathon canning session? Did he eat something special to achieve a consistency optimal for canning? The artist is venerated for the process by which he or she creates, because the value of art traditionally derives in part from the uniqueness of the talent that created it. But while art is thus prized as an intimate portrait of the artist's soul, *Merda* may offer more intimacy than most art patrons can stomach. One wonders if collectors asked Manzoni the same kinds of questions about technique they asked of Jackson Pollock, whose paint-splattered canvases were compared by unappreciative critics to the aftermath of certain bodily functions. There have been many studies of Pollock's creative process, but no one followed Manzoni into the stall to examine his.

Merda d'Artista mocks those who criticize conceptual art as facile while mocking the value systems of art and of commerce. By pegging the price of his poop to gold, Manzoni contrasts the worthlessness of poop with that of both art and precious metals, and makes the viewer think twice about coveting either. After all, which of the three are of any use to the owner? Is art really more relevant to the life of the collector than poop? Is gold? "The contrast between the most precious substance known to men and the most worthless, which they reject as waste matter," said Freud, "has led to this specific identification of gold with feces."

Did Manzoni really do it?

Speculating on the complexities one might encounter in canning one's own poop, you may question whether Manzoni actually went to all the trouble. A more philosophical question is whether it matters—would *Merda d'Artista* be less valuable if it didn't actually have forty-year-old feces in it? But the practical answer has been discovered to the chagrin of numerous collectors: forty-five of the original ninety tins have reportedly exploded, spraying artist's shit (and the bacteria and gasses that had been fermenting in it) all over the collectors' galleries. Of course, that still provides no assurance that the poop was actually Manzoni's, and not his friends' or his dog's. No collector has yet been so concerned about the origin of these feces as to commission DNA tests.

Manzoni is remembered and influential today for forcing museum-goers to question the premises underlying the value they ascribed to art. Since Manzoni, many other artists have incorporated poop into their work. Few, however, have deliberately intended to invoke the symbolic meanings of poop. Most have instead used poop as a symbol of gender or sexuality. In these cases, the symbolic meanings of poop are overwhelmed by the anus' association with the genitals and sexual symbolism. After *Merda d'Artista*, the art world saw few works involving the idea of poop as Manzoni presented it, until Wim Delvoye created *Cloaca*.

Poop in Modern Art: A Short Catalog of Other Works

In 1999, British artist Chris Ofili scandalized New York and enraged then-Mayor Rudolph Giuliani with *The Holy Virgin Mary* a portrait of a black Madonna with pornographic images and elephant dung. Ofili, who used elephant droppings in many of his works, said dung was symbolic of his African heritage and not meant as an insult. Giuliani nevertheless ordered Brooklyn Museum's public funding revoked, though a judge later ordered it restored and enjoined further sanctions by the city.

Since the late '60s, British art duo Gilbert & George have been creating art together. They're best known for their brightly colored, large-scale photomontages that look like stained glass and frequently feature shocking imagery, including 1994's *Naked Shit Pictures* and 1995's *The Fundamental Pictures*. Both series further the duo's use of bodily functions toexplore themes of shame and vulnerability.

In the mid-1910s, the Italian artist Filippo Tommaso Marinetti famously relabeled Leonardo DaVinci's Mona Lisa (known in Italy as *La Gioconda*, or "The Smiler") as *La Gioconda Purgativa* ("The Purgative Smiler")—implying that her look of satisfaction might also be one of relief.

Yves Klein's creation of a unique pigment of ultramarine, dubbed International Klein Blue, made him famous. For a

---

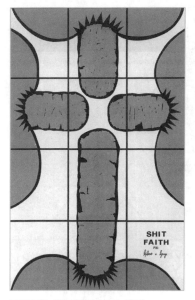

Shit Faith, Gilbert & George, 1982.

The Holy Virgin Mary, Chris Ofili, 1996

1958 exhibition at the Iris Clert Gallery in Paris, he decided to exhibit and sell "immaterial paintings." Opening night crowds arrived to behold empty white walls. They were, however, served cocktails dyed in International Klein Blue to imbue them with the artist's aesthetic sensibility. For several days thereafter, they subsequently experienced the artist's blue aesthetic sensibility every time they went to the bathroom.

In 1992, Kiki Smith sculpted *Tale*, a life-sized figure of a woman on all fours, with a ten-foot long trail of poop coming out of her butt. It was considered important enough to appear in the Whitney Museum of American Art's exhaustive exhibition *The American Century: Art and Culture 1900–2000*.

In the 1960s and 1970s, many German and Austrian performance artists incorporated poop into their work. Günther Brus, for instance, in a single performance, took off his clothes, urinated into his hand, drank it, vomited, and then defecated and smeared his poop on his naked body while singing the Austrian national anthem.

Austrian actionist Otto Muehl shits on stage, 1971.

Film Still from *Santa Chocolate Shop*,
Paul McCarthy, 1997.

Film Still from *Santa Chocolate Shop*,
Paul McCarthy, 1997.

The surrealist Salvador Dali was reportedly fascinated by poop. "The excrementitious palette," he raved, "enjoys infinite variety, from gray to green and from ochers to browns." 1929's *Lugubrious Game* is his first painting to depict poop, showing a man in the foreground wearing poop-stained shorts.

In 1995, German artist Anton Henning debuted *Meatballs, Gherkins, Beetroot, Potatoes, Watermelon, Lemon Juice, Riesling, and Large Brownie.* You can guess what he used for paint. He coated his finished canvas with resin to eliminate odor.

In the mid-1990s, artist and critic Todd Alden asked 400 art collectors to send him cans of their poop. As a "historical rethinking" of *Merda d'Artista*, Alden called his work *Collector's Shit.* He noted that Manzoni's cans were selling for tens of thousands of dollars; as a courtesy to each collector, he offered to sell their own poop back to them at half the initial offering price. Alden initially claimed 81 participants, but the *New York Observer* debunked the hoax, reporting that only one collector actually sent in poop.

CLOACA

Wim Delvoye's *Cloaca* is actually a series of five increasingly complex machines that turn food into poop. The first, *Cloaca Original*, debuted in 2000, followed by *Cloaca—New & Improved* in 2001, *Cloaca Turbo* in 2004, *Cloaca Quattro* in 2005, and a fifth *Cloaca* in 2006. As described in the first chapter, each machine demonstrates continuing progress in the biology, technology, and aesthetics of turning food into poop. *Cloaca Original* was a relatively inefficient exploration of the concept, taking forty hours to convert a meal from food into poop. Subsequent iterations improved production, adopting more of the chemical and bacterial interaction natural to the human digestive processes and allowing curators to time digestion and defecation to coincide with museum hours, down to as little as six hours from food to poop. Future versions of *Cloaca* are expected to churn out poop faster than any human digestive system could ever hope to achieve.

Cloaca is intended to be not a literal representation of the human digestive system, but an abstraction from digestion. When designing the first iteration, Delvoye originally thought along literal lines, experimenting with mechanical components that looked like the biological organs they approximated. But he abandoned this execution in favor of a more conceptual approach, eventually building the system out of glass containers, plastic tubes, and metal frames that in no way suggested the organic processes they encompassed. One can learn about the intricacies of the body from *Cloaca*, but a biology lesson is not the artist's intention. Delvoye has turned down invitations to exhibit *Cloaca* in science museums.

Cloaca is not science, but an exploration of a simple concept: exhibiting poop in a museum. But for Delvoye to realize this concept at its simplest, the work had to avoid distracting notions of identity, gender, or sexuality. Therefore it could not be Delvoye's poop, or anybody's. This is why Delvoye chose to create a pooping machine with no face, identity, or hint of personality. If Delvoye had simply placed poop on a pedestal, the medium would distract from the message. Is it real poop? Whose poop is it? How did it get there? The focus would be on the origin of the poop, not its implications, and not on the provocative question for the viewer: Why am I standing here looking at poop?

Cloaca engenders much of the same discourse as did *Fountain* and *Merda*. Many were disgusted by it, and immediately associated the contagion of poop with its viewers, exhibitors, and especially its creator—what kind of disgusting man would study, invest, and revel in a machine that makes poop? Fortunately for Delvoye's career, most museumgoers and critics are able to get past this and explore *Cloaca* in a deeper way.

Before *Cloaca*, Delvoye had an eclectic career spanning a variety of media and formats. He tattooed intricate designs into the skin of live pigs, commissioned a full-sized cement truck carved from Indonesian wood, and created terrazzo floor tiles with patterns resembling sandwich meats and human poop. Unlike *Fountain* and

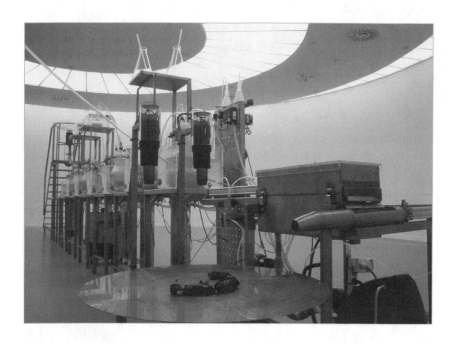

Photos of *Cloaca* and its product. Courtesy Wim Delvoye.

Merda, *Cloaca* was not a poop-specific extension of an established oeuvre, but rather a freestanding work. This is one of *Cloaca*'s greatest strengths as a medium for communication: it requires no knowledge of art history or the artist's past work to understand.

You go into a museum and see a machine pooping. You spend very little time admiring the aesthetics of the product before you begin to wonder why you and all these other people are standing around looking at poop. That begins the line of thought upon which Delvoye most likely intended museum-goers to embark.

Much conceptual art questions the roles of artist, museum, and viewer in validating art, but few works do it as quickly and viscerally as *Cloaca*. Is a pooping machine art simply because an artist says so and a museum agrees? That logic implies that aesthetics have less to do with art than the faith we've placed in its institutions. But how can those institutions be trusted? The *Cloaca* viewer's trust in the museum and the artist puts him nose-to-orifice with a machine pumping out boneless brown trout. And if artist and museum have validated this shit, is the Pollock painting in the next room any better?

This is a perfect example of the Symbolic Meaning of Poop #1: the high of art corrupted by the low of poop. Art is the purest expression of civilization; poop is its most worthless. When the high of art and the low of poop meet, the viewer is forced to be suspicious of the artist and museum as venerable institutions.

Some people will nevertheless continue to accept the judgment of these institutions, and thus see *Cloaca*'s poop as something worth spending time and money to stare at. Some collectors have even spent thousands of dollars to own some of the poop that the machine created. Like *Merda d'Artista*, this calls into question the value system of modern art. If the system encourages people to pay $1000 a pop for a piece of poop vacuum-sealed in a clear plastic bag and accompanied by a certificate of authenticity describing what the machine ate to create it, then perhaps the system is flawed.

Or perhaps $1,000 for a piece of machine-created poop is a reasonable price to pay. Delvoye estimates that each poop from *Cloaca Turbo* represents $200 in resources such as the chemical pancreatin and other enzymes required to produce it (though the live bacteria are cheap, especially if the artist inoculates the machine with his own culture). Beyond that are the fixed costs of machine parts and research amortized across each individual log. Then again, that these poops cost money to produce does not mean they have value. *Cloaca* collectibles bring their owner no tangible benefits beyond pride of ownership and perhaps potential return on investment.

But what are the tangible benefits of a Jackson Pollock painting, or the *Mona Lisa*? This, again, leads the viewer to contemplate that circular fallacy of museum and artist: collectors buy art not for aesthetic reasons, but because of institutional validation. *Cloaca* demonstrates that in modern art, cachet overshadows aesthetics. This is exactly why The Big Show was organized by the Society of Independent Artists to have no jury and no awards: they believed that the institutions of art had become stifling; they wanted to allow the art to speak for itself. Delvoye accomplished the opposite, forcing the artistic institutions to reveal their contradictions by validating as art the most absurd thing possible: poop. *Argumentum a fortiori.*

Fortunately for the institution of art, not every interpretation of *Cloaca* so deeply alienates the viewer. One can believe that poop lowers art, or one can believe that *Cloaca* elevates poop. Behold the machine: huge, complex, unfathomable, with advanced computers required to monitor complicated chemical processes beyond the comprehension of the museum-goer watching the turtlehead emerge—all this to recreate what happens in our gastrointestinal tract! How wonderfully mysterious and intricate is the human body! How remarkable that a process requiring so much equipment and electrical power and money and real estate happens so effortlessly inside our abdomens in an area the size of a basketball! *Cloaca* has pushed art, technology, and biology to their extreme, but the human body easily outpoops it.

So why shouldn't poop be in the museum? Art celebrates and criticizes humanity, after all, and what are humans but six-foot-tall pooping machines? Is anything more relevant to the human condition than the poop we all experience? Is anything a better representative of the species? We build great temples to preserve the output of a few artists (the *Mona Lisa*, for instance, is seen by six million people each year in a a $6.1-million, 9,149-square-foot climate-controlled room in the Louvre, displayed in a bulletproof, non-reflecting, temperature and humidity-controlled airtight glass case), but we spend billions and billions more to dispose of that which every human being produces every day. Art or poop: which weighs more in human affairs?

Whether *Cloaca* makes you see its poop as the paragon of civilization, the destroyer of art, or something in between depends on your personal interpretations of the symbolic meanings of poop. Every person sees poop differently. But regardless of the conclusion, it's important to note what is probably missing from your interpretation. Delvoye succeeded in removing anxieties about sexuality, gender, nudity, and health from *Cloaca*. *Cloaca* is not a peep-show. Unlike what performance artist Gunter Busch's audience must have felt when he defecated on stage, observing *Cloaca* does not cause the discomfort or titillation normally associated with such a breach of privacy. Many artists have explored poop—their own or others'—but few have separated it from identity, gender, and sexuality. Poop functions as an extension of the body in the same way that blood, semen, urine, and mucus do; coming from a person's butt, poop is thus a sexualized extension of the body. Even *Merda d'Artista* forces contemplation of the male pooping butt. But *Cloaca* is a machine. It has no body, no butt. Its poop is pure, signifying nothing beyond itself. For the first time in the history of modern art, poop has been completely separated from the butt.

From this separation we can infer *Cloaca*'s ultimate lesson: that poop, isolated by abstraction, has no meaning of its own. Rather, poop shifts focus away from itself to its context. The reason *Cloaca* makes you question the museum and the artist and your own attendance is because there's nothing in the poop to contemplate. Poop is either where it belongs or matter out of place—but either way, it makes you think about *where* it is, not *what* it is. Each of the symbolic meanings of poop outlined in the last chapter is about poop in a context. What does poop mean in the context of an insult? In the context of protest? In the context of a baby's diaper? In that sense, *Cloaca* proves that the Symbolic Meaning of Poop #12—negativity at the extreme—is the basis of its other meanings.

CHAPTER 8

THE MEDIUM IS THE MESS

ANGELA RICCELLI TEACHES at Stanford University's School of Medicine. In addition to her private practice, she consults with numerous medical facilities as a specialist in encopresis, a psychological disorder that leaves children unable to control their bowels, even though they're past the age of potty training. For these children, their continually messy pants and the associated social and parental condemnation create a vicious circle: the more stressful pooping is, the more the child tries to hold it in; the more a child holds it in, the messier the outcome.

It's a serious problem, and widespread. One children's health website reports that 25% of all visits to pediatric gastroenterologists are due to chronic constipation and encopresis. Encopresis frustrates parents and children alike: the parents wonder what they're doing wrong, and the children lose confidence and self-esteem. Riccelli has seen time and again the damage encopresis can cause to a child and his or her family, but also the joy and relief when a child is cured. She knows how important her work is. Nevertheless, it was a shock for her to be greeted by a new five-year-old patient with the words, "Are you the poop lady?" "The question took me aback," she wrote in a 2003 casebook. "Am I? Do I even want to be?"

This is the problem with poop: even in the most innocent of circumstances, its negative image can overwhelm all else. Riccelli has dedicated herself to the health and well-being of children, and still has to worry about being contaminated by proximity to poop. Though she concludes that she's proud of her moniker—her essay is even entitled "Memoirs of a 'Poop Lady'"—she knows all too well how people react to poop in even wholly inoffensive manifestations.

This is so for anything—a joke, a movie scene, a news report—that invokes poop: people immediately pass it through a set of filters based on their interpretation of society's mandates for fecal denial. As with any encounter with matter out of place, they want to figure out where it belongs. They want to know where contamination lies, so as to avoid it. Your reactions to this book are no exception. You may have been impressed so far that poop's influence on art, literature, and culture could inspire such lucid and insightful writing. On the other hand, you may have been feeling queasy since the moment you read, "The poop slid out of the mechanical anus." But at least you have an opinion. Who knows how many people, upon seeing the title, declined to pick it up the book at all, either because they were disgusted by the subject, or because they worried about what others might think about someone holding a book about poop?

This is the problem to which Angela Riccelli alludes in her essay. Even though her work with poop is wholly altruistic, she nevertheless suffers from the stigma of association. So did the artists described in the last chapter. But they accepted the stigma intentionally. They recognized the power of poop to send their message, knowing it would illuminate their themes and at the same time make their work's impact more visceral. They were willing to accept that many people would instantly hate their artwork simply because of its association with poop, but they also knew that others would find its meaning much more accessible for that same reason. In a marketplace that rewards controversy, they were happy to elicit reactions at both extremes.

But what happens when you want to invoke poop without invoking the stigma that goes with it? Maybe you're a company selling toilets, or the evening news reporting on an exhibition of *Fountain*, or a doctor discussing colon health on a talk show. Unlike an avant garde artist, you don't want controversy; you want only to please your audience. How do you present pure negativity in a positive way, without associating yourself with its contamination? For another example: how could one write a book about poop that people would actually want to read?

Some people wouldn't buy a book about poop no matter how it was presented. Others would buy it no matter how graphic it was. Seeking the broadest appeal to the readers, critics, distributors, and retailers between those extremes, the author and the publisher of this book have tried to balance humor and scholarship, sensationalism and civility, marketability and integrity. Too much along one axis and it would lose the shock value that makes people notice it in a sea of competing titles; but too much along the other and nausea would overwhelm curiosity. There's a delicate border between attraction and alienation, between *The Ramifications of Human Waste Matter in Contemporary Culture* and *Shit: The Book*. Like a train wreck, poop grabs people's attention even as it makes them recoil in horror.

It's extremely difficult to know what crosses the line. As such, few people or organizations that need to invoke poop want to explore the limits. Weighing the benefits of success against the costs of alienating their audience, most err on the side of caution. This is why, despite the successes of Duchamp, Manzoni, and Delvoye, relatively few artists have addressed poop in their work. Whole movements dedicated to the faithful representation of reality have come and gone without, as Van Gogh and Courbet lamented, any depiction of the one facet of reality human beings relate to the most. So it is in literature. In *Aspects of the Novel*, E.M. Forster wondered why no one goes to the bathroom in books, suggesting that this omission strips literature of authenticity. While Forster's generalization has exceptions, few authors have been so concerned with authenticity as to subject their characters to the indignity of the alimentary. Perhaps these authors and artists worry that a poop scene would cause controversy. Perhaps they worry that it would strip their work of its artistic integrity. Or perhaps they worry that the stench of a single bathroom scene would contaminate the rest of their work.

Those worries are all legitimate. The absence of poop from art and writing indicates the strategies of each artist and author aiming to position the work for public consumption. Even though its integrity may suffer in the eyes of those who accept poop as part of life, it remains intact in those who would find poop alienating. To most people and organizations invoking poop, the conservative approach beats risking contamination by association.

But the more relevant poop is to a message, the more strained and ludicrous the attempt to communicate without confronting it. This is the challenge facing toilet paper manufacturers: to market a product that exists wholly to wipe off smeared poop without inviting the consumer to picture its use. In selling a product that exists only because we poop, toilet paper marketers take ridiculous detours through fluffy clouds and the land of teddy bears to avoid making buyers think of their product as something that wipes up poop.

WIPING WITH THE INVISIBLE HAND

The imbalance between what your butt does (poop and stink) and society's sanitary ideal (it should do neither) has created demand for a number of products: toilets, toilet paper, disposable diapers, wet wipes, plungers, and more. Unsurprisingly, the markets for these products are worth billions of dollars a year. From the smell of your feet to the pimples on your face, corporate America swarms over any imbalance created by social pressure, relentlessly marketing products and services purporting to neutralize the sources of self-consciousness. What is surprising about the markets for solutions to the problems under your underpants is that they have evolved differently from nearly every other product category in the American marketplace. These product categories suffer from stunted growth because advertisers refuse to address their products' relevance to the consumer's experience. For example, Noxzema demonstrates in its advertising how a few swipes sweep your pimples away. Charmin would never dare show a corresponding feat.

The marketers responsible for butt products fear alienating those consumers benighted by fecal denial who find anyone invoking poop disgusting by association. No company wants its customers to associate it with poop; an excess of repression is the resulting norm. Even though their products exist only because people poop and only because people's butts stink, the companies that market them nevertheless avoid any direct acknowledgement of poop at all. The evidence for this and the damage it causes are visible in the toilet paper aisle at the supermarket. Most product categories are dominated by brands that have systematically marketed ever more specialized versions of their products, each version appealing to relatively narrower groups of people, a process known as segmentation. Think of all the different kinds of shampoo offered by Pantene Pro V—from Classically Clean and Smooth & Sleek to Purity Clarifying and Daily Moisture Renewal. Think of all the different flavors of Mountain Dew—from Code Red and Baja Blast to Pitch Black and LiveWire. Each new brand extension is intended to create a smaller group of customers more loyal to the variation (which they perceive to be formulated specifically for their needs) than they ever would be to the original (which they now perceive as generic and pedestrian). Companies sacrifice sales from the original brand to wring more money from those loyal to the variation.

The deodorant category is a model of this kind of segmentation. Deodorant makes armpits sweat and stink less. This seems like a simple proposition—how different can one armpit be from another? And yet this category features choices aimed at dozens of different lifestyles and preferences. Right Guard is for athletes. Speed Stick is for athletes. Degree is for businesspeople. Old Spice is for frat boys. Arrid is for Middle America. Axe is for cool people who get laid. Secret is for ladies. Dove is for older ladies. Mitchum used to be for old people, but now it's for cool people who get laid. Each brand is further segmented by functionality (antiperspirant, deodorant, both), form (stick, spray, gel, roll-on), and scent ("Polar Blast," "Deep Freeze," "Cool," "Fresh," unscented, hypoallergenic). Each permutation targets a different segment of the population, which is why many brands are owned by one corporate parent. While one brand may cannibalize another in the corporate family, the combined profit of a few narrowly targeted brands is greater than what would be generated by a single brand alone.

Segmentation necessitates either functional differentiation in conjunction with brand image, or variation in brand image alone. Segmentation has its risks: the brand variation is by definition less relevant to more people. The price of increased loyalty in some is the alienation of others. The marketers at Unilever, the corporate parent behind Axe deodorant, know that their overtly sexual advertising would alienate soccer moms and retirees. They're willing to sacrifice Axe's share of more prudish consumers for the rewards offered by increased loyalty among those more prurient. Of course, those consumers offended by Axe can perhaps turn instead to Unilever's Dove line, a genteel and feminine alternative. Dove's brand positioning alienates men, but generates enough loyalty from women to make up for it. This sacrifice is the hallmark of product segmentation: alienating some in order to resonate with others. And this is exactly what is missing in products for the butt.

Few Americans can imagine life without toilet paper. Nearly every American uses this product every day; most of us have learned the hard way to check for toilet paper before sitting on the toilet, because we can't comprehend any other way to clean up. This kind of product loyalty creates a market with huge potential. But considering the size of the market, the frequency of product use, the loyalty of the consumer base, and their unimaginativeness about alternatives, it's shocking how little of this potential has been realized.

The leading toilet paper brands in the American market are Charmin, Northern, Scott, Angel Soft, and Cottonelle. Almost without exception, the brands differentiate themselves only along the axis of comfort versus price—the more expensive brands are gentle, infused with medicating lotion and fresh scents; the cheaper brands abrade your anus. In a product category in which a fraction of a percent of market share is worth millions of dollars, there has been no real segmentation—no brand for women, for old people, for three-to-nine-year-olds with their sensitive young anuses, or for athletes with their rugged but rank brown starfish. There is no brand specifically engineered for scrunching, or for folding. And there is no brand for cool people who get laid. Segmentation, a hallmark of the American marketplace, is completely absent from the toilet paper category.

Nor has it happened for toilets. Many toilet manufacturers have built global brands based not on what their product does but on inoffensive, intangible, and irrelevant attributes like "innovative design" and "beautiful form." Most people buy toilets not to possess an art object but because they want something that can spirit away last night's chiliburger. And even though recent years have seen more substantial advertising promises (American Standard's Champion toilet is sold under the claim that you'll "never plunge again"), old habits are yet hardy—the Champion's website still gave equal weight to "a sleek Euro-style" that matches "the old-world elegance of our Bordeaux vanity and mirror". Where is the Jeep of toilets, that mud-splattered workhorse that can send your man-sized crap to the brownest depths of hell? Where is the environmentally friendly flush toilet with the kind of holistic outlook that appeals to hybrid car owners? Where is the toilet for cool people who get laid?

They don't exist, because any attempt to position butt-related products in ways more relevant to the consumer experience would involve acknowledgement of poop, which would immediately alienate those who don't want to be seen as people who poop, much less consumers of poop-related products. Marketers have no problem alienating consumers on the bases of age, gender, income, or most other conceivable points of differentiation, but poop is off-limits. Marketers care less how much profit potential exists in a brand that accepts the reality of poop than about the opinions of those who would be offended by it. Not every executive in every company necessarily has such a well-defined justification, but fecal denial is the aggregate reality of the marketplace. And its cost is a lack of segmentation—an inefficient market too constrained by taboo to realize its profit potential.

In the case of toilet paper, businesses compete not to address customer needs, but to create the cutest brand image: Charmin has cartoon bears, Angel Soft adorable babies, and Quilted Northern the "Quilters," an animated trio of sassy ladies who chat about how much they love their bathroom tissue. Smiling toddlers and fluffy clouds and teddy bears are darling, but few households are buying toilet paper because they think it's cute. Similarly, Americans look to their toilets to choke down the burritos we eat and the beer we drink, but toilet manufacturers feign to think that each of us is an interior designer at heart, more concerned about color scheme than with colon scum.

There are few signs of hope. A handful of high-end European boutiques have introduced chic toilet paper aimed at those who want their bathrooms to impress. Huggies recently aired some fairly brazen depictions of pooping and wiping to promote their Clean Time suite of children's products; perhaps they felt that the cuteness of babies negates the yuckiness of poop. And Scott Tissue launched its Halftime Flush promotion for the 2006 Super Bowl, banking on the urban legend that 90 million people are going to the bathroom simultaneously during halftime of the big game to promote its brand's dispersibility (that is, how well it disintegrates in water, helping avoid clogs during high-traffic times). Dispersibility is nice, but it's only a minor benefit of toilet paper. They're still avoiding the major ones.

BRANDS FOR THE DISCRIMINATING POOPER

Most toilet paper marketing features irrelevant brand claims and innocuous images that do shameful shitters the favor of allowing them to buy poop-related products in public without embarrassment—since the ads essentially deny the purpose of the product, so too can he who would otherwise be too self-conscious to buy it. Shameless shitters aren't necessarily alienated by these corporate strategies. Nor, however, are they emotionally invested in them. These strategies of denial provide little upon which a shameless shitter can develop any brand loyalty, which creates a huge opportunity for the first brand to come along and speak directly to the needs of those who are open enough to acknowledge them.

Imagine the success awaiting the first toilet paper to market itself on its utility—the first brand to honestly and straightforwardly tout its ability to wipe clean even the most matted chocolate wreath. The brand would advertise in good taste, of course—shameless shitters are neither exhibitionists nor perverts. They are simply people who would respond to a product describing its functionality without sensationalism or evasiveness. A toilet paper ad campaign needn't be disgusting to be relevant. But no major toilet paper manufacturer has yet discovered how many people are willing to hand over how many dollars for handfuls of a paper that promises, with no hemming and hawing, to clean one's hole without chafing. Visual artist Jed Ela, however, has.

Jed Ela's ShitBegone.

Ela created ShitBegone brand toilet paper in 1999. With its bright and intentionally derivative package printed with the cheery platitude "pillow soft," the only thing that distinguishes ShitBegone from Charmin or Cottonelle is its name. While "Charmin" is surely the brainchild of marketing mavens and focus groups, "ShitBegone" derives entirely from what the product does. ShitBegone is an unexceptional toilet paper, a peer of such brands as Scott Tissue in terms of texture and cleanup prowess. It is art, but different from Duchamp's readymades. Whereas readymades are mass-produced goods appropriated by the artist as art, ShitBegone is mass-produced art appropriated by the artist as a consumer good. You can look at it in a gallery, you can read about it in art magazines, but ultimately it's intended for you to buy in a store and use to wipe your butt. ShitBegone does not fully function as art until it's on a store shelf next to brands evoking teddy bears and fluffy clouds. In that context, ShitBegone highlights the inanity and irrelevance of the other brands' marketing, and every other way corporate America avoids acknowledging poop. Seeing ShitBegone on the shelf, you laugh at first; then you see through the elaborate artifice built on the fear of acknowledging poop.

Is ShitBegone more shocking because of its profanity or because of its honesty? The name alienates many of the consumers who encounter it on a shelf, but attracts others. "Pillow Soft Tissue" would have a wider appeal, but it would not generate the fervent excitement and loyalty that ShitBegone did. Not everyone who bought ShitBegone in the New York area stores that sold it knew it was art; many simply appreciated the name. As Ela puts it, selling toilet paper with fluffy clouds and teddy bears is bullshit; ShitBegone is being sold with honest shit.

ShitBegone will never be a million-dollar brand or a significant player in the toilet paper industry. The profanity in its name relegates it to the market for novelties. ShitBegone does, however, reveal a market segment that wants a simple solution for a simple problem. Some day a large corporate paper mill will meet this demand, creating a ShitBegone without the profanity—a brand that ably cleans without chafing, that tackles your mess while shielding your fingers. There will be controversy, of course. Legions of indignant consumers will organize boycotts and protests and go on Larry King to predict the downfall of society. But it will be worth it—from the consumer's perspective (more choice), from the corporation's perspective (more profit), and especially from society's perspective (less shameful shitting).

Less shameful shitting will happen because simply addressing poop will help clarify the rules surrounding it. Today poop is trapped in a vicious circle of invisibility—corporate America won't speak of it, which encourages people to perceive it as unmentionable, which encourages corporate America not to speak of it. Those embarrassed by their asses have no sign that there's any other socially acceptable way to feel. The epidemic of shameful shitting is worsened by corporate America's refusal to acknowledge poop. But we are all human, and we all poop. The first major brand to break the silence on that will help millions of oppressed poopers come to terms with their brown burden.

Advertising is only one aspect of culture influencing and influenced by shameful shitting. The news media are others. They have the same trepidations about poop, and the same fear of negative reactions by the public. And so the news media also cover up the role of poop. Just as this mitigation requires businesses to abandon their core principle (the pursuit of profit), so do the news media abandon their own core principles in their attempts to whitewash poop in the news.

ALL THE NEWS UNFIT TO PRINT

Recall the choice in 2004 by critics, artists, dealers, and curators of Duchamp's *Fountain* as the most influential artwork of the twentieth century. The event made the news. "World's best art piece? A urinal" was CNN.com's headline. "Duchamp's urinal tops art survey," proclaimed the BBC. "Picasso masterpieces beaten by a toilet" is how Reuters put it. The Age of Australia punned off a Commonwealth colloquialism for a practical joke: "Masterpiece or piss-take?"

Though news organizations purport to report the news without bias, these headlines dripped with opinion. The bodies of the articles were informative to various degrees, depending on the media outlet—CNN and the BBC attempted to contextualize *Fountain*, to explain its meaning and describe why so many in the art world might hold it in such regard; the tabloids were naturally less informative and more sensational. The AP was admirable in its even tone and lack of puns, but many media outlets ran the AP's dispatch in the context of "odd news." FoxNews.com, for instance, placed it in their "Out There" section, leading into it with stories of a granny arrested for taking police on a medium-speed chase and of two men accused of a crime for dumping dirt in a national forest. The AP's dispatch was most widely read in the syndicated "News of the Weird" column, appearing in that trivializing context in over 250 newspapers in the United States and Canada.

A journalist's responsibility is to convey facts objectively and transparently. Reporting of the Turner Prize survey almost universally treated the event with disdain or bemusement—that is, through the filter of opinion. The headlines aimed not to highlight the salient facts but instead to shock and arouse prurient interest. The copy made liberal use of puns. And the articles were placed in judgmental contexts—it matters little how serious or factual an article is if it's presented as "News of the Weird."

An isolated incident? Perhaps. Maybe the pomposity of modern art brings out the indignant everyman in the mainstream news media. Then again, maybe this is but one example of a consistent pattern of unprofessional treatment of poop in the news. Take as another example the reporting on the annual World Toilet Summit. With the primary goal of drawing attention to the implications of public toilets for humanity's health and happiness, the World Toilet Summit convenes each year to address issues important to any human being who's ever had to poop outside the home. A few lecture titles from the 2005 gathering: "Managing Out Crime in Public Toilets," "Public Toilet Excellence—The Singapore Model," and "Meeting the Millennium Development Goals on Sanitation." These matters affect people around the world, from cholera outbreaks in the third world to the environmental impact of sewer systems in the first; from diarrheal illnesses estimated to cause 12,600 child deaths in Asia, Africa, and South America every day to the more unquantifiable damage of shameful shitting (although they don't call it that). The importance of what's on the agenda, however, isn't quite what the news media focus on.

"World Toilet Summit lifts lid on public hygiene," said Reuters, leading into the story (placed in its "Oddly Enough" news section) with puns on the words "flush" and "sitting" in the first paragraph. "World Toilet Summit more than a wee bit important," punned the *Irish Examiner*. "Summit flushes out smelly toilets," declared CNN.com of the 2004 gathering. In most cases, tone or context made it impossible to take seriously any subsequent details the articles presented.

Poop can be funny, serious, or significant in human affairs. Everyone, nearly every day, experiences it. Governments spend billions and risk environmental catastrophe to capture and dispose of it. But the news media inevitably craft their reporting of poop along two major themes: extreme negativity (Symbolic Meaning of Poop #12) and contamination (Symbolic Meaning of Poop #5). The news media should report on the significant and the unusual. But by seeing poop as the extreme of negativity, they *a fortiori* treat poop as more negative—and thus more significant—than the other aspects of a story in which it appears. That invariably gives poop and its associated symbols (urine, toilets, etc.) more consequence than their involvement in the story may objectively merit. The primary focus of the World Toilet Summit is public health, for instance, but this is overshadowed in the stories by poop.

In December 2005, inventor Dean Kamen introduced a water filtration system that can purify any tainted liquid using only 2% of the energy required by traditional distillation. His system would be a lifesaver for the 1.1 billion people in the world who don't have clean water, but the AP's dispatch on the article ran with the headline "Urine business," because Kamen demonstrated the machine's capabilities by drinking distilled pee. This bias is most clearly illustrated when the BBC writes "Duchamp's urinal" in one sentence and "Picasso's *Les Demoiselles d'Avignon*" in the next. Why not "Picasso's five naked women"? Even the legendarily objective *New York Times* is not immune. A May 2006 article entitled "$1.4 Billion Deal for Bus-Stop Toilets Nears Approval" described an agreement between New York City and a Spanish company to create 3,500 bus-stop shelters and 330 newsstands—and only 20 public toilets.

Of two stories with other all facts being of equal importance, the one that involves poop will get wider coverage. The Turner Prize survey certainly wouldn't have been reported as widely had *Les Demoiselles d'Avignon* been the honored artwork. The March 2006 story that two maids at the Siesta Motor Lodge in North Charleston, South Carolina, got into a fight over mutual accusations of stealing toilet paper from each other's carts wouldn't have made it into 128 different publications worldwide (according to Google News), including the Miami *Herald* and the *Independent Online* of South Africa. And no one would have known that poor Bob Dougherty of Nederland, Colorado, once got glued to a toilet seat in a Home Depot bathroom.

It happened in October 2003. After twenty harrowing minutes, during which he suffered a panic attack as the Louisville, Colorado, Home Depot's employees ignored his calls for help (they thought he was joking), Dougherty was rescued by paramedics, who had to unbolt the seat from the toilet so they could finally get him free. His story came to light when he sued Home Depot in late 2005, seeking damages for post-traumatic stress that triggered diabetes and heart trouble (although not blaming the company for the glue on the seat). Dougherty's story was national news twice—first when the story broke, and then a few days later when someone came forward accusing Dougherty of having made claims of getting glued to toilet seats before. (The fact that Dougherty passed his lie detector test denying that charge was less widely reported.)

At least 235 personal injury lawsuits have been filed against Home Depot in federal court since 2001—everything from getting hit on the head by a falling box, to being hit by an employee falling from a ladder, to being beaten up by an employee. In 1998 Home

Norwegian politician Joakim Lund.
Photographs by Glen Musk.

Depot averaged as many as 185 customer injury claims per week. Between 1998 and 2002, the federal Occupational Safety and Health Administration recorded nine deaths among Home Depot employees. No recent figures exist for the total number of customer injuries or deaths at Home Depot, but a Houston attorney whose lawsuits against the company comprise about half his practice calls Home Depot "the most dangerous store in America." And yet the most widely reported cause of legal action against Home Depot was getting glued to a toilet.

The news media can report only a few of the thousands of potential stories taking place every single day. Media outlets evaluate reportable events by a variety of criteria, weighing each one's relevance and distinctiveness against the resources available to cover it. Because decision makers see poop as the extreme negative of the story, poop stories stand out above the rest. So, in spite of consistently disconcerting statistics and anecdotes about safety from Home Depot, thousands of editors in newsrooms across the country decided that the issue was of interest to their readers only when a toilet was involved.

Many media-savvy organizations take advantage of the fact that poop makes news. Organizers of the World Toilet Summit know that "The World Public Sanitary Health Summit" wouldn't get nearly as much press; they must feel the publicity the name generates is worth the tone by which it's delivered. The First Church of God in Pendleton, Oregon, lit up the AP Wire in January 2006 with the news that it was raising money for a mission to Costa Rica by selling Angel Soft toilet paper. And in September 2005, two Norwegian politicians used poop to get their names and pictures all over the world. Norway's Oppdal party member Joakim Lund bet his colleague Håvard Holden that he would "shower in shit" if Holden's Center Party won more than six percent of a particular vote. When the Center Party did indeed achieve that milestone, Lund honored his end of the bargain by standing under a manure pump on a Norwegian farm wearing only snorkeling gear and a swimsuit—a disgusting fate, but earning worldwide media attention.

But while the media will eagerly report poop in the news, no media outlet wants to be associated with news about poop. When confronted with an ambiguous manifestation of poop—as when a urinal is honored as great art—the news media worry about what their readers may think of them for reporting such a story. So they take great care to distance a poop story from their other reporting—linguistically, by writing in a tone that communicates their contempt for the subject; contextually, by putting the stories in the "wacky news" section so readers know the media outlet sees this story differently; and professionally, by analyzing the facts less critically then they would for less taboo subjects. Their fear is not that an equal footing would elevate poop, but that the contamination of poop would drag down all their other work.

With society divided as to whether it is or is not acceptable to admit that one poops, the media must hedge their bets. They can report poop, but must distance themselves lest they alienate the poop-aversive. The media respond to (and exacerbate) poop's confused role in society by ensuring that any validation it provides to a poop story is moderated with superficiality or even scorn.

Perhaps the best example of how widespread—and shallow—mainstream media reporting of poop is comes from Erie,

Pennsylvania. In the post-9/11 anxiety, it sometimes seems as though bomb squads and SWAT teams are called out every time someone leaves his groceries unattended for five minutes. Such occurrences rarely make it beyond the local news anymore—unless the parcel in question is a plastic bag containing feces-encrusted blue jeans. Then the whole country hears about it.

On the morning of May 26, 2004, eighteen-year-old Erie resident Troy Musil pooped his pants. He had mild flu and couldn't quite make it to the bathroom. So Musil borrowed some pants from a friend, put his own in a plastic bag, and (in a moment of bad judgment he'd regret) threw the bag over a fence, on the other side of which was the 33-million-gallon Sigsbee Reservoir from which Erie draws drinking water. Unfortunately, Musil forgot to take the keys out of his pocket. A day later, he hopped the fence to retrieve them. Somebody spotted him. The HAZMAT team, the bomb squad, the Erie police, and the FBI were scrambled. Musil left the scene before they arrived, but they diligently tracked him down and arrested him. Though the innocent nature of Musil's crime soon became clear, officials nevertheless spared no expense in its exhaustive investigation.

Musil's story made national news, and everyone had a good laugh. But for Musil, things soon got worse. First he was fired from his construction job. "I don't need this kind of attention," Musil's boss told him after the authorities came around asking questions. A few weeks later, Musil appeared in court. Pleading guilty to the charges of defiant trespassing, he was told to expect a $100 fine—and was shocked when the court ordered him to pay $5,000 to help the city recover costs spent dispatching so many resources to prevent his poopy pants from poisoning Erie. If he couldn't pay $500 a month for the next ten months, Musil would go to jail. But with no job and no savings, he really didn't have much choice. Although PoopReport.com tried to raise money for him, its $567.01 donation came too late. He was arrested in late July 2004, for criminal trespassing and five counts of theft after getting caught stealing bikes and other items out of Erie garages.

Was Musil a bad egg, or just an unlucky kid driven to desperation by a fine he couldn't afford to pay? Only he knows. Musil defaulted on his payments and paid his debt to Erie in time spent behind bars.

The story was a paragon of post-9/11 hysteria, but the presence of poop ensured that it would not be reported as such. Though Musil's escapade was news all over the world (he was mocked on the Internet and late night TV, and Keith Olbermann even named him a "top-three newsmaker" that June), his hardships went uninvestigated. What about Musil's civil rights—did his boss unfairly fire him? Even worse, Musil told PoopReport that he didn't have a lawyer at the time—aren't all defendants entitled to court-appointed representation? No one investigated. And what about Musil's punishment? Was $5,000 or jail an appropriate punishment for littering and trespassing? Should Musil have been held responsible for the government's knee-jerk assumption of the worst-case scenario?

But because the news media view poop as an extreme negative and a contaminant, issues of justice and human suffering were trivialized into wacky soundbites. The news media eschewed critical analysis of this story. Musil was laughed at and forgotten. Because they involved poop, the serious issues raised by this incident, including the humiliation and imprisonment of a young man for a relatively trivial offense, were ignored.

But what made Troy Musil different from June Edmonds? In September 2003, acting on a tip, authorities entered her home in Osteen, Florida, and discovered a horrifying sight: four children living in filth. A two-year-old girl was sleeping with three dogs in a urine-soaked playpen. The kitchen and living room floors were covered in human and dog poop. A portable toilet with no running water had been set up in the kitchen. In April of 2004, a judge stripped Edmonds of her parental rights as she awaited sentencing on charges of criminal neglect. The headline on Central Florida's WKMG-TV's website read, "Mom Loses Custody Battle after Kids Found in Feces."

No punny headlines, no judgmental contexts—just straightforward reporting of the atrocities committed by Ms. Edmonds and her punishment. Is this an exception to the news media's pattern of distancing themselves from the poop in poop stories? The answer is no. Poop is still a contaminant in this story, and still the most negative aspect—that is, a story like Ms. Edmonds' gets more attention from an editor than a poop-free story of child abuse. The difference is that, in a story such as Ms. Edmonds', the news media needn't worry that the contamination of poop will taint the messenger. Though there is confusion about the acceptability of publicly admitting that one poops, there is no doubt in contemporary culture that poop belongs in toilets, and not on kitchen and living room floors. So while the media feel compelled to distance themselves when reporting on poop in an ambiguous position, there is no such pressure when poop is clearly out of place. Everyone agrees that children aren't supposed to live in houses filled with poop, and everyone knows what to think of parents who subject their children to such conditions.

The news media use puns and judgmental contexts when poop arises in a grey area. A urinal on display in a museum, for instance: the media don't know whether to report it from the perspective of the common man in condemning the urinal or of the museum in sanctioning it. Troy Musil's story engendered a similar problem: join the police in taking the poop seriously, or the common man in laughing at it? The news media commit to neither side, instead using puns and dismissive contexts to remind the reader that the media are appropriately disdainful of poop.

But when poop manifests in an utterly unambiguous way, the media have no need to rearticulate its perspective. "Malnourished men found in feces-filled house," reads a headline from Georgia's *Gwinnett Daily Post*. "Woman's body found in feces-strewn house with 37 animals," reports KOB-TV of Albuquerque. "Police: Man killed over toilet paper," CNN.com reports to its readers. For such stories, only one judgment is possible, and the media report with the confident expectation of that judgment by its readers.

Mary Douglas theorized that society finds something dangerous if it is "matter out of place." Poop on the kitchen and living room floors seems to qualify for Douglas's concept. But such poop is, in fact, quite comfortably in its place—in that we know exactly how to react to it. Poop on the floor is neatly categorized. It's ambiguous manifestations of poop, such as its being displayed in a museum, that cause problems and force the media to assert their purity. The Victorians actively denied their own poop even as they fretted about the pooping conditions of the masses. This wasn't hypocritical, because they believed poop was something that only happened to other people. It was, in fact, what made other people other people. This sort of categorization enables the news media to report certain stories about poop without puns and without judgment. When poop is perfectly recognizable as "matter out of place," it is already clearly contaminating something else. Judgmental contexts and techniques aren't necessary because judgment is built-in.

THE WIPED MAN'S BURDEN: CONTAMINATION AND POWER

Something contaminated is by definition at odds with the standards of civilized society; society's typical response is to shun it. But sometimes society decides to do something about it. In 1898, as part of Spain's surrender at the end of the Spanish-American war, the U.S. paid $20 million for a number of Spanish territories, including the Philippines. The war had begun as an intervention by the U.S. to stop the Spanish from committing atrocities in their colony. After its victory, however, liberator quickly became colonizer. The Filipinos were not happy to trade one ruler for another; toughened by fighting for their independence against Spain since 1896, they simply turned their guns against the Americans. Fourteen years of guerrilla warfare ensued.

At home, there was considerable resistance to the war, including anti-imperialists who felt the U.S. had betrayed its noble intentions in entering the war, and writers (such as Mark Twain) who wrote persuasively that the U.S. was violating the ideals of democracy by making the Philippines its client state. Given this opposition, it was clearly in the government's best interest to warm Americans to the occupation. According to Warwick Davis in his essay "Excremental Colonialism," one thing the government used for this purpose was poop, as figure for the contrast between the pure American body and the grotesque Filipino. If the Filipinos were filthy, the logic went, it was Americans' burden to clean them up, whether they liked it or not.

We can see evidence of the official attitude toward native Filipinos in writings by doctors, scientists, government representatives, and highly placed civilians. A typical example comes from Emily Bronson Conger's 1904 *An Ohio Woman in the Philippines*: "It does not matter which way you turn you see hundreds of natives at their toilet. One does not mind them more than the caribou in some muddy pond, and one is just about as cleanly as the other." Dr. Thomas R. Marshall's wrote in his 1904 *Asiatic Cholera in the Philippine Islands* that "[t]he Filipino people … should be taught that … promiscuous defecation is dangerous and should be discontinued." The editor of the influential *Cable-news-American* was even more to the point, declaring that the "lower classes of natives" could be made to avoid germ-laden food and drink "only by force."

And that's just what happened. With the pretext of sanitizing the filthy masses, the Americans justified their remaking of Filipino society. Marshes were drained. Traditional marketplaces were replaced with American-built ones. "Disinfection squads" numbering in the hundreds of men were dispatched upon whole neighborhoods to spray dwellings with carbolic acid. Children were trained to avoid "raw vegetables, impure water, poorly ventilated houses, a sedentary way of life, and deformed posture," as Davis describes it. New waste infrastructures were mandated by law, and taxes levied to pay for them. People who resisted sanitary reforms were arrested. In the name of isolating disease-carriers, the Americans would analyze natives' poop and quarantine people based on the results, separating them from their friends and family and forbidding them from going to work until the Americans decided otherwise.

Through the lens of modern standards, the Americans were arguably improving the sanitary conditions in the Philippines. But from the perspective of the natives, these could only have been seen as acts of oppression. As Davis writes, the Americans would tell them in one breath that they needed to treat their "evacuated intestinal contents as a poison" and that poop possessed "dangers that would kill uninitiated men"; at the same time, the Americans would obsessively collect poop from cesspools and privies. We can guess today that the Americans were taking samples to study outbreaks of disease, but to the natives, these must have seemed like hypocritical fecal mandates that the scientists themselves flouted. But native resistance was not tolerated. In the name of sanitation, the Americans did whatever they wanted.

Natives are dirty, even when they're not.

An outbreak of typhoid in Army barracks in November 1909 illustrates the belief in the filthy native put into action. During the typhoid crisis, the chief surgeon of the Philippines Division searched natives working in the camp for carriers of the disease. None were found. Nevertheless, as Davis describes, the surgeon issued orders "forbidding natives, laundrymen, etc., to sleep under barracks... Natives were prohibited from touching or eating from any dish used by soldiers." Even when the outbreak was traced to contaminated water, exonerating the Filipinos who worked in the barracks, the surgeon still concluded that "natives are uncontrolled as to their personal hygiene and are undoubtedly a source of disease."

This marginalization of the Filipinos by such influential official sources as doctors and scientists created a divide between Us and Them, between civilized and savage, to justify the use of power by Us for the betterment of Them (whether They liked it or not). This was best articulated by U.S. Secretary of the Interior for the Philippines Dean C. Worcester in 1914. After the fourteen-year war that killed 4,324 American soldiers and an estimated 16,000 Filipino soldiers, and during which 250,000 to 1,000,000 civilians died of war-bred famine and disease, Worcester defended the US presence as "the regime of civilization and improvement which started with American occupation and resulted in developing naked savages into cultivated and educated men."

Using contamination to justify force is not limited to the postwar Philippines. It also occurred in English justifications of their colonization of India. A representative statement comes from sanitary evangelist Frank Lugard Brayne, describing the hygienic lives of a typical child from the areas in and around Delhi in 1927: "His early youth was spent playing in the dust on the village muck heap and in what might best be described as the latrine-cum-rubbish-heap area. His eyes and nose were often running and flies settled in dozens on them and on his mouth. He was rarely if ever washed and never taught clean habits. He was much neglected." In America, the sanitary reformer Jacob Riis' 1890 book *How the Other Half Lives* provided vivid images of filth and contamination in American inner cities, spurring widespread government action to alter the conditions of the urban poor.

Contamination is used to justify the use of power even today. Before the U.S. invasion of Iraq in 2003 and during the first few months of the occupation, the country's crumbling sanitary infrastructure was invoked as yet another reason for the U.S.' decision to invade (well behind terrorism and WMDs, of course). Similarly, the contamination left by the receding waters in New Orleans after Hurricane Katrina was invoked by officials in their refusal to allow rebuilding in certain neighborhoods. And the Federal Communications Commission used the pretext of contamination in 2003 and 2004 to issue fines to broadcasters for Howard Stern's antics on his radio show and for Janet Jackson's infamous nipple slip during the Super Bowl. Their rationale: the public found these incidents "filthy," so it was the FCC's job to clean it up.

All this isn't to say that fear of the state's power is the direct cause of the media laughing at stories such as Troy Musil's. Rather, this is to demonstrate the power ascribed by the civilized to contamination, and to underscore the reasons for avoiding it. Mary Douglas theorized that we judge everything we encounter by its place on the continuum between clean and dirty. If you travel toward the dirty end of the spectrum, people will shun you; travel even further, and they may decide to do something about you.

From this perspective, it's fairly easy to believe that filth is the basis for state control of the individual. That's what Frenchman Dominique Laporte claimed in his 1978 book *The History of Shit*: that the toilet being assigned as the mandatory fecal infrastructure represented a power grab by the state deeper into the private life of the individual than ever before in history. Using the lan-

guage of sanitary science, he says, the government justifies regulating the water that flows into your house and that which rides
it out. Such language sanctifies the oppression of those who don't
rise to the benchmarks of civilization—taxes, fines, even loss of
property and freedom in the extreme cases. This is the ideology
echoed in each breathlessly reported discovery of a woman living
with fifty cats and their accumulated feces, for instance. Acknowledgement of contamination is all the justification necessary to
take away her cats and throw the woman in an institution.

Whether Laporte is right or not, the threat of contamination is
powerful indeed. This threat is yet another influence on shameful
shitters. They see how society treats the contaminated. They see
how contamination becomes a pretext for the use of force. They
see how institutions such as advertisers and the news media
strive desperately to avoid contamination. And seeing all this,
they see no reason to invite contamination upon themselves,
which is what they fear they'd be doing if they were to poop when
and where others would be aware of it. Fear of contamination
keeps the shameful shameful.

Contamination is so powerful, in fact, that it's a danger even
to civilization itself. As the media fear when they report poop stories, and as Angela Riccelli feared when someone called her "The
Poop Lady," and as the French guard proved when he farted in the
general direction of King Arthur and his men in *Monty Python and
the Holy Grail*, contamination is contagious. The rules of civilization that assign contamination have an Achilles Heel:
contamination can be transferred back even to them.

Images of François Rabelais' Gargantua.

CHAPTER 9

BROWN COMEDY: HUMOR, SATIRE, AND THE CARNIVALESQUE

WOMEN ARE SOBBING. Men are screaming. Two Jews are pummeling a priest. Bodies fly every which way as hippie tree-huggers, devout Christians, and everyone else in town pulls hair, yanks ears, and generally beats the hell out of each other. Political correctness is tearing this quiet little white-bread redneck mountain town apart.

The occasion was the elementary school's happy, inoffensive, nondenominational Christmas play (with music and lyrics by New York minimalist composer Philip Glass), and it was supposed to be a time of joy. The play had been written and choreographed in accordance with the townspeople's desire that absolutely no individual or group find anything offensive in the production. Since Jesus offends the Jews, He was out; so was any reference to God, since that would offend those who desire separation of church and state. Santa Claus was taboo because he offends the Christian fundamentalists, blinking lights because they offend epileptics, and the little flaps on coffee lids because they offend the guy who thinks that if you don't want to spill your coffee you shouldn't be driving with it.

Inoffensive is what they got. Children in monochrome leotards writhed abstractly. Glass played atonal melodies as he chanted metronomic nonsense. It was perfectly innocuous, and perfectly awful. Horrified at the monstrosity they had created, the town turned upon itself, each group blaming the others for creating the vortex of political correctness that sucked down all that was good and wholesome about an elementary school Christmas play. Anger turned to violence, and blood began to spill.

On stage, the children stopped their performance and watched in horror as their town plunged into anarchy. Suddenly, a piercing whistle cut across the bedlam, and a high-pitched voice began to speak. The fighting stopped as the townspeople, stunned into silence, turn toward its source. "Come on, gang," the voice implored, "don't fight. You people focus so hard on the things wrong with Christmas that you've forgotten what's so right about it. Don't you see? This is the one time of year we're s'posed to forget all the bad stuff, to stop worrying and being sad about the state of the world, and for just one day say, 'Aw, the heck with it! Let's sing and dance and bake cookies!'"

Fists and chairs were lowered as the townspeople looked around in uncertainty. Then a man began to clap. And then another, and then the whole town was cheering, crying, embracing, forgiving. Christian, Jew, hippie, mayor, police officer, veteran, Chef—they remembered the true meaning of Christmas, and they united in joyous song. All thanks to Mr. Hankey, the Christmas Poo, that smiling, six-inch talking turd in a Santa hat who comes out of the toilet every year to give presents to everyone who has lots of fiber in their diets. Mr. Hankey delivered that moving speech; it is to him the people of *South Park* owed their freedom from the evils of political correctness.

SCATOLOGICAL HUMOR

Despite its wicked reputation, *South Park* is an emphatically moral show. It set a new standard for challenging American taboos from the moment it first aired on Comedy Central in 1997, and immediately earned the ire of critics across the spectrum. Created by Trey Parker and Matt Stone, the show chronicles the adventures of four elementary school boys in the small town of South Park, Colorado. Most episodes place the boys in outrageous or controversial situations that end with them learning a valuable lesson. *South Park*'s negative reputation comes from how those lessons are taught. First, each episode's lesson typically hinges on exposing the hypocrisy of one or another social group—the left, the right, the church, celebrities, the media, the rich, the poor, and all points in between. Second, the narratives that develop the lessons are written to maximize shock.

Parker and Stone have fully embraced the taboo as a tool to criticize people, groups, trends, and ideas. They tell their stories with bad language (one episode featured the word "shit" 162 times in thirty minutes), scandalous situations (another episode centered around a woman with a dead fetus attached to her head), and, of course, liberal use of poop (like the episode in which eating food with your butt and pooping it out of your mouth was somehow a parable about atheism). The shows' endlessly creative breaches of taboo can obscure their redemptive messages. This is why the show is perpetually condemned—for blasphemy, for being offensive, and for its fanatical devotion to scatological humor.

Scatological humor can get a laugh from just about anyone—in small doses, of course, and in the proper context, and couched in sufficiently tame language. Many have embraced it, from Aristophanes to Seinfeld. But every audience has its limit, and excessive mining of this vein of humor is likely to be condemned as juvenile. To some, scatological humor like *South Park*, *Dumb and Dumber* and Howard Stern represents the first step in the breakdown of civilized society.

While advertisers and the news media strain to avoid the contaminating association of poop, shows such as *South Park* wallow in it. To its critics, *South Park* is filth that contaminates its creators, the network that broadcasts it, and advertisers who support it. Critics are contemptuous of its fans, too, but think they can be redeemed. They decry the show's immaturity as a corrupting influence on the young men who are its biggest audience, as if they would be reading Virgil and Frost if only the show were cancelled. These critics don't realize that *South Park* is not introducing its audience to something new, but giving them something they seek—and not immaturity, but rebellion.

In their 2004 collection *Fecal Matters in Early Modern Literature and Art*, scholars Jeff Persels and Russell Ganim define scatology as "the representation of the process and product of elimination of the body's waste products (feces, urine, flatus, phlegm, vomitus)." In the prospectus for her doctoral dissertation on scatology, Marisol Cortez refines that definition, pointing out that scatology doesn't just represent bodily waste, but does so in a way that invokes disgust. Scatological humor, then, invokes the disgust surrounding the body's waste products for laughs. That laugh is an act of rebellion.

The link between scatological humor and rebellion was best explained by French sociologist Pierre Bourdieu. Discussing the difference between high culture and popular culture, he described the latter as "a refusal of the refusal which is the starting-point of the high aesthetic." In other words, high culture is based on the exclusion of things like poop; the fun of low culture comes from the refusal to refuse them. Although Bourdieu wasn't talking specifically about scatological humor, his analysis applies: laughing at scatological humor means rejecting the mandate to reject poop. In potty training, you learned that the rules of society sometimes require the rejection of the desires of the body. To reject this rejection, you're rebelling against the potty-training-instilled foundations of the rules of society.

But what exactly does that mean? Who laid down the rules of society?

The categorizations Mary Douglas described aren't made by divine proclamation or governmental decree. They are taught to us via ideological apparatuses: the schools, the media, the church, and parental advice, to name just a few. Watching TV, hearing sermons, listening to our parents, we are given cues as to how the world is categorized. Take farts, for example. We see how our parents react to farts, how the media depict them, how they are received in church. These experiences unite as the categorizing voice of civilization.

Each of us interprets the voice of civilization in his or her own way, based on uniquely personal encounters with ideological apparatus. That's why one person will announce, "I have to pee" while another will euphemize, "I have to use the bathroom"—differing interpretations of the voice of civilization. But though we all have nuanced views, there is generally agreement on the broadest categories. We all agree that farting is acceptable in the bathroom and unacceptable in church. If you accept something knowing it's unacceptable, you're refusing the refusal that the rules of society mandate. Scatological humor presents poop in situations in which you know you're supposed to refuse it. Laughing at a fart in church is a refusal of that refusal. It's a rebellion against the voice of civilization—against society.

This is why scatological humor typically appeals to teenagers, especially males: not because they're immature, but because they're rebellious. And this is why older people and people in authority decry scatological humor: because it challenges the order that gives them their power. Scatological humor is really only funny to those who identify with the challenger. Seeing Lieutenant Proctor humiliated on that porta-potty by the *Police Academy* gang is funny because we've grown to hate him, but Proctor's mother would think differently. On the other hand, seeing the pitiable Dawn Wiener humiliated in the bathroom by Lolita isn't funny because we feel sorry for Dawn. Perhaps the most personal example to most Americans: the Bible tells us that the crowd mocked Jesus at his crucifixion by smearing his face with the same kind of vinegar-soaked sponge they would use to wipe their butts. To the crowd, Jesus represented a political order that they hated or feared; to his followers, Jesus represented a political order they loved. You can see why the crowd found it funnier than the faithful did.

From this perspective, it's clear why *South Park* is notorious. Its unprecedented embrace of scatological humor is an unprecedented rebellion against the voice of civilization, not just by the writers, but also by the network that broadcasts it, the advertisers who support it, and the fans who watch it.

SCATOLOGICAL SATIRE

Early in the *South Park* episode in which Mr. Hankey made his debut, the children are rehearsing for their Christmas play when they see through the window that it's begun to snow. Overjoyed, they rush outside to catch snowflakes on their tongues. First Wendy catches one, then Kyle, and then even the embittered Cartman delights in the pure innocence of this game. But when Kenny gapes up, a passing eagle poops into his mouth. Cartman howls in laughter.

Contrasting the eagle pooping in Kenny's mouth with the character of Mr. Hankey, it becomes clear that *South Park* uses scatological humor in a couple of different ways. The eagle doesn't seem to add much to the plot other than a quick laugh; Mr. Hankey, however, has resonance beyond the appeal of a singing and dancing turd. Parker and Stone could have made their point about political correctness in any number of ways, but they decided a singing and dancing turd would be the most poignant way to teach the people of South Park—and, by extension, the audience—their lesson. In the case of the eagle, poop makes you laugh; in the case of Mr. Hankey, poop makes you laugh and then makes you think. *South Park* isn't just thirty minutes of meaningless poop jokes; it uses poop to satirize. And for the same reasons that Duchamp's urinal is a more powerful ready-made than his bottle rack or dog comb, satire is more powerful when it's scatological.

Where scatological humor provides a laugh in the face of the voice of civilization, scatological satire channels that laugh into a critique of it. A satirist uses wit, humor, or irony to either bring down a political order or force a political order to accept something it rejects. Because poop is so universally rejected, it is the perfect tool to dramatize rejection.

The technique predates *South Park* and Howard Stern, Piero Manzoni and Marcel Duchamp, James Joyce and Geoffrey Chaucer, dating at least as far back as ancient Greek dramatists such as Aristophanes, who punctuated his plays with fart jokes. But the writer most closely linked with scatological satire in English is Jonathan Swift, author of *Gulliver's Travels*. First published in 1726 and never out of print since, *Gulliver's Travels* chronicles the journey of Lemuel Gulliver through a series of strange and fantastic lands, including Lilliput, where he towers over the six-inch-tall inhabitants; Brobdingnag, where the seventy-two-foot inhabitants tower over him; Laputa, a flying island devoted to arts and sciences but wholly unable to make practical use of them; and finally the land of the Houyhnhnms and the Yahoos. The former are a species of intelligent horses; the latter are hideous and savage creatures who, Gulliver grows to realize, are really human beings at their most degenerate. Scatological humor and satire pervade the book.

While the image of Gulliver tied to the ground by the Lilliputians has been made famous in countless cartoons and children's books, less known is the moment when he pees while in his bonds: "I was able to turn upon my Right, and to ease myself with making Water; which I very plentifully did, to the great Astonishment of the People, who conjecturing by my Motions what I was going to do, immediately opened to the right and left on that Side, to avoid the Torrent which fell with such Noise and Violence from me." Later, as the Lilliputians grow more accepting of Gulliver, he employs two servants with wheelbarrows to dispose of his poop. In Brobdingnag, he tries to jump over a giant cow pie and lands right in the middle of it; after his rescue the story is told to the queen and her court, and Brobdingnagians laugh at him for days. The Yahoos greet Gulliver by showering him with their poop from the trees.

But beyond the fantasy and the humor, *Gulliver's Travels* is a work of complex satire, criticizing contemporaries of Swift from politicians and royalty to physicians and everyday people. Even Gulliver is, at the end, shown to be a pompous jerk. Scatology plays a crucial role in communicating Swift's satirical purposes. To criticize science, Swift writes of the ridiculous experiments Gulliver observed in the Grand Academy, including an "operation to reduce human excrement to its original food" as well as a study of how the poop of suspicious individuals can be analyzed for evidence of conspiracies against the government. To depict the corruption of man, Swift describes how sycophantic Yahoos who fall out of favor in their social structure are pooped on, one at a time, by every member of society.

Gulliver describes one of the experiments observed at the Grand Academy on the floating island of Laputa.

"Another Professor shewed me a large Paper of Instructions for discovering Plots and Conspiracies against the Governments. He advised great Statesmen to examine into the Dyet of all suspected Persons; their times of eating; upon which side they lay in Bed; with which hand they wiped their Posteriors; take a strict View of their Excrements, and from the Colour, the Odour, the Taste, the Consistence, the Crudeness, or Maturity of Digestion, form a Judgement of their Thoughts and Designs. Because Men are never so Serious, Thoughtful, and Intent, as when they are at Stool, which he found by frequent Experiment: For in such Conjunctures, when he used meerly as a Trial to consider which was the best way of murdering the King, his Ordure would have A Tincture of Green, but quite different when he thought only of raising an Insurrection or burning the Metropolis."

Scatological satire is one of the main ways in which the Yahoos are presented as filthy and repugnant, which makes it more meaningful when the enlightened Houyhnhnms condemn Gulliver as a Yahoo himself. This is one of the most poignant messages of the book: that no human being is above his nature as a disgusting, stinking, pooping Yahoo.

Though Swift uses scatology regularly across his body of work, that last example in particular seemed to exemplify Swift's beliefs in the eyes of his critics. For almost three hundred years, critics have derided Swift's "excremental vision," describing his poetry and prose as "an extreme of vulgarity and obscenity" and denouncing him for harboring a "physical nausea of mankind." Aldous Huxley accused him of having a "hatred of the bowels." Such criticism, of course, directly complies with civilization's mandate to reject poop. These critics are trying to contaminate Swift by associating him with the poop he writes about, as though one who writes about poop were inseparable from his subject. But if one ignores the proddings of the voice of civilization and analyzes scatological satire, not as a measure of a writer's character but instead objectively as a legitimate literary tool, a different pattern emerges. Swift uses scatology to turn the judgmental voice of civilization against itself, to associate the voice of civilization with that which it reviles the most.

The danger scatological satire poses to the voice of civilization is of turning the contamination of poop against the very authority that gives poop the power to contaminate. Critics decrying Swift's excremental vision are trying to defend the voice of civilization from his attacks, to put the contamination-by-association back on Swift's shoulders where they feel it truly belongs. Critics who decry *South Park*'s excremental vision are similarly trying to protect the voice of civilization from the threat of contamination.

In the right hands, scatological satire has the power to contaminate any aspect of the voice of civilization but one. Scatological satire transfers the contamination of poop from one source to another, but poop itself is portrayed no differently in scatological satire than by the news media. Poop is still the extreme negative, still a contaminant. The scientists on Laputa, for instance, are contaminated with poop because they give so much attention to such an unseemly subject. By drawing a parallel between real-life scientists and the scientists on Laputa, Swift is pointing the contamination of poop at them. He's not associating poop with the lofty goals of science, but bringing science down to the level of poop. Scatological satire may flaunt the mandates of fecal denial, but it does nothing to challenge the underlying philosophy.

But Mr. Hankey does challenge this philosophy. He doesn't bring political correctness down to the low of poop—he elevates the townspeople above it. He is poop, but he is not negative. Mr. Hankey is poop that is redemptive.

The concept of redemptive poop was explored by Mikhail Bakhtin, a Russian philosopher and scholar. But before we can understand Bakhtin's theories, we need to go further back in time, two hundred years before Swift, to a series of five books written in the sixteenth century about two giants who pooped a lot.

THE CARNIVALESQUE: SCATOLOGICAL REDEMPTION

François Rabelais' *Gargantua and Pantagruel* chronicles the adventures of a pair of giants, father and son, who are concerned only with indulging the desires of their bodies: eating, drinking, having sex, and pooping. The book elegantly describes the eponymous duo's legendary feats and equally legendary excretions. Poop is integrated into the plot from the first (the narrator attests to the truth of his story by threatening the reader with diarrhea: "If you do not believe it, I wish your bum-gut fall out and make an escapade") to the last (the final scene in the initial book in the series describes how Pantagruel cured constipation by swallowing sixteen miners to clear out the massive turd lodged in his nether regions). Numerous characters, from the members of the Paris Parliament to the regents at the Sorbonne, mess their britches in Pantagruel's imposing presence. In a scene early in Book I that may have inspired Swift, Gargantua causes a bit of mischief upon arrival in Paris: "Then smiling, he untied his fair braguette, and drawing out his mentul into the open air, he so bitterly all-to-bepissed them, that he drowned two hundred and sixty thousand, four hundred and eighteen, besides the women and little children."

Gargantua and Pantagruel, Book I, Chapter XIII*:* in which young Gargantua, aged five, demonstrates his intellectual acuity by recounting his quest for the perfect bum fodder.

"...I wiped my bum, said Gargantua, with a kerchief, with a pillow, with a pantoufle, with a pouch, with a pannier, but that was a wicked and unpleasant torchecul; then with a hat. Of hats, note that some are shorn, and others shaggy, some velveted, others covered with taffeties, and others with satin. The best of all these is the shaggy hat, for it makes a very neat abstersion of the fecal matter.

"Afterwards I wiped my tail with a hen, with a cock, with a pullet, with a calf's skin, with a hare, with a pigeon, with a cormorant, with an attorney's bag, with a montero, with a coif, with a falconer's lure. But, to conclude, I say and maintain, that of all torcheculs, arsewisps, bumfodders, tail-napkins, bunghole cleansers, and wipe-breeches, there is none in the world comparable to the neck of a goose, that is well downed, if you hold her head betwixt your legs. And believe me therein upon mine honour, for you will thereby feel in your nockhole a most wonderful pleasure, both in regard of the softness of the said down and of the temporate heat of the goose, which is easily communicated to the bum-gut and the rest the inwards, in so far as to come even to the regions of the heart and brains."

The excesses of *Gargantua and Pantagruel* are understood today to be a satire on contemporary French society. The scatology it employed made it as controversial when the book was published as you might imagine. The Catholic Church came out against it, and it was condemned by the academics at the Sorbonne and even briefly banned by the French Parliament (neither of whom could have been amused by what Rabelais depicted happening in their pants). But in spite of all this official opposition, the books sold well in France and beyond its borders, earning Rabelais the distinction as one of the most widely read sixteenth-century French authors. It has been studied by scholars for its examples of the literary techniques and religious views of the time ever since. But in the mid-1960s, *Gargantua and Pantagruel* took on a whole new life when Bakhtin published *Rabelais and His World.*

Originally written during World War II as a dissertation for a doctoral degree—which, perhaps owing to the controversial ideas presented, was denied—*Rabelais and his World* didn't find a publisher until 1965. In it, Bakhtin explored the laughter, parody, and "grotesque realism" *Gargantua and Pantagruel* used in critiquing French society. The church at the time of the book's publication vilified eating, pooping, and having sex (the "lower body stratum," as Bakhtin put it), and the official response to the book told Bakhtin that the church saw the book as a dire threat. That reminded Bakhtin of another threat to the church at the time: the medieval carnival.

Also known as the Feast of Fools, the medieval carnival was widely celebrated in many European countries through the fifteenth century. The annual festivities were more than just wild eating and drinking; they included rituals that turned normal class hierarchies and social values upside-down. Celebrants would openly mock official culture, satirizing religious and royal ceremonies, portraying heroes as clowns and clowns as heroes, and indulging their most degenerate desires as they cross-dressed or ran naked, eating, drinking, and making merry. These were times of release, in which people were momentarily liberated from their toil and given brief freedom to enjoy life as they wished. Think of such events as Mardi Gras, Burning Man, or spring break in Florida as the medieval carnival's distant descendants: the public drinking, the partying, the breast flashing, and the wild debauchery are clearly against the rules, but authorities grudgingly allow it for a week or two, after which things go back to normal. The Feast of Fools was similar, a brief social upheaval that inverted everything but ultimately changed nothing, a revolution with an expiration date. The church was always strongly against it, of course, but it took them until as late as the seventeenth century in some places to fully stamp it out.

Bakhtin saw *Gargantua and Pantagruel* as the medieval carnival in book form. It engendered the same liberating laughter, the same vicarious release from the repression of the lower bodily stratum. Because it turned poop into something positive, it was different than scatological humor or scatological satire. It was what Bakhtin called "carnivalesque," a scatological redemption. Still extreme, still contaminating, but in this case contaminating with redemption. It is something you *want* to be contaminated with. It's still *argumentum a fortiori*—but instead of the most extreme negative, it is the most extreme redemption.

The carnivalesque has the power to redeem both the oppressors and the oppressed. As an example, consider this: you hear a fart in church. A packed church, a moment of silent prayer, and then a sudden, explosive, juicy fart that sputters and spits for a matter of seconds. You don't know who did it, but you know everyone heard it—your parents sitting sternly at your side, the other parishioners, the choir, even the priest. You want to laugh, but you know what will happen if you do: your parents will kill you, your Sunday school teacher will discipline you, and even God will probably make note of your disrespect. All around you, no one reacts. Heads remained bowed. Brows remained furrowed. And then the priest starts laughing. His shoulders shake, his eyes tear up, and then he just gives up and lets loose. That's it for the rest of you. The choir, the parishioners, your Sunday school teacher, and even your parents—you all drop your inhibitions and let the laughter fly, not mocking the person who farted, just reveling in the pure comedy of the fart. It's funny that someone bebopped on the butt trumpet in the middle of church, and because anyone there could have been responsible. This is what Bakhtin meant by carnivalesque laughter: when those with authority and those with none are marveling equally at the universal absurdity of the human body. While scatological humor rebels against the voice of civilization, and scatological satire turns the voice of civilization against itself, the carnivalesque exposes the impossibility of the ideals the voice of civilization mandates. This laughter isn't mocking; it's inclusive.

The ideal body, if you believe the voice of civilization, is James Bond's or Lara Croft's—always dignified, never humbled by stomach cramps. It is, in other words, a total fiction. Carnivalesque laughter acknowledges this lie—you admit that your body is flawed, and you acknowledge that all bodies are flawed, and you realize that this doesn't make all humanity equally bad—this makes all humanity equally good. Bakhtin called this the "material bodily principle." It's the understanding that we all answer to a lower power. And it's the refutation of shameful shitting.

Gargantua and Pantagruel does not evoke in us today the passion it generated in sixteenth-century France—no governments are banning it, no churches are condemning it, and very few of us are inspired to reject the conventions of polite society just by reading it. Today our kids grow up reading books such as *Walter the Farting Dog* and *The Adventures of Captain Underpants*, so it's hard for us to see what the big deal was about *Gargantua and Pantagruel*. But Bakhtin is not suggesting that utopia would be achieved if only everyone read it. Rather, he is pointing out that the potential for the carnivalesque exists in each culture.

Jonathan Swift met the carnivalesque potential of his particular culture in his poem *Strephon and Chloe*, discussed in Chapter Six. In it, the newlyweds' awkwardness and discomfort evaporate only when they realize that they needn't hide their bodies from each other, because both of their bodies are equally disgusting. They were unhappy trying to maintain the rules of decorum as mandated by the voice of civilization, and they find happiness only when they embrace the material bodily principle. To some critics, of course, this was a presentation of the degeneration of man just like Swift's condemnation of humanity as Yahoos. In fact, Swift's message is quite the opposite: because no one is especially sublime, we are all equally sublime. Aldous Huxley was wrong about Swift; he doesn't hate the bowels. He hates the way society forces us to experience them.

It might be easier for us to appreciate *Strephon and Chloe*, but it isn't going to shake contemporary society, either. What is carnivalesque is relative to culture. In sixteenth-century France, books were relatively rare, so it must have been astonishing to find so many precious pages devoted to matters of the butt. In Swift's time, in an Ireland of rigid social roles and stringent rules of decorum, such frank talk about the earthly nature of the angelic archetypes Chloe and Strephon touched a nerve. But today, inundated with media and desensitized to scatology, we find neither pooping giants nor uninhibited newlyweds stirring.

Bakhtin's key observation is that each culture contains the potential for the carnivalesque to uproot, even for a moment, the divisions and hierarchies normally accepted as given. *Gargantua and Pantagruel* was a carnivalesque threat to sixteenth-century French pretense. *Strephon and Chloe* posed a similar threat to eighteenth-century Ireland. With Bakhtin as our guide, we can seek the contemporary carnivalesque—that which threatens the Victorian legacy of fecal denial that drives our views of bodily functions and the epidemic of shameful shitting.

We can see hints of the carnivalesque in Mr. Hankey. After the Christmas play, the voice of civilization had led the people of South Park into an all-out war. The only thing that could refute the voice of civilization was the one thing all agreed that civilization condemned. Thus Mr. Hankey did not contaminate the idea of political correctness with the negativity of poop; rather, he "contaminated" the people of South Park with redemption. He didn't bring political correctness down, but brought the people up.

Mr. Hankey is, alas, not purely carnivalesque. Though he provided a positive portrayal of poop, he did not get the people of South Park nor the viewers at home to realize that all our butts are equally stinky. Mr. Hankey was redemptive, but did not communicate the material bodily principle. True carnivalesque is rare, even in today's glut of scatological media. It's absent from scatological movies such as *Dumb and Dumber*, which are more about mocking laughter than inclusive laughter. It's absent on Howard Stern's show, which is more about pushing against taboos simply because they are there. And it's not present even in *South Park*, which is more focused on exposing hypocrisy and shaming those in power than on getting the powerful and the powerless to acknowledge that their farts are equally smelly.

The carnivalesque is a wonderful vision. The idea that redemptive laughter unifies sounds magical, much more appealing than the anxieties and neuroses engendered by fecal denial. So why is the carnivalesque so rare? Because fecal denial has great PR.

THE PROPAGANDA OF THE POOP-FREE WORLD

The philosopher Thomas Hobbes described mankind's lowest conceivable moment as the "war of all against all." In this "state of nature", as it's now known, there are no laws and no government, and people are motivated only by their desire for power and their fear of others. They use whatever means are necessary to satisfy the former and alleviate the latter. Hobbes' chilling vision of mankind at its worst is consistently depicted in movies, television, and the arts, and in these depictions, poop often gets a prominent role. *Lord of the Flies* is one vision of the state of nature. In it, between moments of violence, misery, and fear, the shipwrecked children flaunt their freedom from authority by pooping wherever they feel the urge. The specification of a place for them to poop is shown as a step back toward civilization and order, and their subsequent abandonment of the site is symbolic of their descent back into anarchy.

HBO's *Deadwood* provides an even better example. In this Gold Rush-era town, there are no laws—you work, you drink, you curse, and you kill. This state of nature is saturated with filth and bodily fluids: the roads are paved with horse shit, and the characters poop and pee with no decorum. In *Deadwood*, filth is as much a part of the fall of man as is suffering and death.

This association isn't limited to fantasy, either. New Orleans after Hurricane Katrina was nearly a real-life state of nature, a vacuum of authority in which people did what they needed to survive. As America watched in horror during that awful week, reports of violence and suffering were inseparable from the filth of a whole city suddenly wrenched from the bathroom infrastructure upon which our civilization relies. The bathrooms at the Superdome were depicted as ground zero for the fall of man, from the toilets overflowing with unflushed poop to rumors of murderers and sexual predators lurking in the stalls. Though the worst of the reports were later debunked, that the rumors were plausible confirms what fictional states of nature have envisioned: when man descends into the abyss, he descends into poop.

Opposed to our poop-encrusted visions of hell are our poop-free visions of the ideal world. Pope John XXIII is said to have returned the blueprints for a new building on Vatican grounds to the architect with no comment but a marginal notation: *Non sumus angeli*—"We are not angels." The architect puzzled over this until he realized that he had neglected to include bathrooms, having envisioned the Vatican as a citadel whose occupants were too perfect to poop. As Milan Kundera pointed out in *The Unbearable Lightness of Being*, behind any faith—secular, political, or religious—lies a belief in an ideal world that only can be brought about only by living life according to the faith. To some, this utopia is Heaven; to others, it's the American Dream, or *The Andy Griffith Show*, or the *Communist Manifesto*. Everyone has his own vision of utopia, but we all see one thing in common: in the ideal world, there is no matter out of place.

That alone does not automatically exclude poop. After all, poop is only matter out of place in certain circumstances. But these visions of the ideal world exist in the real world and are subject to evaluation through filters of categorization. We reject anything that we categorize as contaminated—including a vision of utopia. So, just like toilet paper advertising, visions of utopia must be presented so as to avoid being categorized as contaminated. Fear of alienating an audience excludes poop from utopian visions. If a preacher, a television show, or a political leader were to describe a carnivalesque utopia in which everyone poops in blissful, shameless equality, he would inevitably estrange some of his followers. It might be that in Heaven or in Mayberry everyone poops and no one is embarrassed about it; but even faith is subject to the rules of the marketplace. Some adherents might alter their beliefs to accept this new detail about their ideal world, but many more would associate this new vision with the contamination of poop, and reject it accordingly. Just as no toilet paper advertiser wants to alienate its customers by associating its product with the poop they use it to wipe up, no faith—be it secular, political, or religious—wants to alienate its followers by describing the role of poop in the utopia.

So in the worst of all worlds, we see poop. In the best, we see none. That could seem to mean that no one poops in utopia, or that the rules of poop are the same in utopia as in the real world. Either way, the result is that we're offered no guidance as to when poop is good. We only see poop when it is bad.

There's no carnivalesque in visions of the ideal world because there is no carnivalesque in the real world. And if there's no carnivalesque in the real world, there won't be carnivalesque in visions of the ideal world. The status quo of pooping in our society is maintained wholly by inertia. Fecal denial became part of our culture side-by-side with the Victorian-inspired flush toilet, the private bathroom, and a rule that any acknowledgement of one's own poop is uncivilized. That rule has made fecal denial self-sustaining, because any presentation of a more candid fecal philosophy immediately thereby condemns itself as uncivilized. Fecal denial is maintained wholly by this built-in rejection of any alternative.

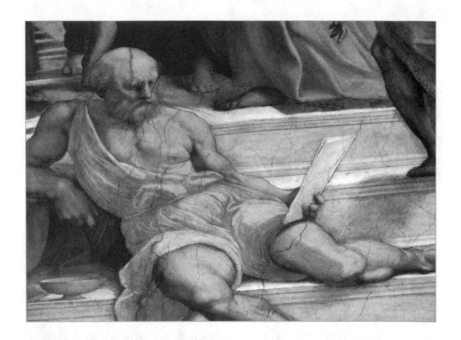

Diogenes of Sinope.

CHAPTER 10

FREE YOUR HIND:
THE TAO OF POO

ONE FINE DAY FOUR HUNDRED YEARS before Christ was born, Diogenes of Sinope crapped in the Athens marketplace. As a Cynic, Diogenes rejected social customs as vanity. He believed that man's attempts to distance himself from the animals were self-deceptions. Fine clothes, gourmet food, formal rituals, the pursuit of beauty—all were narcissistic attempts to deny our nature. Why should there be things you can do in private but not in public? If human necessity is in accordance with nature, isn't it in accordance with nature no matter where it is addressed?

And so, to make his point, he walked into the marketplace, lifted his cloak, squatted on his haunches, and dropped a steaming souvlaki right there where everyone else was shopping. Anyone who was shocked was, by his logic, in denial of his human essence.

Athenians may have spent a few days gossiping about Diogenes, but they ignored his message and kept on dressing in their nicest robes and combing their hair and perfuming their bodies and restricting their poop to the places and times deemed appropriate by society. And two-and-a-half millennia later, we're still elevating society over biology. We use deodorant to change how we smell, make-up to change how we look, and bathrooms and toilets to keep our poop out of the sight, smell, and hearing of everyone else, even though our poop all looks, smells, and sounds equally bad.

If Freud is right, Diogenes' fight for fecal acceptance was actually directed against an instinct far more entrenched than mere vanity. Freud believed that our aversion to the smell of poop developed when our ancestors adopted an upright posture. Before then, humans hunched over like gorillas, knuckle-dragging and relying on smell as much as any other animal, and probably casually sniffing each other's butts just as other animals do. But our evolution into the upright posture pulled our noses away from where all the smells are strongest: on the ground, and in others' genital regions. Since we relied on it less, the sense atrophied. Whereas before humans used smell to understand the world, now only the most intense smells mattered: those involved with eating, sex, and, of course, pooping. Fecal aversion arose in part, Freud postulated, because poop was one of the few odors strong enough for our much-weakened sense of smell to recognize.

It doesn't matter if Freud is right, or even whether man evolved or was created in accordance with biblical teachings. Either way, the facts are stacked against Diogenes: for whatever reason, fecal aversion is a constant in Western civilization. Evidence for it has been appearing in writing for at least 2,500 years. Few writers actually took the time to describe their culture's feelings about poop, but the contexts in which writers invoke poop reveal those feelings. In the sixth century B.C., for example, Pythagoras forbade his followers from eating beans, as farting was unphilosophical. The fart jokes Aristophanes made in his fourth-century B.C. plays could only have been funny if farts were considered stinky and vulgar. The Roman poet Juvenal, who lived in the first and second century A.D., worried about people dumping their poop from their upper-story windows and "wounding the unwary wretch who walks below." In *The Divine Comedy*, Dante portrays poop floating in the river Styx and in the moat around the inner part of Hell, and describes the flatterers damned to the eight circle of Hell as wallowing in it. Most significant in *The Divine Comedy* is when Dante and his guide Virgil make it to the very center of Hell, where Satan, trapped in ice, is chewing on Judas, Brutus, and Cassius for all eternity. The duo climb down Satan's ragged fur to Hell's lowest point, "where the huge thighbone / Rides in its socket at the haunch's swell": that is, the devil's ass, the worst place to be in all of hell. Some scholars interpret Dante to suggest that the two then climbed through Satan's asshole to escape Hell, emerging on the far side of the Earth in time for Easter Sunday. In Chaucer's fourteenth-century *Canterbury Tales*, the Miller's Tale portrays its main characters farting in each other's faces. In his 1516 *Utopia*, Sir Thomas More describes chamber pots made of gold and silver, reflecting the contempt his imaginary society had for formerly precious metals. And the Marquis de Sade explored the disgust associated with poop to a horrifying degree in his 1785 book *120 Days of Sodom.*

In the Bible, there are very few direct references to poop; most manifest in contexts that imply that even its Inventor finds it gross. In Malachi 2:3, God threatens to spread poop on the faces of priests who do not glorify his name. ("Behold, I will rebuke your seed, and will spread dung on your faces, even the dung of your feasts.") In II Kings 9:37, the indignity of the dead lying unburied is compared to dung on the field. In Ezekiel 4:1–15, God instructs Ezekiel to foretell the siege of Jerusalem by enduring a number of hardships, including eating bread cooked with dried human poop as fuel. Ezekiel protests this indignity, and God relents by allowing him to use dried cow poop instead. The most significant appearance of poop in the Bible is the Gospels, of course, in that final insult to Jesus on the cross, as previously discussed.

Only a few passages in the Bible provide any direct guidance about poop. I Samuel 24, for instance, hints at rules of pooping decorum. In it, Saul leads 3,000 men into the wilderness of En-Gedi, where he ducks into a cave to "cover his feet," as some more modest translations put it. We aren't told why he chose to poop in privacy—out of shame? A desire for privacy? Because he didn't want to poop in his camp? The passage offers no further details, focusing instead on King David, who is hiding with his men in the cave, and his decision not to slay Saul as his butt runneth over.

The most detailed biblical reference to poop comes in Deuteronomy 23:12–14, part of a series of passages numerating rules for armies on the march. "Thou shalt have a place also without the camp, whither thou shalt go forth abroad. And thou shalt have a paddle upon thy weapon; and it shall be, when thou wilt ease thyself abroad, thou shalt dig therewith, and shalt turn back and cover that which cometh from thee. For the Lord thy God walketh in the midst of thy camp, to deliver thee, and to give up thine enemies before thee; therefore shall thy camp be holy: that he see no unclean thing in thee, and turn away from thee." In this passage, God tells us that he doesn't like it when you poop where you eat and sleep. He doesn't say, however, that you should hide your shovel behind your back and slink out of camp when no one is watching; he just says to take your business elsewhere. Since these rules were written for military situations, their application to behavior at home is debatable. Some rabbis believed that they applied to people in Jerusalem, which was also called "the Camp of the Lord." Pity the poor Jewish Jerusalemite: the trip to the outskirts of the city was longer than the distance of travel permissible on the Sabbath. On holy days, then, they just had to hold it in.

Outside of the Bible, the most noteworthy references to poop in the Christian tradition appear in the writings of Martin Luther. At many points in his work, Luther detailed his chronic constipation that led to many hours spent deep in thought on his privy, struggling with a stubborn demon he described as symbolic of his inability to escape his own inner evil. The history of Western civilization wouldn't have been the same if Luther had eaten more fiber. His argument that salvation is granted through faith, not deeds—the fundamental basis of the Reformation—came to him, he wrote, during one such battle against his stubborn intestines: "This knowledge the Holy Spirit gave me on the privy in the tower." Though some Lutheran scholars have tried to deny the digestive details of Luther's divine message, suggesting that the tower was "metaphorical," Luther himself had no problem reconciling the bathroom as a place of holy inspiration.

IT'S IMPOSSIBLE to prove that Western civilization has always exhibited fecal aversion. But there's no denying that fecal aversion is a constant theme, beginning in the Bible, continuing through classical antiquity, spreading into medieval Europe and through the Renaissance, and lasting until this very day. And where there's fecal aversion, there are rules and rituals surrounding poop.

These rules and rituals develop uniquely in every society based on factors including population density, technology, wealth, geography, and climate. Some societies developed very strict rules regarding poop, while others were more lax—the ancient Romans, for instance, were compelled to build public toilets and massive sewers to handle their waste, while the poorer citizens of Paris in bygone centuries were content to simply toss the contents of their chamber pots out the window. In many societies, these rules and rituals endowed poop with symbolic, almost magical power.

Poop's symbolic meanings also develop uniquely in every society. This can help explain observations that might otherwise discredit fecal aversion's universality. Consider stories of peasants at the medieval Festival of Fools who partied in poop. This comes to us from John Bourke's 1891 *Scatologic Rites of All Nations*, in which the author recounts legends of actors on dung-carts throwing poop at the crowds enjoying the medieval carnival, laughing as they sang scatological songs. This doesn't mean that the medieval peasants had no instinct to avoid poop—rather, it means that in some contexts the symbolic meanings of poop can overshadow fecal aversion. We see this even in today's poop-phobic society, as when teenagers stuff poop into the mailboxes of kids they don't like—it's not that these bullies possess no sense of fecal aversion, but rather that the meaning of poop in their ritual can outweigh the revulsion they feel.

So fecal aversion is a baseline in human history. Throughout history, men and women have wrinkled their noses when they smelled poop, stepped over it if they saw it on the street, reviled the vermin and insects it attracts, and did what they needed to do to keep it separate from the rest of their lives. So it is today, only more so. Thanks to the flush toilet, humanity is disassociated from its own poop more than ever before.

THE FOUL OF MAN

In his book *A Sociological History of Excretory Experience*, David Inglis said it best: "From a position whereby the filth of the proletariat had positive ramifications, there emerged a situation whereby such filth became dysfunctional vis-à-vis the interests of the bourgeois order." His point, though hard to understand, is spot-on: poop occupies a different position in today's society from any it ever has occupied before.

The vilification of poop is nothing new. A few centuries after Christ's death, for instance, the Gnostic Christians taught that Jesus Christ ate and drank like normal men, but that he did not defecate. To them, the idea that the Son of God would poop was too much to bear. Similarly, in 831 A.D., a monk, Paschasius Radbert, caused an uproar when he argued that the communion host (which, according to Christian belief, is the actual body of Christ), is subject to digestion—and, of course, that to which digestion leads. Radbert and his followers were contemptuously labeled Stercoranists, after Sterculius, the Roman god of manure. Considering the history of responses to blasphemy, after suggesting that the body of Christ turns into poop in the stomach, they got off pretty easy.

The Victorians were hardly the first to find poop inconsistent with man's more lofty ideals. But they did give us two innovations: they instilled the view that poop should be denied across all classes, and they enabled such denial through a society-wide infrastructure. The Victorians upped the ante on toilet practices as a means of social differentiation at a fortuitous time: the beginning of the Industrial Revolution, when technology was evolving so rapidly that inventors were soon realizing thitherto-impossible antifecal ideals. Thanks to their new flush toilet, the elite could now pull a chain and make their poop disappear. It was as though they didn't poop at all. But the cheap labor most fortunes ultimately relied upon was living in squalor, and scientists had finally connected squalor to epidemic. If they were to survive to work, the workers had to be clean. The Victorian elite faced a unique quandary: if they wanted to keep their own standard of living, they had to improve everyone else's. And they did. Flush toilets and sewers for everyone.

While the flush toilet was spreading across England, it was growing popular in America as well, but for different reasons. Before the Civil War, Americans of all classes embraced the toilet as a sign of progress and modernization, and eagerly built upon the technology arriving from England with their own innovations. The result was a chaotic and haphazard infrastructure of poor plumbing and unsanitary waste disposal. In the 1870s, scientists realized that the health danger posed by the average American's plumbing infrastructure equaled in scope the crisis confronting the English masses a few decades earlier. Thus America was in the same situation as England: to survive, people needed uniform waste management. Toilets may have been a symbol of progress before, but now they were a symbol of health.

In theory, this meant flush toilets, modern plumbing, and municipal sewers. But in practice, it involved something more: an ideology. The toilet had been created so Victorians could achieve fecal denial; and the philosophy hadn't been separated from the apparatus. So when the plutocracy in England and the state in America determined that the toilet would be the only acceptable receptacle for pooping, they were mandating fecal denial right along with it.

Fecal denial had existed among elites before. But never before had it been the official ideology of the entire society—and never before had it been supported by an infrastructure that made the impossible ideal achievable.

So here we are. After over a century with the toilet as the crown of a universal pooping infrastructure, fecal denial is still the dominant influence on society's bathroom outlook. Though it is not without its dissenters —the ranks of shameless shitters are considerable—the philosophy of fecal denial is nevertheless the one reflected and reinforced by the media and other ideological apparatuses. Fecal denial has introduced a third duality of poop. The first duality of poop is between pleasure and pain: the more it hurts before it comes out, the better it feels once it finally escapes. The second duality is between the individual and society: that poop is a problem for the individual until it comes out, at which point it becomes a problem for society.

Fecal denial has forced onto us a third duality, a dichotomy between biology and psychology. Poop is natural to our bodies but unacceptable to our minds.

Shameful shitting is one of the most widespread problems this causes. Every one of us agrees that poop is supposed to go in a toilet, and every one of us agrees that a toilet is supposed to be in a private place. But life does not always present us with such cut-and-dried situations. On the border between public and private are public bathrooms, and the hallways leading to them—places in which our very presence implies the need to poop, and in which the sounds and smells of our pooping mingle with those of others'. How do the rules of fecal denial apply to such an ambiguous location? Shameless shitters see the answer clearly; shameful shitters struggle with it. They incur stress trying to hold it in, constipation if they're too successful, and humiliation if they can't live up to their impossible standards.

The bathroom infrastructure represents other problems, such as the strange fact that we all use toilet paper. In a cleanliness-obsessed society, it's shocking that the method of choice to clean poop off our butts is paper that simply smears it into finer and finer layers. Water makes much more sense and would probably be a better use of resources than the incalculable deforestation needed to make the estimated 26 billion rolls of toilet paper we use every year. But if we can't even address that issue, how can we address the greater costs of the toilet infrastructure? Although the flush toilet is superior to any other waste management method in human history in terms of safely separating man from the dangers of his poop, we can see today that it's not superior enough: not only do we waste 1.6 gallons of water every time we flush, and waste billions of taxpayer dollars on sewage treatment plants to separate this water out of the poop at the other end, but we're also left with millions of tons of toxic sludge waiting to haunt us. Our poop is sequestered from its proper place in the food chain, and chemical fertilizers introduced to make up for it. Our excretory lives are based upon an archaic, 150-year-old infrastructure, but the infrastructure is tied so strongly to the ideology that we can't imagine doing it any other way.

Then there are psychological problems. Fecal denial promotes the repression of anally-fixated desires which, as Freud said, are channeled into neurosis and anxieties that plague millions. And according to Norman O. Brown, society as a whole suffers in the same way. Brown saw anal psychopathologies diverting society's energy into the most destructive aspects of capitalism and the lust for power. In Brown's utopia, the lower bodily strata are accepted, anxiety and apprehension disappear, and society is freed from its neurosis for more benevolent and holistic pursuits. But in our reality, the strength of fecal denial allows for no abatement of repression.

Fecal denial even creates religious problems. Christians believe that God created man in His image; and while that does not necessarily mean that God poops, He at least is responsible for our doing so. Why do we find uncivilized the bodily functions that He created in us? Do we believe that He created us in an unacceptable manner? To those who are adhere to both Judeo-Christian scripture and fecal denial, this contradiction must be a horrible cross to bear. In *The Unbearable Lightness of Being*, Kundera described their predicament: to them, "the daily defecation session is daily proof of the unacceptability of Creation."

What can be done?

CLEANING UP: THE DOWN SOUTH SHALL RISE AGAIN

By now, you understand poop's role in contemporary society. You know what it's made of and how it forms and what happens when you flush it down. You know what it does to our psyches and how it manifests in art, culture, media, and our everyday interactions with others. You recognize that society suffers under fecal denial. You know that the only way to overcome fecal denial is through the carnivalesque: the lesson that everyone's butt makes the same funny sounds and the same nasty smells, and that's what makes us all human. And you know that fecal denial perpetuates itself through circular logic: anyone who poops is uncivilized, therefore anyone who argues for an alternate fecal philosophy automatically discredits himself by acknowledging in his argument that he poops.

You know that fecal denial is the problem, and the carnivalesque the solution. But you don't know how to apply the latter to the former. Neither do I.

How do you change a culture? Do you organize protests? Run an ad campaign? Lobby the government? Write letters to the editor? Sponsor carnivals? Turn to Howard Stern or Trey Parker and Matt Stone and hope they do something about it? Smash your toilets and burn your toilet paper? Stage theater productions of *Gargantua and Pantagruel*? Drop your pants and crap in the marketplace? Buy this book for everyone you know?

While the last option sounds good, I have no answer. I do know, however, that people have overcome fecal denial through participation on PoopReport.com. The site's early days were a directionless foray into an unexplored universe. None of the participants had ever had engaged in such deep and extended thought about the world of poop, a world so big and so rich that we were overwhelmed by how much there was to contemplate and laugh about. From bathrooms at work to the different ways we wipe, from the courtesy flush to how we avoid touching nasty toilet seats, from the best brands of toilet paper to the worst bathrooms we'd ever seen, it was a glorious cacophony of shapeless discourse and laughter. And then, on August 17, 2001, I published this letter from a PoopReporter named Doniker:

> I know we have been though this time and time again, but I want to again applaud those people known as the "shameless shitters."
>
> There I was in the bathroom at work, peeing in the urinal, when a co-worker I barely know walks in, happy as can be and says "how you doin'!" He then enters a stall, pulls down his pants, sits down on the can and starts farting away! Then there is the sound of splashing as his turds hit the water. He's 100% shameless!
>
> If I had been in his shoes and had entered the bathroom looking to take a dump and seen someone at the

urinal, I would have walked up to another urinal and faked a pee. If I am already in a stall and somebody enters, I am quiet as a mouse until they leave.

I wish I could be a shameless shitter, it would take a lot of stress out of my endless daily ritual of holding it in or trying to find the right time and place to shit.

Though we may not have realized it right away, we had a new way of categorizing the poop experience. Patterns began to emerge. The great unexplored world of poop began to organize itself as the chaotic swirl of individual experience and opinion coalesced around two main camps, shameful and shameless. Suddenly everything began to make sense: why some people could stroll into a bathroom with their head held high while others could only slink in when no one was looking, why some would hide on a toilet until everyone else had left the bathroom while others would carry on grunt-laced conversations with anyone in the next stall. We learned why pooping was so enjoyable for some and so traumatic for others, and why so many people refused to even talk about it.

Both shameful and shameless shitters participated on PoopReport. Freed by anonymity from the fear of their shoes being recognized by the person in the next stall, the shy added their opinions to those of the outgoing. We shared our stories, not just of pooping at the office, but about the overall pooping experience that most of us, shameful and shameless alike, simply had never been able to discuss in our offline relationships. And as we laughed at each other's stories of success and failure alike, we all laughed together with the knowledge that side by side in a public bathroom, any two human beings are stripped of their differences and reduced to their most basic essence: a quartet of feet sticking out below the stalls, and a pair of butt trumpets performing a greasy symphony to celebrate humanity's nonnegotiable deference to the call of the vile.

As time went on and PoopReport grew more popular, people began to convert. Shameful shitters learned for the first time that there is another way. Before discovering the site, they had no idea that they could acknowledge their own poop without condemning themselves in the eyes of others; for these people, it was an epiphany to discover alternate fecal philosophies. They realized the absurdity of holding in their poop all day because they were ashamed to be seen using the office toilet. It was healing for them to read others' stories, and cathartic to share their own. And the proof is scattered across the site—in comments from people who are shameful but are trying not to be, or who once were shameful but now are not. This is not self-aggrandizement. It is truly the case. Without intending to, we created a utopia of the carnivalesque, and people have brought the carnivalesque into the real world. We have broken the circle.

Our utopia is not pooping anarchy. All PoopReporters exhibit fecal aversion—we believe that poop is stinky and gross, and should be confined to a particular time and place. But we reject the mandates of fecal denial. We see pooping not as something at odds with civilization, but rather directly in line with it. We envision not a nation of stinking perverts or turd terrorists, but a world in which the wonderful things for which man strives are easily reconciled with the stinky thing that comes out of our butts.

In the second century A.D., the Roman physician and philosopher Galen taught that the control of the bowels was one of the distinguishing features of the higher orders. He pointed out that the sphincter is the only organ in the digestive system governed by reason—and without this "instrument of the psychic soul," he said, "the residues flow out involuntarily and inopportunely, showing clearly how shameful and gross would be our life if from the beginning Nature had not planned something better." We couldn't possibly pursue the lofty ideals of philosophy and medicine, he said, if our butts didn't have the capacity to keep poop from interrupting the conversation. We retain; therefore, we think.

Five hundred years after Diogenes, Galen credited our ability to keep poop inside until a convenient time as the foundation of an enlightened society. Two hundred years ago, the Victorians decided that the enlightened did not poop at all. One hundred and fifty years ago, they bequeathed their outlook to English society; soon after that, it was adopted in America as well. But while they cursed us with the ideology of fecal denial, they blessed us with an infrastructure that saved countless lives and enabled cities to thrive free of water-borne epidemics. The next step is to rehabilitate the Victorian infrastructure with the Galenic outlook: to apply our enlightened society to the betterment of the manifestations of poop. To improve the infrastructure as we abandon its ideology for a new one in which pooping is not a filthy act, but a cleansing ritual. You enter the bathroom with the impurities of your body gathered in your rectum, you poop those impurities out, and you exit the bathroom at your cleanest, purest, and most civilized.

Pooping as a cleansing ritual: this is truly the triumph of the carnivalesque.

WORKS CONSULTED

2006 Water and Sewer Tap Fee Schedule. City and Community of Arvada, 2005.

Adams, Cecil. "Does Flushing the Toilet Cause Dirty Water to Be Spewed Around the Bathroom?" *The Straight Dope*, 16 Apr. 1999 <http://www.straightdope.com/classics/a990416.html>.

The Air up There. Dir. Paul Michael Glaser. 1994.

Alley, Mark, and W.G. Wysor. "Fertilizer in 2005." *Crop and Soil Environmental News* Feb (2005). <http://www.ext.vt.edu/news/periodicals/cses/2005-02/fertilizer.html>.

Along Came Polly. Dir. John Hamburg. 2004.

American Chemical Society. "Watts From Wastewater: New Device Produces Power While Treating Sewage." *Science Daily,* 2 Nov. 2004 <http://www.sciencedaily.com/releases/2004/10/041030205626.htm>.

American Splendor. Dir. Shari Springer Berman. 2003.

Anderson, Warwick. "Excremental Colonialism: Public Health and the Poetics of Pollution." *Critical Inquiry* 21 (1995): 640–669.

Anspaugh, Kelly. "Powers of Ordure: James Joyce and the Excremental Vision(S)." *Mosaic* 27 (1994): 73–100.

Anspaugh, Kelly. "Ulysses Upon Ajax: Joyce, Harington, and the Question of 'Cloacal Imperialism.'" *South Atlantic Review* 60 (1995): 11–29.

Arachnophobia. Dir. Frank Marshall. 1990.

Aristotle, W. Rhys Roberts, and Ingram Bywater. *Rhetoric*. 1st ed. New York: Modern Library, 1984.

Austgen, Laura, R.A. Bowen, and Melissa Rouge. *Pathophysiology of the Digestive System*. Colorado State University. 1998 <http://www.vivo.colostate.edu/hbooks/pathphys/digestion/index.html>

Bakhtin, M.M. *Rabelais and His World*. 1st Midland Book Ed. Bloomington: Indiana UP, 1984.

Barney, Richard A. "Filthy Thoughts, or Cultural Criticism and the Ordure of Things." *Genre* 27 (1994): 275–294.

Beder, Sharon. "From Sewage Farms to Septic Tanks: Trials and Tribulations in Sydney." *Journal of the Royal Australian Historical Society* 79 (1993): 72–95.

Bell, Michael Mayerfield. "Deep Fecology: Mikhail Bakhtin and the Call of Nature." *Capitalism, Nature, Socialism* 5 (1994): 65–84.

The Beneficial Uses of Biosolids/Sludge. Ithaca, New York: Cornell Waste Management Institute, 1996.

Betacourt, Michael. *The Richard Mutt Case: Looking for Marcel Duchamp's Fountain*. Art Science Research Laboratory <http://www.artscienceresearchlab.org/articles/betacourt.htm>.

Biever, Celeste. "Poop Power: Plugging Into the Power of Sewage." *New Scientist* 11, Mar. 2004 <http://www.newscientist.com/article/dn4761.html>.

"Bill Introduced to Repeal Low-Flow Toilet Requirement." *U.S. Water News Online,* Nov. 1999 <http://www.uswaternews.com/archives/arcpolicy/9bilint11.html>.

Boeree, C. George. "Sigmund Freud." Shippensburg University. 12 Feb. 2006 <http://www.ship.edu/~cgboeree/freud.html>.

Bourdieu, Pierre. *Distinction a Social Critique of the Judgement of Taste.* Cambridge, Mass: Harvard UP, 1984.

Bourke, John Gregory, and Louis P. Kaplan. *The Portable Scatalog: Excerpts From Scatalogic Rites of All Nations, a Dissertation Upon the Employment of Excrementitious Remedial Agents in Religion, Therapeutics, Divination, Witchcraft, Love-Philters, Etc., in All Parts of the Globe.* 1st ed. New York: W. Morrow, 1994.

Bowles, Wallace. *The Sitting Toilet—an Inconspicuous 'Carcinogen'?* Australian Vegetarian Society <http://www.veg-soc.org/html/articles/sitting-toilet.html>.

Bracha, H. Stefan. "Does 'Fight or Flight' Need Updating?" Oct. 2004. *Psychosomatics* 45 (2004) 448-449.

Brighton Beach Memoirs. Dir. Gene Saks. 1986.

Brooke, James. "Japan Engineers Focus on Bottom Line." *The New York Times,* Oct. 2002.

Brown, Norman Oliver. *Life Against Death: The Psychoanalytical Meaning of History.* 2nd ed. Scranton, PA: Distributed by Harper & Row, 1985.

Bulletproof. Dir. Ernest R. Dickerson. 1996.

Caddyshack. Dir. Harold Ramis. 1980.

Cameron, Dan. *The Thick of It* <http://www.cloaca.be/thick.htm>.

Camlot, Jason. "The Victorian Postmodern." *Postmodern Culture* 13 (2002).

Canning, Susan M. "The Ordure of Anarchy: Scatological Signs of Self and Society in the Art of James Ensor." *Art Journal,* Fall 1993.

Cast Away. Dir. Robert Zemeckis. 2000.

Census Bureau. United States Department of Commerce. *Median Duration in Residence is 5.2 Years; Majority Move in June Through October, Census Bureau Says.* 1998.

Chattahoochee. Dir. Mick Jackson. 1989.

Chun, Allen. "Flushing in the Future: the Supermodern Japanese Toilet in a Changing Domestic Culture." *Postcolonial Studies* 5 (2002): 153–170.

"Church Selling Toilet Paper to Raise Money." *CBSnews.com,* 3 Jan. 2006.

Chu, Petra Ten-Doesschate. "Scatology and the Realist Aesthetic." *Art Journal Fall* (1993).

City of New York, Department of Environmental Protection. *North River Wastewater Treatment Plant.* 15 Feb. 2002. <http://www.nyc.gov/html/dep/html/northri.html>.

Clark, John R. *The Modern Satiric Grotesque and Its Traditions.* Lexington, KY: UP of Kentucky, 1991.

Clark, William. "Katherine Dreier and the Société Anonyme." *Variant* 14 (2001).

Cockburn, T. Aidan. "Infectious Diseases in Ancient Populations." *Current Anthropology* 12 (1971): 45–62.

Coe, Malcolm. Review of Ralph A. Lewin, "Merde: Excursions in Scientific, Cultural, and Socio-Historical Coprology." *Nature,* 20 May 1999.

Cohen, William A., and Ryan Johnson. *Filth: Dirt, Disgust, and Modern Life.* Minneapolis: U of Minnesota P, 2004.

Collings, Matthew. *This is Modern Art.* London: Seven Dials, Cassell & Co, 1999.

"Colorado Man Glued to Toilet Seat, Sues Store." *NineMSN,* 11 Nov. 2005.

Composting Toilet Demonstration: Feasibility Study. Smart Water Fund, 2003.

Constipation. Jackson Gastroenterology <http://www.gicare.com/pated/ecdgs07.htm>.

Cook, David. "Red Bank High School—What Vandalism Can't Erase." *The Chattanoogan* 22 Aug. 2005, sec. Opinion.

Cortez, Marisol. *"A Lot of Things Going in and Out of Holes": 'Jackass' and the Logic of Scatological White Masculinity.* UC Davis. 2004.

Cortez, Marisol. "Brown Meets Green: the Political Fecology of PoopReport.com." *Reconstruction* 5 (2005) <http://reconstruction.eserver.org/052/cortez.shtml>.

Cortez, Marisol. *Is Abjection Necessary?* UC Davis. 2004.

Cortez, Marisol. *Reading Shit: From Textuality to Materiality (Working Title).* UC Davis.

Cortez, Marisol. *Reading Shit: The Ecological Politics of the Scatological in Contemporary U.S. Culture.* UC Davis.

Cortez, Marisol. *Waste Treatment: Narratives of Accumulation in Locke and Marx.* UC Davis. 2003.

Crockett, Jonathan. *Assessing the Feasibility of Alternative Sanitation Systems.* Enviro 2000 Conference. Sydney AWA, 2000.

Crockett, Jonathan, Sarah Oliver, Clair Millar, Michael Jefferson, Buzz Burrows, and Kim Jacques. *Feasibility Study for a Dry Composting Toilet and Urine Separation Demonstration Project.* Enviro 04 Conference and Exhibition. Sydney, 2004.

D'amato, Eric. "Mystery of Disgust." *Psychology Today,* Jan.–Feb. 1998.

Dannatt, Adrian. *Lav Lab* <http://www.cloaca.be/lab.htm>.

Dante Alighieri, C.H. Sisson, and David H. Higgins. *The Divine Comedy.* New York: Oxford UP, 1993.

Dawson, Jim. *Who Cut the Cheese? A Cultural History of the Fart.* Berkeley, CA: Ten Speed Press, 1999.

Delvoye, Wim. *What is Cloaca Turbo?* <http://www.cloaca.be/turbo.htm>.

Diarrhea. Jackson Gastroenterology. <http://www.gicare.com/pated/ecdgs28.htm>.

The Digestive System. University Medical Center, Ohio State University <http://medicalcenter.osu.edu/patientcare/healthinformation/diseasesandconditions/digestive/digestivesystem/>.

Dimmer, Christine, Brian Martin, Noeline Reeves, and Frances Sullivan. "Squatting for the Prevention of Haemorrhoids?" *Townsend Letter for Doctors & Patients* 159 (1996): 66–70.

Ditmann, Melissa. "Eww, Gross! Psychologist Paul Rozin Offered Insights Into the Science of Disgust." *Monitor on Psychology* 34 (2003).

Douglas, Mary. *Purity and Danger: An Analysis of Concepts of Pollution and Taboo.* New York: Routledge, 2002.

Dundes, Alan. *Life is Like a Chicken Coop Ladder: A Study of German National Character through Folklore*. Detroit: Wayne State UP, 1989.

Dutton, Michael, Sanjay Seth, and Leela Gandhi. "Plumbing the Depths: Toilets, Transparency and Modernity." *Postcolonial Studies* 5 (2002): 137–142.

Eddy, Natalie. "India Pays Homage to the Toilet." *Small Flows Quarterly* 5 (2004): 30–33.

Esty, Joshua D. "Excremental Postcolonialism." *Contemporary Literature* 40 (1999): 22–59.

"Europe's Most Acclaimed Artists: Wim Delvoye and Daniel Richter." *Artsnews* 29, Mar. 2004 <http://www.absolutearts.com/artsnews/2004/03/29/31919.html>.

Ferenczi, Sandor. "The Ontogenesis of the Interest in Money." *Contributions to Psycho-Analysis* (1916): 269–279.

Fight Club. Dir. David Fincher. 1999.

Folwell, Amory Prescott. *Sewerage: The Designing, Construction, and Maintenance of Sewerage Systems*. 8th Ed. London: Chapman & Hall, Limited, 1918. 1–12.

"Food for Thought: Paul Rozin's Research and Teaching at Penn." *Penn Arts & Sciences*, Fall 1997.

Fools Rush In. Dir. Andy Tennant. 1997.

Forster, E.M. *Aspects of the Novel*. New York: Harcourt, Brace, 1956.

Francblin, Catherine. *An Encounter Between Bataille and Doctor Frankenstein* <http://www.cloaca.be/encounter.htm>.

Friedin, B.D., and Helene K. Johnson. "Treatment of a Retarded Child's Faeces Smearing and Coprophagic Behavior." *Journal of Mental Deficiency Research* 23 (1979): 55–61.

Freud, Sigmund. *Civilization and Its Discontents*. New York: Dover Publications, 1994.

Gandy, Matthew. "The Paris Sewers and the Rationalization of Urban Space." *Transactions—Institute of British Geographers* 24 (1999): 23–44.

Geest, Sjaak Van Der. "The Night-Soil Collector: Bucket Latrines in Ghana." *Postcolonial Studies* 5 (2002): 197–206.

Gerling, Daniel. *Kitsch: Theory and Art*. U of Texas, Austin.

Gershon, Michael D. *The Second Brain: The Scientific Basis of Gut Instinct and a Groundbreaking New Understanding of Nervous Disorders of the Stomach and Intestine*. 1st ed. New York: HarperCollins Publishers, 1998.

Ghaziuddin, Neera, and Carrick McDonald. "A Clinical Study of Adult Coprophagics." *British Journal of Psychology* 147 (1985): 312–313.

Goodland, Robert, and Abby Rockefeller. "What is Environmental Sustainability in Sanitation?" *UNEP-IETC Newsletter*, Summer 1996.

Goodwin, Doris Kearns. *Lyndon Johnson and the American Dream*. 1st ed. New York: Harper & Row, 1976.

Gray, Harold Farnsworth. "Sewerage in Ancient and Medieval Times." *Sewage Works Journal* 12 (1940): 939–946.

Greed, Clara. "Public Toilets in the 24-Hour City." 2003 World Toilet Summit.

Hahn, Tim. "Much Ado about Nothing." *Erie Times-News* 28 May 2004.

Haidt, Jonathan, Paul Rozin, Clark McCauley, and Sumio Imada. "Body, Psyche, and Culture: The Relationship Between Disgust and Morality." *Psychology and Developing Societies* 9 (1997): 107–131.

Harrison, Jeff. "UA Study Shows Leaks in Conservation Theory Behind Low-Flow Toilets." *UANews.org,* 31 Oct. 2000 <http://uanews.opi.arizona.edu/cgi-bin/WebObjects/UANews.woa/wa/MainStoryDetails?ArticleID=2525>.

Hart-Davis, Adam. *Thunder, Flush, and Thomas Crapper: an Encycloopedia* [sic]. North Pomfret, VT: Trafalgar Square Pub., 1997.

Hawkins, Gay, and Stephen Muecke. *Culture and Waste: The Creation and Destruction of Value.* Lanham, MD: Rowman & Littlefield, 2003.

Hawkins, Gay. "Plastic Bags: Living with Rubbish." *International Journal of Cultural Studies* 4 (2001): 5–23.

Heavens, Al. "Tackling Low-Flow Toilet Woes." *Realty Times,* 8 Aug. 2002 <http://realtytimes.com/rtcpages/20020808_lowflow.htm>.

Henderson, Amy. "Media and the Rise of Celebrity Culture." *OAH Magazine of History* 6 (1992).

Henley, Jon. "Smiles All Round as the Mona Lisa Settles Into Her New Home." *The Guardian* 6 Apr. 2005.

Hepner, Gershon. "Scatology in the Bible." *Scandinavian Journal of the Old Testament* 18 (2004): 278–295.

"High Altitude Hijinks: First Class Drunk Loves Liquor, Linen." *The Smoking Gun* <http://www.thesmokinggun.com/altitude/monday1.html>.

History-Timeline—Scott Brands <http://www.scottbrand.com/us/history/timeline1.asp>.

Hollmann, Mark, and Greg Kotis. *Urinetown: the Musical.* 1st ed. New York: Faber and Faber, 2003.

Horan, Julie L. *The Porcelain God: a Social History of the Toilet.* Secaucus, NJ: Carol Pub. Group, 1996.

Horn, Matt. "Scheisse N' Dice." *Spielboy* 4 <http://www.spielboy.com/scheissanddice.php?page=1#42>.

How Does the Sense of Smell Work? What Causes a Smell? <http://science.howstuffworks.com/question139.htm>.

Inglis, David, and Mary Holmes. "Toiletry Time: Defecation, Temporal Strategies, and the Dilemmas of Modernity." *Time & Society* 9 (2000): 223–245.

Inglis, David. *A Sociological History of Excretory Experience: Defecatory Manners and Toiletry Technologies.* Lewiston, NY: Edwin Mellen P, 2001.

Inglis, David. "Dirt and Denigration: the Faecal Imagery and Rhetorics of Abuse." *Postcolonial Studies* 5 (2002): 207–221.

Isbit, Jonathan. "Doctors Don't Know Squat." *Chet Day—Health and Beyond* <http://chetday.com/squattingtoilet.htm>.

Isbit, Jonathan. "Squatty Training." *PoopReport.com,* 1 July 2002 <http://www.poopreport.com/Techniques/Content/Nature/squatty.html>.

Jenkins, Joseph C. *The Humanure Handbook: A Guide to Composting Human Manure.* 2nd ed., Completely Rev., Expanded and Updated. Grove City, PA: Jenkins Pub., 1999.

Johnson, Steven. *The Ghost Map: The Story of London's Deadliest Epidemic—and How It Changed the Way We Think About Disease, Cities, Science, and the Modern World.* New York: Penguin Group, 2006.

Jones, Amelia. *Mr. Clean.* MargaretMorgan.com <http://www.margaretmorgan.com/articles/jones/>.

Jun'ichiro, Tanizaki. "One Thing and Another on the Privy." Trans. Thomas Harper. *Postcolonial Studies* 5 (2002): 147–151.

Juni, Samuel. "The Psychodynamics of Disgust." *The Journal of Genetic Psychology* 144 (1984): 203–208.

Josephus, Flavius, and William Whiston. *The Wars of the Jews*. New York: E.P. Dutton & Co., Inc., 1928.

Jurassic Park. Dir. Steven Spielberg. 1993.

Kimball, John W. *Sewage Treatment*. 2003 <http://users.rcn.com/ jkimball.ma. ultranet/BiologyPages/S/SewageTreatment.html>.

King, Chris. "High Marks for Low-Flow Toilets." *Plumbing & Mechanical,* May 2000 <http://www.pmmag.com/CDA/Archives/7a436155b6fc7010VgnVCM100000f9 32a8c0____>.

Kleeblatt, Norman L. "MERDE! The Caricatural Attack Against Emile Zola." *Art Journal,* Fall (1993).

Kristeva, Julia, and Kelly Oliver. *The Portable Kristeva*. New York: Columbia UP, 1997.

Kundera, Milan. *The Unbearable Lightness of Being*. 1st ed. New York: Harper & Row, 1984.

Laporte, Dominique. *History of Shit*. Cambridge, Mass: MIT Press, 2000.

Largey, Gale Peter, and David Rodney Watson. "The Sociology of Odors." *American Journal of Sociology* 77 (1972): 1021–1034.

Lasley, D. Marty. "Anything Goes: The Art Crap Flaps." *American Wasteland* 30, Mar. 2000 <http://www.americanwasteland.com/anythingoes.html>.

The Last Emperor. Dir. Bernardo Bertolucci. 1987.

Lee, Jae Num. *Swift and Scatological Satire*. 1st ed. Albuquerque: U of New Mexico P, 1971.

Levine, Lawrence W. *Highbrow/Lowbrow: The Emergence of Cultural Hierarchy in America*. Cambridge, Mass: Harvard UP, 1988.

Lewin, Ralph A. *Merde: Excursions in Scientific, Cultural, and Sociohistorical Coprology*. 1st ed. New York: Random House, 1999.

Llanos, Miguel. "Poop Power? Sewage Turned Into Electricity." *MSNBC,* 19 July 2004 <http://www.msnbc.msn.com/id/5335635/>.

Lovel, Jim. "Accidents Claim Lives of Home Depot Shoppers." *Atlanta Business Chronicle,* 21 Feb. 2003.

Mack, Mehammed Amadeus, and Joshuah Bearman. "Katrina in Words." *LA Weekly*, 5 May 2006.

The Madness of King George. Dir. Nicholas Hynter. 1994.

Malen, Lenore. "Postscript: An Anal Universe." *Art Journal,* Fall (1993).

"Man Glued to Toilet Passes Polygraph Test." *ABC11tv.com,* 11 Nov. 2005.

Markowitz, Michael. "The Sewer System." *Gotham Gazette,* 10 Oct. 2003 <http://www.gothamgazette.com/print/569>.

Marks, Jay W. "What is Constipation?" MedicineNet.com <http://www.medicinenet.com/constipation/article.htm>.

Marston, Wendy. "On Germ Patrol, At the Kitchen Sink." *New York Times,* 23 Feb. 1999, sec. Health.

Mason, Thomas. "Managing Protest Behaviour: From Coercion to Compassion." *Journal of Psychiatric and Mental Health Nursing* 7 (2000): 269–275.

Mason, Thomas. "Scatolia: Psychosis to Protest." *Journal of Psychiatric and Mental Health Nursing* 3 (1996): 303–311.

Matthew, Collings. *This is Modern Art.* London: Seven Dials, Cassell & Co, 1999.

May, Margaret Tallmadge, and Galen. *Galen on the Usefulness of the Parts of the Body.* Ithaca, NY: Cornell UP, 1968. 240–242.

Mayer, Peter W., David M. Lewis, and William B. Deoreo. *Seattle Home Water Conservation Study: the Impacts of High Efficiency Plumbing Fixture Retrofits in Single-Family Homes.* Seattle Public Utilities/the United States Environmental Protection Agency. Boulder: Aquacraft, Inc. Water Engineering and Management, 2000.

McAmant, Caroline Hinkle. *Diapers and Toileting.* Families.com, 12 Feb. 2006 <http://parenting.families.com/diapers-and-toileting-269-271-ecc>.

McClintock, Mike. "An Update on Low-Flush Toilets." *The Plumber.com,* 14 Oct. 1999 <http://www.theplumber.com/lowflowupdate99.html>.

McKenzie, John. "Bums, Poos and Wees: Carnivalesque Spaces in the Picture Books of Early Childhood. or, Has Literature Gone to the Dogs?" *English Teaching: Practice and Critique* 4 (2005): 81–94.

Middlemist, R. Dennis, and Eric S. Knowles. "Personal Space Invasions in the Lavatory: Suggestive Evidence for Arousal." *Journal of Personality and Social Psychology* 33 (1976): 541–546.

Miller, John. "The Fig Leaf Was Brown: Classifications of Scatological Art." *Art Journal Fall* (1993).

Miller, Karen. "Harnessing the Power of Poop." *Space.com,* 19 May 2004 <http://www.space.com/businesstechnology/astronaut_electricity_040519.html>.

Miller, William Ian. *The Anatomy of Disgust.* Cambridge, Mass: Harvard UP, 1997.

Mink, Janis, and Marcel Duchamp. *Marcel Duchamp, 1887–1968: Art as Anti-Art.* Köln: Benedikt Taschen, 1995.

"Mom Loses Custody Battle after Kids Found in Feces." *Local6.com,* 19 Apr. 2004.

Monty Python and the Holy Grail. Dir. Terry Gilliam. 1975.

Morgan, Margaret. *Porcelain.*

Morgan, Margaret. "The Plumbing of Modern Life." *Postcolonial Studies* 5 (2002): 171–195.

Mosquera, Gerardo. *Notes on Shit, Art, and Cloaca* <http://www.cloaca.be/notes.htm>.

"Mr. Hankey, the Christmas Poo." *South Park.* Comedy Central, 17 Dec. 1997.

Murphy, Cullen. "Something in the Water: One Man's Pursuit of Microbial Mayhem." *The Atlantic Online,* Sept. 1997 <http://www.theatlantic.com/issues/97sep/water.htm>.

Nelson, Emily. "The Tissue that Tanked: Marketing Miscues Hobble a Much-Hyped Toilet Paper Product." *The Wall Street Journal Classroom Edition,* Sept. 2002.

"New Toilets Wave of Future." *Sapa-AFP,* 10 Sept. 2003 <http://www.theplumber.com/newtoiletswaveoffuture.html>.

Nunhuck, Ayesha. "Shit Scared." *StudentBMJ* 11 (2003): 206–207.

Ogle, Maureen. *All the Modern Conveniences: American Household Plumbing, 1840–1890*. Baltimore: Johns Hopkins UP, 1996.

"Packers' Davenport Gets into Load of Trouble in Miami." *ESPN.com,* 8 July 2002.

Parasympathetic Nervous System (PaNS). The Foundation of Good Health <http://www.drmacdc.com/health/pans.html>.

Persels, Jeff, and Russell Ganim. *Fecal Matters in Early Modern Literature and Art: Studies in Scatology.* Burlington, VT: Ashgate, 2004.

Persels, Jeff. "'Straitened in the Bowels', or Concerning the Rabelaisian Trope of Defecation." *Etudes Rabelaisiennes* XXXI (1996).

Phillips, Grania T., and Jane E. Smith. "The Behavioural Treatment of Faeces Retention: An Expanded Case Study." *Behavioural Psychology* 14 (1986): 124–136.

Pieper, Werner. *Das Scheiss Buch.* Berlin: Der Grüne Zweig 123, 1988.

Pietras, Jamie. "Everyone Poops. But Not Everyone Gets Arrested for It." *New York Press*, Volume 17, no. 46.

Pines, Maya. *The Mystery of Smell: Finding the Oderant Receptors.* Seeing, Hearing, and Smelling the World: A Report from the Howard Hughes Medical Institute. 1997 <http://hhmi.org/senses/>.

Plank, William G. *The Psycho-Social Bases of Scatological Humor: the Unmasking of the Self.* Montana State U, Billings <http://www.msubillings.edu/bplank/humor.htm>.

Police Academy 4: Citizens on Patrol. Dir. Jim Drake. 1987.

Poonurse. "Diarrhea on My Mind." *PoopReport.com,* 21 Jan. 2004 <http://www.poopreport.com/Doctor/Content/diarrhea.html>.

Poonurse. "Rabbit Pellet Poop." *PoopReport.com,* 6 Feb. 2004 <http://www.poopreport.com/Doctor/Content/rabbit.html>.

Pops, Martin. "The Metamorphosis of Shit." *Salmagundi* 56th ser. (1982): 26–61.

Rabelais, François. *Gargantua and Pantagruel.* New York: Knopf, 1994.

Reid, Donald. *"History of Shit* (Review)." *Bulletin of the History of Medicine* 77 (2003): 463–464.

"Rev Henry Moule and the Earth Closet." *JLDR.com,* 31 Mar. 1997 <http://www.jldr.com/henrymoule.htm>.

Riccelli, Angela. "Memoirs of a Poop Lady." *Families, Systems & Health,* Mar (2003).

Riis, Jacob A. *How the Other Half Lives.* New York: Dover, 1971.

Roach, Mary. "Ladies Who Spray: If You Sprinkle When You Tinkle, Cut It Out!" *Salon,* 19 May 2000 <http://archive.salon.com>.

Rockefeller, Abby A. "Civilization and Sludge: Notes on the History of the Management of Human Excreta." *Capitalism, Nature, Socialism* 9 (1998): 3–18.

Roelstraete, Dieter. *Back to the Toilet: Truth and Fiction in Wim Delvoye's Cloaca* <http://www.cloaca.be/back.htm>.

Rushdy, Ashraf H.A. "A New Emetics of Interpretation: Swift, His Critics and the Alimentary Canal." *Mosaic* 24 (1991): 1–32.

Sabbath, Dan, and Mandel Hall. *The First Taboo.* New York: Urizen Books, 1977.

Sakamoto, Saiko, and Atsuhiro Katsumata. *The Next Generation Toilet and Its Maintenance.* Japan Toilet Association Maintenance Study Institute.

Schülting, Sabine. "Pray, Did You Ever Hear of Pears' Soap?": Soap, Dirt, and the Commodity in Victorian England." *Journal for the Study of British Cultures* 8 (2001): 137–156.

"Sewage Disposal." *Encarta*, 1993. Microsoft Corporation <http://encarta.msn.com/encyclopedia_761565852/Sewage_Disposal.html>.

"Sewerage." *The Columbia Encyclopedia*, 2001. Columbia UP <http://www.bartleby.com/65/se/sewerage.html>.

"Shameless Shitters." *PoopReport.com*, 17 Aug. 2001 <http://www.poopreport.com/Shameless/Content/Shameless/shameless.html>.

Shea, Sheila. "Everything You Ever Wanted to Know about Hemorrhoids." *Chet Day— Health and Beyond,* June 1998 <http://chetday.com/hemorrhoids.html>.

Silk, Gerald. "Myths and Meanings in Manzoni's Merda D'Artista." *Art Journal Fall* (1993).

Silver, Maury, Rosaria Conte, Maria Miceli, and Isabella Poggi. "Humiliation: Feeling, Social Control and the Construction of Identity." *Journal for the Theory of Social Behavior* 16 (1986): 269–283.

Smith, Paul. *The Book of Nasty Legends*. Boston: Routledge & Kegan Paul, 1983.

Smith, Steve, and Eric Sticken. "Aging Low Flows." *Plumbing & Mechanical* 27, Feb. 2001 <http://www.pmmag.com/CDA/Archives/dadac940b9fc7010VgnVCM100000 f932a8c0___>.

Spinrad, Paul. *The RE/Search Guide to Bodily Fluids*. San Francisco, CA: RE/Search Publications, 1994.

Steinfeld, Carol, and Claire Anderson. "Water-Wise Toilets." *Mother Earth News,* June–July 2002.

"Survival of the Primmest." *BBC Science and Nature* <http://www.bbc.co.uk/ science/humanbody/mind/articles/emotions/disgust.shtml>.

Swartz, David. *Culture & Power: The Sociology of Pierre Bourdieu.* U of Chicago P, 1997.

Swift, Jonathan, and Huw Parker. *Gulliver's Travels to Lilliput and Brobdingnag.* Hauppauge, NY: Barron, 1999.

Swift, Jonathan. *Strephon and Chloe*. 1734.

Tan, Sarah. *Think Before You Flush or Brush*. Bryn Mawr College, 2002.

Tarr, Joel A. *The Search for the Ultimate Sink: Urban Pollution in Historical Perspective*. 1st ed. Akron, Ohio: U of Akron P, 1996.

Teters, Michael. "The New Art of Digestion." *The Lancet* 359 (2002): 986.

"The Evolution of Disgust: Tunbridge Wells Strikes Back." *The Economist,* 17 Jan. 2004: 78.

Tisdall, Jonathan. "Political Dispute Ends in Muck." *Aftenposten* no. 30, Sept. 2005.

ToiletPaperWorld.com: Historical Facts. ToiletPaperWorld.com <http://www.toiletpaperworld.com/tpw/encyclopedia/navigation/funfacts.htm>.

ToiletPaperWorld.com: Manufacturers. ToiletPaperWorld.com <http://www.toiletpaperworld.com/tpw/encyclopedia/navigation/manufacturers.htm>.

"Toilet Training." *Families.com,* 13 Feb. 2006 <http://parenting.families.com/toilet-training-835-836-ecc>.

Tomes, Nancy. "The History of Shit: an Essay Review." *Journal of the History of Medicine and Allied Sciences* 56 (2001): 400–404.

Toyama, Noriko. "Developmental Changes in the Basis of Associational Contamination Thinking." *Cognitive Development* 14 (1999): 343–361.

TV Timeline. Parents Television Council <http://www.parentstv.org/ptc/facts/tvtimeline.asp>.

Ue, Koo. "Can Sewage System [sic] Survive in the 21st Century?" Japan Toilet Association. 2003 World Toilet Summit.

Unforgiven. Dir. Clint Eastwood. 1992.

USA, National Digestive Diseases Information Clearinghouse, National Institute of Health. *Diarrhea* <http://digestive.niddk.nih.gov/ddiseases/pubs/diarrhea/>.

USA, National Center for Infection Diseases, CDC. *An Ounce of Prevention: Keep the Germs Away* <http://www.cdc.gov/ncidod/op/handwashing.htm>.

USA, National Digestive Diseases Information Clearinghouse, National Institute of Health. *Constipation* <http://digestive.niddk.nih.gov/ddiseases/pubs/constipation/>.

USA, Water Use Efficiency Program, EPA. *Low Flow Toilets* <http://permanent.access.gpo.gov/websites/epagov/www.epa.gov/OWM/water-efficiency/toilets.htm>.

Vancheri, Barbara. "These Shows Broke Barriers." *Pittsburgh Post-Gazette,* 11 Dec. 2003.

Van Der Ryn, Sim. *The Toilet Papers: Recycling Waste & Conserving Water.* White River Junction, VT: Chelsea Green Pub. Co., 1999.

Van Gogh, Vincent. "Letter to Theo." 30 Apr. 1885. Van Gogh Museum.

Von Meier, Kurt. *A Ball of Twine: Marcel Duchamp's "with Hidden Noise"*. California State U, Sacramento <http://www.csus.edu/indiv/v/vonmeierk/noise.html>.

Waring Jr., George E. "The Draining of a Village." *Harper New Monthly Magazine,* June 1879: 132–135.

Water and Sewer Tap Fees. City of Federal Heights, 2006.

Weisberg, Gabriel P. "In Deep Shit: the Coded Images of Travies in the July Monarchy." *Art Journal,* Fall (1993).

Welcome to the Dollhouse. Dir. Todd Solondz. 1995.

"What Happens When You Take the A Train." *Gothamist.com,* 31 Jan. 2006 <http://www.gothamist.com/archives/2006/01/31/what_happens_wh.php>.

Wheeler Jr, Cyrenus. "Sewers: Ancient and Modern; with an Appendix." Cayuga County Historical Society. Cayuga County, NY, 14 Dec. 1886.

Wilson, Elimna T. United States of America. Department of Agriculture. *Modern Conveniences for the Farm Home*. Farmers' Bulletin #270, 1906.

Wilson, John. "You Stink, Therefore I Am: Philosophers Ponder the Meaning of Disgust." *Boston Globe,* 2 May 2004 <http://www.boston.com/news/globe/ideas/articles/2004/05/02/you_stink_therefore_i_am?pg=full>.

Wim Delvoye: Cloaca—New and Improved. The Power Plant, 2004 <http://www.thepowerplant.org/exhibitions/spring04_Cloaca/info.htm>.

Wolf, Buck. "Great Moments in Toilet Paper History." *ABCnews.com,* 11 Apr. 2001 <http://abcnews.go.com/Entertainment/story?id=93597>.

Wood, Beatrice, and Lindsay Smith. *I Shock Myself: The Autobiography of Beatrice Wood*. Rev. Chronicle Books ed. San Francisco, 1988.

Also From Feral House

JIM GOAD'S GIGANTIC BOOK OF SEX
**An Oversized, Jaunty, and Highly Colorful Compendium
Containing Over 100 Articles and Essays**

Flip through the vibrant colors and gorgeous layouts nestled between the covers, and you'll realize there is no other book like this one. This book is CONTROVERSIAL! EXCITING! SCABROUS! BONER-INDUCING! VAGINA-LATHERING!

It delivers ULTIMATE READING SATISFACTION! This book is indisputably gigantic—eleven inches long and eight-and-a-half inches wide. If that's not enough to satisfy you, go see a doctor.
8.5 x 11 • 224 pages • ISBN: 978-1-932595-20-8 • $22.95

PRISONER OF X
20 Years in the Hole at Hustler Magazine
by Allan MacDonell

"Allan MacDonell gets vocal about his 20-year tenure as foil to hillbilly horndog Larry Flynt." — *Vanity Fair*

"Few books open a chapter with 'Visions of anus were plaguing me' and mean it literally." — *Spin*

"Luridly witty ... often strikes gold" — *Rolling Stone*

6 x 9 • 312 pages • ISBN: 1-932595-13-9 • $16.95

BIG DEAD PLACE
Inside the Strange & Menacing World of Antarctica
by Nicholas Johnson

"Johnson's savagely funny story of life 'Inside the Strange and Menacing World of Antarctica' is a grunt's-eye view of fear and loathing, arrogance and insanity in a dysfunctional, dystopian closed community. It's like *M*A*S*H* on ice, a bleak, black comedy." — *The Times of London*

6 x 9 • 276 pages • 16-page color insert • ISBN: 0-922915-99-7 • $16.95

TO ORDER FROM FERAL HOUSE:
Individuals: Send check or money order to Feral House, P.O. Box 39910, Los Angeles CA 90039, USA. For credit card orders: call (800) 967-7885 or fax your info to (323) 666-3330. CA residents please add 8.25% sales tax. U.S. shipping: add $4.50 for first item, $2 each additional item. Shipping to Canada and Mexico: add $9 for first item, $6 each additional item. Other countries: add $11 for first item, $9 each additional item. Non-U.S. originated orders must include international money order or check for U.S. funds drawn on a U.S. bank. We are sorry, but we cannot process non-U.S. credit cards.
www.feralhouse.com